VB/VBA Developer's Guide to the Windows Installer

VB/VBA Developer's Guide to the Windows Installer

Mike Gunderloy

SYBEX®

San Francisco • Paris • Düsseldorf • Soest • London

Associate Publisher: Richard Mills
Contracts and Licensing Manager: Kristine O'Callaghan
Acquisitions & Developmental Editor: Denise Santoro-Lincoln
Editor: Rebecca Rider
Associate Editor: Patrick Peterson
Senior Production Editor: Lisa Duran
Technical Editor: Walter Ritscher
Book Designer: Kris Warrenburg
Graphic Illustrator: Tony Jonick
Electronic Publishing Specialist: Bill Gibson
Proofreaders: Camera Obscura, Laurie O'Connell, Alison Moncrieff
Indexer: Nancy Guenther
Cover Designer: Design Site
Cover Illustrator/Photographer: Jack D. Myers

Library of Congress Card Number: 00-101444

ISBN: 0-7821-2745-2

Manufactured in the United States of America

10 9 8 7 6 5 4 3 2 1

For my parents, who taught me to live and who encouraged me through all the changes of life that followed.

FOREWARD

Windows Installer is Microsoft's new way of delivering software on the Windows 98 and Windows 2000 platforms (and legacy platforms like Windows 95 and Windows NT 4.0).

It's important. So important that Microsoft has made using it a requirement for the Windows 2000 logo. But that's not why you should be using it—you should be using it because doing so makes your applications look better in your customer's eyes.

Applications installed using the Windows Installer are more robust because they will repair themselves if they get damaged. If a critical file is deleted from the system, the next time the application is run, it can detect this and re-install the missing file. You'll get fewer support calls and your customers will have fewer problems.

This book is an excellent, detailed discussion of the Windows Installer technology for the developer. You'll learn to understand how Windows Installer works and how you can use it to make your applications robust and self-healing. You'll also learn how to make them configure themselves according to your user's needs.

Michael Day
Visual Studio Installer Program Manager
Microsoft Corporation
March 2000

ACKNOWLEDGMENTS

I'd like to thank the editorial team who took my manuscript and turned it into a book: Denise Santoro-Lincoln, acquisitions and developmental editor; Rebecca Rider, editor; Patrick Peterson, associate editor; Lisa Duran, senior production editor; and Walter Ritscher, technical editor. Denise especially helped me fight hard for this book at a time when no one, in the publishing industry or elsewhere, really understood why we should care about the Windows Installer. And, of course, no book would happen without the careful people who make up the rest of the book team: Bill Gibson, electronic publishing specialist; Camera Obscura, Laurie O'Connell, and Alison Moncrieff, proofreaders; and Nancy Guenther, indexer.

Various folks on the Windows Installer Internet mailing lists have helped with bits of useful code and information, even though they didn't know I was collecting them for a book. I'd like to particularly thank Stefan Kreuger and Darwin Sanoy for maintaining valuable Internet resources on the subject.

Jim Sturms at Microsoft deserves the credit for introducing me to the Windows Installer during an early stage in its development and for staying up late with me trying to make it work before there was any substantial documentation available.

Of course, none of these people are responsible for any errors that snuck into this book despite their best efforts.

And, as always, thanks to Dana Jones for helping to feed chickens, nurse sick animals, cook dinner, clear brush, stack firewood, chase loose llamas, and do all the other million and one things necessary to keep a small farm running. Without a partner like you, I could never complete a single book.

CONTENTS AT A GLANCE

TABLE OF CONTENTS

INTRODUCTION

A year ago, no one outside of Microsoft had ever seen the Windows Installer Service.

A year from now, it will be available on millions of computers.

That's the sort of market penetration a new technology can achieve when it's a part of both Microsoft Windows 2000 and Microsoft Office 2000.

The team of people behind the Windows Installer started with a simple question: what could be done to make installing applications on Microsoft Windows a better experience for the end user? Working in concert with the Office and Windows teams, they've come up with a number of substantial innovations. These innovations include the following:

- "Install-on-demand" leaves bits of an application on the source media until they're actually needed.
- Advertisement makes it look to an end user as if an application is installed without actually putting it on their computer.
- A new set of rules for creating and installing component puts an end to "DLL Hell" scenarios in which installing one application breaks five others by upgrading some shared component.
- Self-repairing software repairs much accidental damage.

You'll learn about these features, and many others, in this book.

Who Should Read This Book?

Perhaps you picked up this book because you want to understand how to modify the Office 2000 installation process. Or perhaps you want to create an application that's eligible for the Windows 2000 logo. Or perhaps you just figure that if Microsoft is pushing this technology, you'd better find out what it's about. No matter what your question or approach, you'll find a complete overview of the Windows Installer here with an emphasis on understanding the complex database that drives the software installation process. With the help of this book and a good editing tool (I'll discuss several of these in Chapter 12, "Installer Editing Tools"), you should be able to create modern and robust setup programs for your own software.

I was privileged to work with the Windows Installer during the Office 2000 development process, before it was released to the world. During that time, I watched it change from a shaky internal beta through version 1.0 to the version 1.1 release that ships with Windows 2000. Although working with it has been at times tedious and confusing, I'm glad I stuck with it. The end result of understanding Windows Installer technology is comprehending a software installation process that vastly increases the chances of your application working the first time on a wide variety of target computers. If you stick with it through the learning curve, you'll agree with me.

How This Book Is Organized

The Windows Installer Service is brand new in the software world, so I don't assume that you're already an expert with this technology. The first three chapters of the book will introduce you to the promise of the Windows Installer, show you how to install applications with it, and acquaint you with the basic concepts and terminology used in this software.

Chapters 4 through 7 are focused on the Installer database. The actions of the Windows Installer Service are completely database-driven. To customize the Windows Installer to do what you want it to do, you need to create a database and make the proper entries into that database. These chapters will show you how to do this.

Chapters 8 and 9 cover ways that you can use the Windows Installer Service from within your own applications, either through the public application programming interface (API) or through the Installer object model. Understanding the material in these chapters will help you make full use of the Installer's powerful capabilities to install software interactively and repair missing or damaged components.

Chapters 10 and 11 cover some advanced uses of the Windows Installer. They cover how to customize products using patch packages (for upgrades), merges (to use components from other developers), and transforms (to customize the components installed in particular circumstances).

Chapter 12 is a survey of the available tools for editing Windows Installer databases, and Chapter 13 discusses the use of validation to make sure that you haven't made a mistake when editing those databases.

Finally, the Appendix to the book looks at the current requirements for the Microsoft Windows logo, and it shows how the Windows Installer Service fits with those requirements.

Generally speaking, this book is meant to be read in order. You should read the first three chapters to familiarize yourself with the basic terminology and concepts of the Windows Installer Service, and then you should at least skim the next four chapters to become familiar with the Windows Installer database. You can tackle the more advanced concepts in the remaining chapters as you need them. If you picked up this book because you suddenly find yourself responsible for creating an Installer package, you might want to skip ahead to Chapter 12 to see what your choices are for editing software.

What Hardware/Software Is Required

The Windows Installer Service is a native part of Windows 2000. It's also available as a redistributable update for Windows NT 4.0, and Windows 9*x* (I'll discuss this in more detail in Chapter 1). Once you've installed this update, you should be able to work with the Windows Installer on any computer that runs any 32-bit version of Microsoft Windows.

Release Dependency

This book was written in late 1999 and early 2000 using the then-current versions of the software it discusses:

- Windows 2000 RC3
- Visual Basic 6.0 with Service Pack 3
- Windows Installer Service 1.1

Inevitably, there will be updates, service packs, and release versions that change this software. With luck, all of the samples will keep working, but if anything doesn't work, I'd appreciate it if you'd let me know. My e-mail address is MikeG1@mcwtech.com, and I'm always happy to hear from my readers.

What Kind of Code Is in This Book?

Although the example code in this book is entirely written in Visual Basic, the Windows Installer itself can be used from any language that's capable of writing Windows applications. I chose Visual Basic because many developers can follow VB code, because it's widespread, and because my own expertise lies in that area. But the Windows Installer is designed for developers working in any language, and so is this book.

About the Web Site

You'll notice that there's some Visual Basic code in this book, but there's no CD-ROM. That's because all of the code is available on the Sybex Web site. Just go to www.sybex.com, look up this book (you can search by title, author, or ISBN from the Catalog page), and click the Downloads button. Accept the license agreement, and you'll go straight to a Web page where you can download any of the sample projects discussed in this book. I'll also use the Web site to post any necessary additions and corrections to the book.

chapter 1

Introduction to the Windows Installer

- Issues with Older Setup Software

- Solutions from the Windows Installer

- Getting the Windows Installer

- The Windows Installer SDK

- The Windows Installer Clean Up Tool

Starting with the release of Office 2000 in early 1999, the new Windows Installer is Microsoft's preferred way of delivering software to end users. But why should you care? There are several reasons why you should investigate this new technology:

- Using the Windows Installer is a requirement for any application that wants to conform with the new Windows 2000 logo guidelines.
- The Windows Installer makes it less likely that your application will break existing applications by accident. This translates directly into cost savings in troubleshooting and support.
- You can speed up your applications, make the user's experience better, and offer increased flexibility by making full use of the Windows Installer.

In this chapter, I'll introduce the Windows Installer by outlining the problems that it was designed to solve and the solutions that it delivers. Then, I'll let you know how you can get your own copy of this software and introduce you to the Windows Installer Software Development Kit (SDK). I'll use the rest of the book to show you what you can do with this software, both from the command line and from your own applications written in Visual Basic.

Issues with Older Setup Software

Why did Microsoft decide that this was a good time to invest resources in a new way of installing applications? Because existing software installation solutions have grown complex and unreliable. If Windows applications can't be installed and uninstalled without problems, this ultimately reflects poorly on the operating system itself.

Let's take a look at some of the problems with software installation on Windows that existed before the Windows Installer:

- "DLL Hell."
- Setup programs that take forever because they install everything locally.
- Lack of administrative control over end-user installations.
- Software needs administrative rights to install properly.
- Setup programs must use different application programming interfaces (APIs) for different platforms (Windows 95, Windows 98, Windows NT, Windows 2000).
- Software can't be uninstalled completely or without breaking other software.
- Setup programs are unable to repair broken software without a complete reinstall.
- Failed installations could break existing software.

.dll Version Conflicts

The first problem with existing setups is so prevalent that it's gotten its own informal term over the years: "DLL Hell." This refers to the tendency of installation programs to do the wrong things with Windows libraries (.dll files). Sometimes older versions are installed atop newer versions, breaking programs that depend on the newer versions. Sometimes newer versions replace older versions even though they're not 100 percent compatible. Sometimes shared libraries are removed even when other applications are using them. Overall, while shared libraries represent an important part of the functionality of Windows, maintaining them has required far too much time, trouble, and effort.

Too Much Software Installed

Over the years, applications have grown from the 27KB of the original VisiCalc (the first spreadsheet program) to the roughly 1GB of Microsoft Office 2000 Premium with all the bells and whistles installed. Although hard drives have continued to grow and to get cheaper per megabyte, today's applications are huge by any measure. Most people, although they install complete applications, never use most of the functionality of those applications. And even when setup programs provide custom installations that let users pick and choose what to install, the choices often don't make a lot of sense to the non-developer. The net result is that applications routinely install much more software than the user will actually ever use.

Lack of Administrative Control

If you're installing software for yourself, you can keep track of what you've put on your computer and where you put it. But what if you're the administrator for a large network? It's a nightmare trying to maintain a thousand installations of, say, Microsoft Office if every user can choose their own set of features and their own location for the software. Network administrators need the ability to control the installations done by end users. Although some tools, such as Microsoft Systems Management Server, exist to help with this task, there's no standard to allow them to work easily with all installation programs.

Need for Administrative Rights

It's becoming increasingly popular for large organizations to *lock down* user desktops to a greater or lesser extent. The *fiddle factor*, the natural tendency of users to change settings on their computers, to move things around, and to customize their desktops, is reputed to waste significant resources in large organizations. So administrators are inclined to provide a standard environment that the user can't change, often by using

Windows NT Workstation as the operating system and using security to restrict what the user can do.

This leads to problems when installing software, though. Many software packages need to be installed under an account with administrative privileges in order to function properly. If you've locked down your users' desktops, this means that they can't install their own software.

Varying Setup Routines

Windows now includes four major platforms (Windows 95, Windows 98, Windows NT 4.0, and Windows 2000) with over a dozen minor variations. In order to work everywhere, setup programs must take into account the differences between these platforms. Some Registry keys have to be written to different locations on different platforms, some folders are in different places, even some API calls function differently on one platform or another.

This leads to larger setup programs with more complex logic, which inevitably means that there are more bugs in the setup programs and those bugs are harder to fix. It also leads to a substantial testing burden, especially for smaller software developers. How many developers can afford to set up a couple of dozen computers just to test their installation program?

Uninstalls Break Other Software

Some applications today don't treat shared resources properly. A shared resource might be a library (.dll file) in the Windows folder, a Registry key that's used by multiple programs, or an environment setting. Some software removes shared resources when uninstalled, even when those resources should remain. The result is that uninstalling one application can break another application.

Software Isn't Resilient

Things go wrong with software. The user accidentally deletes a critical file, the Registry gets corrupted when the user's hard drive fills, or the user customizes a setting and can't remember how to return it to its default value. Most of today's software can't deal with these problems at all. How many times have you been told by technical support that the answer is to completely uninstall and reinstall the application? Even one time is too many. Good software should be able to repair itself when things go wrong.

Failed Installations Make a Mess

If an application fails to install completely, it can leave the user's computer in an inconsistent state. Perhaps only one of a pair of matched libraries gets updated, or a Registry key gets deleted without a new key being created. Whatever the actual mechanics, it's very difficult to recover from failed installations. In the worst case, not just the new software, but also the existing software, fails to work after such a disaster.

Solutions from the Windows Installer

The Windows Installer acts as a single point of contact for all software that needs to be installed on your computer. Instead of each application making its own calls directly to the operating system to copy files, write Registry keys, and perform other setup tasks, applications call services from the Windows Installer.

Figure 1.1 illustrates this change. In pre–Windows Installer setup programs, the setup program contained both a description of what should be done and the actual programming code to do it. If there was a Registry key to be installed, for example, the setup program contained the name and value for that key. It also contained the code to open the Registry, create a key, and write a value to it. In a Windows Installer setup, the description of the setup is separated from the code to implement that setup. The setup program is now just a large database containing information on, for example, the name and value of Registry keys to create. The Windows Installer Service itself actually contains the code to manipulate the Registry according to the information in the setup program (now called an Installer database).

FIGURE 1.1
Old and new installations

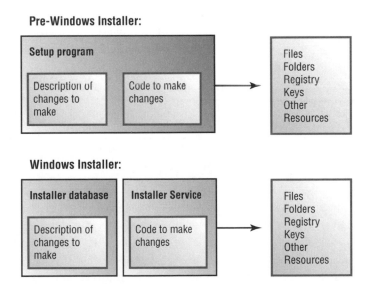

With the Windows Installer, application developers are free to do what they do best (describing the changes that their application should make to the user's computer), while leaving Microsoft free to implement the actual changes.

This allows the Windows Installer to perform several critical functions:

- Versioning and sharing rules for libraries and other components are consistently followed.
- Features can be "advertised" so that they appear to be installed without taking the time to actually install them.
- Administrators can control exactly what gets installed on computers in an enterprise.
- Software can be installed even when the user can't modify the desktop or Registry directly.
- Setup programs use one uniform API on all platforms.
- All changes during setup can be "rolled back" for a clean uninstall.
- Software can be repaired or reinstalled by calling the Windows Installer.
- Failed installations make no changes to the user's computer.

The Windows Installer delivers all of these benefits, but at the moment it's version 1.1 technology. What this means is that you can still expect some problems when trying to use the Installer, and you'll find some features that could stand to be improved. But bear in mind that Microsoft has clearly indicated that this is the way they expect all future software to be installed on Windows. A good reason to trust this statement is that Microsoft requires all applications to use the Windows Installer for their setup programs in order for products to obtain the Windows 2000 "Certified for Windows" logo.

NOTE   For more information on the Windows Logo Program and Visual Basic, see the appendix, "Meeting Windows Logo Requirements."

Enforcement of Setup Rules

Because the Windows Installer does all the actual work of modifying the user's computer, it provides complete and consistent enforcement of the rules of installing applications. For example, the Windows Installer provides a set of versioning rules designed to make sure that no program ever overwrites a library that another program depends on, unless the newer version is 100 percent compatible with the older version. This is accomplished not just by checking the version information contained in the library, but by checking the Component ID of the component containing the library. The Component ID is a unique number (actually, a GUID: Globally Unique Identifier) that developers are required to change whenever a new version is not 100 percent compatible with an old version.

Advertised Features

The Windows Installer Service supports the concept of advertised features and applications. An advertised feature or application is one that has not yet been installed on the user's computer, yet appears to be installed. The first time the user tries to use the feature or application, the Windows Installer takes over and installs the actual components required for the feature or application to function. This is called *installation on demand*.

NOTE   You'll learn more about the difference between components, features, and applications in Chapter 3, "Basic Installer Concepts."

Advertising an application will enable various parts of the application:

- The application's Start Menu entries and icons will be available.
- The application's documents will show in Windows Explorer with their proper icons and shortcut menus.
- The application's MIME (Multipurpose Internet Mail Extensions) information will be registered (so attached files from the application will appear properly in e-mail).

In addition, Windows 2000 supports advertising the classes created by a COM server so that the server is installed when a client tries to instantiate one of its objects.

Administrative Control

The Windows Installer supports modifying an application's Installer database through the use of a *transform*. A transform is a partial Installer database that represents a series of changes that should be made to a second Installer database before it's processed by the Windows Installer Service. Because these transforms can modify any part of the Installer database, they can be used to add or remove components, make default selections in the user interface of the setup process, or even force an installation with no user intervention whatsoever.

Elevated Installation Privileges

Because the Windows Installer Service is a separate service, not a component launched by the user, it can run with a different security context than the logged-on user has. In particular, the Windows Installer Service can start and stop services, and write Registry keys or files, even if the user lacks the privileges to perform these actions.

Uniform Setup API

Although the Windows Installer is provided in two versions (an ANSI version for Windows 9x, and a Unicode version for Windows NT and Windows 2000), both versions use exactly the same API. This allows setup authors to write installations for all supported platforms using a uniform API. In addition, the Windows Installer provides a type library with an automation interface for its major functionality. This way it can be easily manipulated from COM client languages such as Visual Basic.

NOTE   There's more information on the Installer API in Chapter 8, "Using the Installer API," and on the Installer Automation Model in Chapter 9, "Using the Installer Automation Model."

Clean Uninstalls

The Windows Installer keeps track of every action it performs, including the creation of files and folders, the incrementing of shared component reference counts, and more. This record allows the Windows Installer to cleanly uninstall an application it has installed.

In addition, the Windows Installer database contains information that's available to the Windows 2000 Add/Remove Programs Control Panel applet. By clicking the Support Information hyperlink in the Add/Remove Programs dialog box, you'll get an information dialog box similar to the one for Office 2000 Premium shown in Figure 1.2. The information displayed in this dialog box is supplied in the Windows Installer package for Office 2000 Premium.

FIGURE 1.2
Extended support
information

Repair and Reinstallation

The Windows Installer also significantly increases the resiliency of installed applications. It does this through two mechanisms: the Installer API and repair installation.

The Installer API allows applications to query the Installer database for an application directly, even after the installation is over. This can tell an application whether and where a particular component is installed, and it frees the application from depending on static path names.

In addition, the Installer itself can be launched in a reinstall mode. This mode can check the components that have already been installed, and if necessary, it can rewrite Registry keys, files, and other information to repair any damage to those components.

Rollback

While you're using the Windows Installer to install an application, it keeps track of everything it's doing in a log file. It also makes copies of any deleted files in a hidden folder and keeps these copies until the installation is completed successfully.

If there's any problem with the installation, the saved copies, plus the log file, are used to completely roll back the installation. Every change the Installer has made to the computer will be reversed, and deleted files will be restored to their previous locations. The net result is a computer with no changes made at all.

In other words, installation is treated as a single transaction, and it will only succeed or fail as a unit.

NOTE Because it has to keep copies of deleted files, the Installer may require more disk space than the finished application takes up. If you're low on disk space, you can risk installing without the rollback information by using a command-line switch. There's more on command-line switches in Chapter 2, "Running the Installer."

Getting the Windows Installer

The Windows Installer is shipping as a native service in all versions of Windows 2000. As soon as you install Windows 2000, the Windows Installer Service is there. In fact, Windows 2000 uses the Windows Installer Service to manage parts of its own installation.

For older versions of Windows, the Windows Installer Service will be provided as part of a service pack. As of this writing (Spring 2000), though, these service packs had not yet been released by Microsoft.

Because software using the Windows Installer was available before the service packs containing the Windows Installer were developed (for example, Office 2000, which shipped in Spring 1999, makes heavy use of the Windows Installer), there's a bootstrap method that installations can use to install the Windows Installer. This bootstrap amounts to running one of two self-executable files before the installation of the application begins:

- `InstMSI.exe` installs the Windows Installer on Windows 95 or Windows 98. This is the ANSI version of the Windows Installer.
- `InstMSIw.exe` installs the Windows Installer on Windows NT 4.0. This is the Unicode version of the Windows Installer.

NOTE   You may find that both of these files are named `Instmsi.exe` on some software CD-ROMs. If the manufacturer decided to rename the Windows NT version, you'll find them in different directories.

NOTE   You'll learn more about this bootstrapping process in Chapter 2.

Office 2000 included version 1.0 of the Windows Installer. Windows 2000, officially released in February 2000, is the first product to include version 1.1 of the Windows Installer. Version 1.1 is backwards compatible with version 1.0 (that is, Installer packages created with version 1.0 can be read and processed by version 1.1). However, 1.1 adds some additional functionality. In this book, I'll be using version 1.1 of the Windows Installer. If you only have version 1.0, you should upgrade to version 1.1 by running `InstMSI.exe` or `InstMSIw.exe`.

The Windows Installer SDK

If you're going to do any serious work with the Windows Installer, you absolutely need a copy of the Windows Installer SDK. There are two ways to get a copy of this:

- It's included in the Windows Platform SDK, a part of the Microsoft Developer Network, under `Management Services\Setup\Windows Installer`.
- It can be downloaded from the Windows Installer SDK page on Microsoft's Web site at `msdn.microsoft.com/downloads/sdks/platform/wininst.asp`.

Even if you have a copy of the Platform SDK, you'll probably want to download a copy of the SDK from the Web site. The downloadable version includes numerous tools that are not included in the Platform SDK version. The Windows Installer SDK contains these components:

- Bootstrap files
- Help files
- C++ Source, Library, and Header files
- Group Policy Editor file
- Orca Installer database editor
- Installer database validation tool
- Command-line import and export tools
- Command-line merge and install tools
- Cleanup tool
- MsiSpy
- Patch files
- Sample databases

Bootstrap Files

The bootstrap files are both named `InstMsi.exe`. These are the installers for the Installer Service itself. The ANSI version is for Windows 95 or 98 (in the Win9x directory), and the Unicode version, is for Windows NT 4.0 (in the WinNT directory). Of course, there's no version for Windows 2000, which ships with the Windows Installer Service. If you're distributing a setup program that might be run on a platform other than Windows 2000, you need to be sure to include the appropriate bootstrap file.

Help Files

The Installer SDK includes two help files. `Msi.chm` is a hypertext help file for the Windows Installer itself. This is the most essential reference if you're trying to learn all of the ins and outs of the Installer database, the Installer API, and the Installer automation model.

The SDK also includes `MsiTool.hlp`, which is the help file for the other utilities that the SDK includes.

C++ Source, Library, and Header Files

The SDK includes examples for developers who wish to use the Windows Installer APIs directly from C++ programs. These samples won't be used in this book. Instead, I'll include sample code for the Visual Basic developer.

Group Policy Editor File

The Windows Installer SDK includes `Instlr1.adm`, which is a Group Policy Editor administrative template. Group Policy Editor administrative templates allow system administrators to determine which actions end users may perform on systems in a particular domain. Figure 1.3 shows the policies that you can set using this administrative template on a Windows 2000 domain.

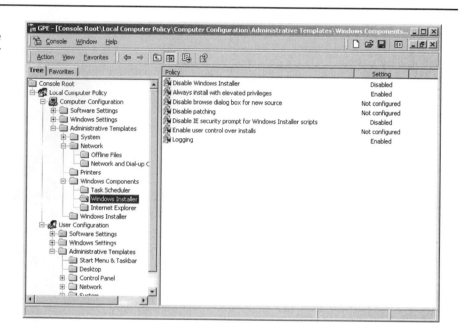

Orca Installer Database Editor

The Installer SDK installs a copy of `Orca.msi` to your computer. This is a Windows Installer package that you can use to install Orca, the Windows Installer database editor. Figure 1.4 shows this editor in action, editing the Installer database for the MsiVal2 utility. Orca provides a simple interface for viewing and editing the contents of any Windows Installer database.

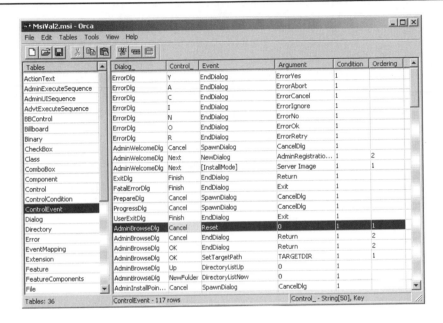

FIGURE 1.4
The Orca Windows Installer
database editor

You'll learn more about Orca, as well as other, more full-featured editors for Windows Installer packages, in Chapter 12, "Installer Editing Tools."

Installer Database Validation Tool

MsiVal2.msi is a Windows Installer package that installs the MSI validation command-line tool. This tool can help you check your Installer packages for internal consistency. Microsoft requires any candidate for the Windows Logo to pass validation. You'll learn more about validating Installer packages in Chapter 13, "Validating Installer Databases."

Command-Line Import and Export Tools

The Windows Installer SDK includes two command-line tools for importing and exporting information from Installer packages. MsiDb.exe is a command-line tool that imports and exports text files from Installer databases. MsiInfo.exe is a command-line tool to set or inspect the summary information that's stored in Windows Installer packages.

While it may seem that command-line tools are unnecessary if you have a graphical editor such as Orca, they can be extremely useful if you're involved in building a large and complex application. That's because command-line tools can be called directly from batch files and used as part of an automated build process.

In addition, MsiDb allows you to import cabinet files, a crucial part of building an Installer database. I'll cover MsiDb in Chapter 12. I won't work with MsiInfo in this book. For more information on its use, see the `MsiTool.hlp` file.

Command-Line Merge and Install Tools

Two other command-line tools help you modify existing Windows Installer packages. The `MsiMerg.exe` tool merges two Installer databases. It's especially useful for inserting merge modules into a new or existing database. The `MsiTran.exe` tool applies transform files to Installer databases. A transform file is a separate Installer database that's designed to pre-select options, add additional components, or otherwise modify an Installer database.

NOTE   You'll learn more about merges and transforms in Chapter 11, "Merges and Transforms."

Cleanup Tool

`MsiZap.exe` is a command-line tool used to remove selected Windows Installer information from a computer. It can also be used to recover from situations in which the Installer information has become corrupted, for example, by a power failure during an installation. However, this tool is both powerful and dangerous, and in most situations, you should use the Windows Installer Clean Up tool, discussed later in this chapter, instead of using `MsiZap.exe` directly.

MsiSpy

`MsiSpy.msi` is an Installer package with a dual role. First, this package is used for many of the examples in the Installer SDK. Second, the utility that it installs, MsiSpy, is a program for listing the components that are being managed by the Windows Installer on your computer. Figure 1.5 shows the information that you can retrieve with MsiSpy.

FIGURE 1.5
MsiSpy in Action

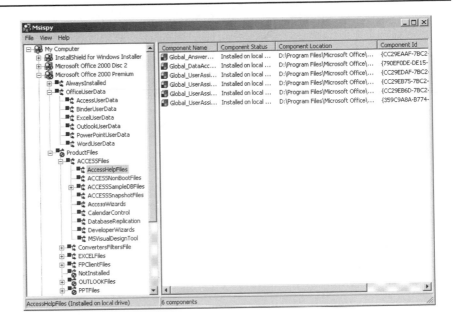

Patch Files

The Installer SDK installs an entire folder of documentation and examples on building patch files. Installer patch files are designed to make minor changes to the functionality of existing products. You'll learn more about patch files in Chapter 10, "Creating and Using Patch Packages."

Sample Databases

Finally, the Windows Installer SDK installs two sample databases that you might want to use as a starting point. Schema.msi is a completely blank Installer database that contains all of the necessary tables needed in any Installer package. UISample.msi contains all of the necessary tables and also enough entries in those tables to create a user interface for the setup program.

The Windows Installer Clean Up Tool

The Windows Installer caches quite a bit of information on your computer when you perform an installation. Some of this information is cached in the Registry and some in disk files. It's possible for this information to get corrupted, in which case, the Installer may not be able to repair or reinstall a particular product or properly service install-on-demand requests. You may also not be able to uninstall a product if the Installer database has become corrupted.

Corruption can result from

- Registry or disk crashes
- User edits to the Registry
- A crash during the installation of a program
- Multiple instances of the Installer running at one time

Microsoft has released the Windows Installer Clean Up tool to help recover from these problems. Figure 1.6 shows this tool in action. It lists all of the products that are known to the Windows Installer on your system and lets you remove any or all of these products along with the cached installation information.

FIGURE 1.6
Windows Installer
Clean Up tool

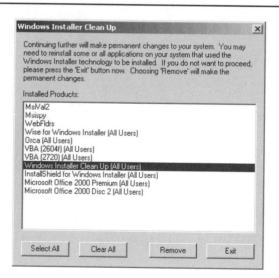

The Windows Installer Clean Up tool maintains a log file of its actions in `Windows\ Temp\msicu.log`. You can use this file to determine what actions the tool has taken. Of course, you'll need to reinstall from the original source media any application that you uninstall with this utility.

To obtain a copy of the Windows Installer Clean Up tool, refer to article Q238413 in the Microsoft KnowledgeBase. You can access this article online at `support.microsoft.com/ support/kb/articles/q238/4/13.ASP`. You can also receive a copy of this article via e-mail by sending a message to `mshelp@microsoft.com` with the subject Q238413. The article contains the latest information on where to download the tool, which comes in separate versions for Windows 95 and Windows NT. The Windows NT version can also be used on Windows 2000.

Using the Windows Installer Clean Up tool should be treated as a last resort for fixing setup problems. But sometimes you'll need to use that last resort.

NOTE   The Windows Installer Clean Up tool works by making calls to the command-line MsiZap utility.

chapter 2

Running the Installer

- Bootstrapping

- Installation Modes

- Installer Options

- Reading Installer Logs

Because the Installer Service is the same for every application that uses the Windows Installer, there are uniformities between the installation of all of these applications. In particular, applications can share the means of loading the Windows Installer Service on a fresh computer, the different modes of setup, and the command-line switches that can be used to modify the operation of the Installer Service. The Windows Installer also maintains standard logs, which can be useful when you need to do some troubleshooting. In this chapter, I'll examine the shared features that are available in all Windows Installer-driven applications.

Bootstrapping

Consider an early adopter of the Windows Installer technology, for example, Microsoft Office 2000. Microsoft Office 2000 uses the Windows Installer for its setup, and it supplies an Installer package containing all of the necessary information to set up the application. Yet it must be capable of being installed on computers that do not yet have the Windows Installer Service itself installed. How can the software resolve this apparent contradiction?

The answer lies in a process called *bootstrapping*. Until the Windows Installer Service is pervasive, any software that depends on the Windows Installer being present must first ensure that the Installer is in fact present. The logic goes like this:

1. User launches `setup.exe` to begin a new installation.

2. The `setup.exe` program checks to see whether the Windows Installer Service is present. If it is, the program skips to step 6. Note that if the program is running on Windows 2000, the Windows Installer Service will always be present because it's installed as part of the operating system.

3. The `setup.exe` program determines what platform is being used.

4. If the platform is Windows 95*x*, `setup.exe` launches the ANSI version of `InstMsi.exe` to install the Windows Installer.

5. If the platform is Windows NT 4, `setup.exe` launches the Unicode version of `InstMsi.exe` to install the Windows Installer.

6. `Setup.exe` constructs an appropriate command line using the `.msi` file in the installation and passes it to `MsiExec.exe`, the actual Windows Installer launcher.

`Setup.exe` is not a part of the Windows Installer itself. Office 2000, for example, uses a version written by the Office team. This version is more sophisticated than the bare-bones outline here. For example, it allows the user to automatically launch an administrative install using a command-line switch. Also, when it performs step 6, it uses a copy of the Windows Installer that's on the Office CD-ROM. This avoids the need to reboot after steps 4 or 5 to activate the Installer Service on the target computer.

If you're using a commercial tool such as InstallShield for Windows Installer or Wise for Windows Installer, the tool will supply a `setup.exe` that you can include with your own installation to carry out this bootstrapping process. Otherwise, you have two choices:

1. Write your own bootstrap application.

2. Include a readme file on your distribution media that instructs the user to run `InstMsi.exe` if necessary.

If you expect most of your users to be running your installation on Windows 2000, you might opt for a simple note in the readme file since there won't be any point to creating a bootstrap application for that platform. Otherwise, in the interest of making the user experience as smooth as possible, you should write a bootstrap application and include it as part of your setup distribution.

Fortunately, writing your own bootstrap application in Visual Basic is fairly simple. You only need to be able to check whether the Installer Service is already installed, and to check the current operating system so you'll know how and whether to install it. The necessary routines are available in the `LaunchInstaller.vbp` sample project, which is available for download at this book's page on Sybex's Web site (`www.sybex.com`). To determine the operating system, you can call `GetVersionEx`, as shown in the `Get-Platform` function in Listing 2.1.

Listing 2.1: Visual Basic Code to Determine the Current Operating System

```
Public Declare Function GetVersionEx _
 Lib "kernel32" Alias "GetVersionExA" _
 (lpVersionInformation As OSVERSIONINFO) As Long

Public Type OSVERSIONINFO
        dwOSVersionInfoSize As Long
        dwMajorVersion As Long
        dwMinorVersion As Long
        dwBuildNumber As Long
        dwPlatformId As Long
        szCSDVersion As String * 128
End Type

Public Const VER_PLATFORM_WIN32s = 0
Public Const VER_PLATFORM_WIN32_WINDOWS = 1
Public Const VER_PLATFORM_WIN32_NT = 2
```

```
Public Enum ePlatform
    plWin32s
    plWin95
    plWin98
    plNT351
    plNT4
    plWin2000
    plUnknown
End Enum

Public Function GetPlatform() As ePlatform
    ' Use GetVersionInfoEx() to determine the current
    ' operating system and return a constant indicating
    ' the result

    Dim typVersionInfo As OSVERSIONINFO

    typVersionInfo.dwOSVersionInfoSize = _
    Len(typVersionInfo)

    If GetVersionEx(typVersionInfo) > 0 Then
        ' Determine the platform type
        Select Case typVersionInfo.dwPlatformId
            Case VER_PLATFORM_WIN32s
                ' This is Win32S on Windows 3.1 (ugh!)
                GetPlatform = plWin32s
            Case VER_PLATFORM_WIN32_WINDOWS
                ' This is one of the consumer platforms.
                ' We can distinguish Win95 from Win98
                ' by checking the minor version
                If typVersionInfo.dwMinorVersion = 0 Then
                    GetPlatform = plWin95
                Else
                    GetPlatform = plWin98
                End If
            Case VER_PLATFORM_WIN32_NT
                ' This is one of the NT platforms. Check
                ' the major version to see which one
                Select Case typVersionInfo.dwMajorVersion
                    Case 3
                        GetPlatform = plNT351
                    Case 4
                        GetPlatform = plNT4
                    Case Is >= 5
                        ' For our purposes, we can treat
                        ' future versions as Windows 2000
                        GetPlatform = plWin2000
                End Select
        End Select
```

```
        End Select
    Else
        ' A zero return value from GetVersionEx
        ' indicates an error. This is too serious
        ' to recover from, so just give up.
        GetPlatform = plUnknown
    End If
End Function
```

GetVersionEx is the Windows API call that returns an OSVERSIONINFO structure filled with operating system information. The GetPlatform function, shown in Listing 2.1, first checks the dwPlatformId member of this structure, which tells us whether the program is running under Win32s, one of the consumer versions of Windows (Windows 9*x*), or one of the Windows NT versions of Windows. In the latter two cases, it checks other members of the structure to retrieve enough version information to make a decision.

To determine whether the Installer Service is present on the computer, you can use the HasInstaller function:

```
Public Function HasInstaller() As Boolean
    ' Determine whether the Windows Installer
    ' is already installed on this system
    Dim oInstaller As Object
    On Error Resume Next
    Set oInstaller = CreateObject _
     ("WindowsInstaller.Installer")
    HasInstaller = (Err = 0)
End Function
```

As you'll learn in Chapter 9, "Using the Installer Automation Model," the Installer automatically installs an automation model when it's installed on a computer. This automation model provides, among other objects, a WindowsInstaller.Installer top-level object. If this object can be created, the code is running on a computer that already has the Installer installed. Note that the use of late binding, by declaring oInstaller as Object, combined with the CreateObject function allows this code to be compiled, even on a computer without the Installer Service.

TIP   The LaunchInstaller.vbp project also contains a form, frmSetup, which demonstrates how you might use these two functions in a bootstrap program.

Installation Modes

The Windows Installer Service is designed to supply all of the installation needs of the applications that use it. This includes four distinct modes of installation:

- Regular installation
- Administrative installation
- Rollback installation
- Maintenance installation

In this section, I'll briefly describe these four different modes and discuss how they fit in with applications.

Regular Installation

Performing a regular installation is the most common use of the Windows Installer. This is an installation that takes information and files from the source media and transfers them to the user's computer to produce a working copy of the software.

The Installer processes a regular installation (and other installations) in two phases:

1. During the *acquisition phase*, the Installer reads from the Installer package, and interacts with the user, to determine what actions need to be carried out. These actions are written to an Installer script.

2. During the *execution phase*, the part of the Installer with elevated privileges executes the script that was created during the acquisition phase.

As you'll learn in Chapter 4, "A Guide to the Installer Database," Installer packages contain a database that tells the Installer exactly what to do. The sequence of events in a regular installation is controlled by entries in the InstallUISequence and InstallExecuteSequence tables. These tables list, in an ordered fashion, all of the top-level actions that the Installer will perform. That might include displaying a dialog or copying selected files to the user's hard drive.

The actions contained in these two tables can be native Installer actions or custom actions. Custom actions can be supplied by creating a DLL with a specific entry point. This allows you to extend the Installer to perform any action you can conceive of, not just those that were allowed for by the team that designed the Installer. You'll learn more about custom actions in Chapter 6, "Installer Actions."

Administrative Installation

An administrative installation does not install an executable application on a user's hard drive. Rather, it installs the entire Installer package and all other files from the original source media to a network drive. The location that the administrative installation transfers files to is known as an *installation point*. Later, users can run the setup program from the installation point to actually install the application to their own hard drive.

Like a regular installation, an administrative installation is table-driven. However, in this case, the tables containing the installation logic are named AdminUISequence and AdminExecuteSequence. The use of a second set of tables for an administrative installation means that this installation can have a completely different appearance from a regular installation.

During an administrative installation, the Installer changes certain properties in the database based on information contained in the original database. In this fashion, software installed from an installation point can be made to have different defaults than the same software installed from the original source media.

An administrative installation can be launched from the command line by using the /a switch.

Rollback Installation

A rollback installation is triggered by the Windows Installer itself, rather than by a user. Actually, you might think of this as an *un*installation. During a regular or administrative installation, the Windows Installer keeps a complete log of all actions performed as well as copies of any files that it deletes. If anything goes wrong with the installation, the Installer uses this log and these file copies to completely remove any changes it has made to the computer. Thus, a rollback installation is designed to leave the computer in the exact state that it was in before the original regular installation was started.

Rollback files are stored in a hidden system directory that's automatically deleted if an installation is completed successfully.

It's possible to completely disable the rollback functionality in the Windows Installer by setting the DISABLEROLLBACK property in an Installer database to True. However, this is a dangerous practice because it can lead to a partially functioning piece of software being left on a computer if anything goes wrong. Unless you expect an application to be installed with extremely limited extra disk space, you should leave rollback enabled.

NOTE   If you're involved in a large development effort, you might want to disable rollback during your beta testing period. If you don't, problems installing beta copies of the software might prevent anyone from testing the parts that do install!

Maintenance Installation

In addition to regular and administrative installations, the Windows Installer is capable of three distinct modes of software maintenance. First, it's possible for the user to choose to install additional software features after the software has been installed or to remove features that they no longer need. Second, it's possible to use the Windows Installer to repair an application that's experiencing problems. Finally, a user might choose to remove the application entirely from their computer.

Generally, you'll want to make all of these capabilities available from the Add/ Remove Programs applet in the Windows Control Panel. For example, when the user chooses Add/Remove Programs in Microsoft Office 2000, the dialog box in Figure 2.1 appears. This dialog box allows the user to choose which of these maintenance modes to enter.

FIGURE 2.1
Choosing a maintenance
mode

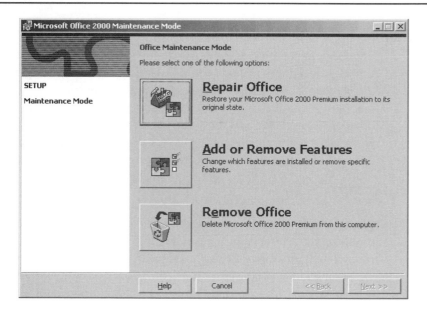

No matter which mode the user chooses, the Installer creates a change script and then uses the elevated privilege portion of the Installer software to execute the change script. Like an installation script, a change script is a list of commands from the Installer to itself, not a file that's available to users.

The Windows Installer actually supports quite a number of options for repairing applications. I'll discuss those options and the command-line switches used to invoke them later in the chapter.

Installer Options

The Windows Installer can be controlled interactively by running the `MsiExec.exe` program. This program will be installed in one of the directories that Windows automatically searches for program to be run (typically the `\Windows\System` directory) the first time you install any application that's written to use the Windows Installer. If you just run `MsiExec.exe` without any options, you'll get a dialog box (shown in Figure 2.2) that will tell you the version of the Installer that's currently installed.

FIGURE 2.2

The Windows Installer version dialog box

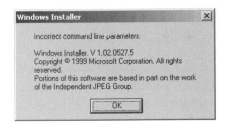

For a more useful Installer session, you will need to enter some arguments on the command line. The general format of a Windows Installer command line follows:

```
msiexec <options> <property settings>
```

For example, the following command line would perform an installation of the package `Test1.msi` from the e: drive, and it would set a public property named COMPANY to the value "Lark Group":

```
msiexec /I e:\Test1.msi COMPANY="Lark Group"
```

In the rest of this section, I'll explain the Installer command line in more depth. You'll learn about three things here:

- Command line options
- Repair options
- Public variables

Command-Line Options

The core Installer program msiexec supports 15 different switches that can be used singly or in combination. These allow you to control the type of the installation, create log files, manipulate the user interface, and handle self-registering libraries.

/i

One command-line option you'll almost certainly want to use is /i. The /i option is used to specify which Installer package should be used for the current session. For example, if you had an Installer package named Test1.msi on your d: drive, you could install it with the following simple command line:

```
msiexec /I d:\Test1.msi
```

NOTE   The command-line options for the Windows Installer aren't case-sensitive. That is, both /i and /I have the same effect.

If you know what it is, you can use the product code in place of the package name. For example, this is a valid command line for the installation of Microsoft Office 2000 Premium:

```
msiexec /i {00000409-78E1-11D2-B60F-006097C998E7}
```

Of course, using the product code is only useful for products that the Installer already knows about (that is, those which have already been installed at least once on your computer).

/a

To do an administrative install, you substitute the /a switch for the /i switch:

```
msiexec /a d:\Test1.msi
```

Unlike the /i switch, the /a switch must be followed by a package name, not by a product code.

/x

To uninstall a product, you can use the /x switch with either a package name or a product code. You may find it more useful to use the product code when you're uninstalling a product, because that can be easier to find than the package name. You can get the product code from places like the Installer automation model (see Chapter 9). For example, this command line tells the Windows Installer to remove Microsoft Office 2000 Premium:

```
msiexec /x {00000409-78E1-11D2-B60F-006097C998E7}
```

/f

To repair a product, you call msiexec with the /f switch (think of "fix" as a mnemonic for this). Here's the command to reinstall Microsoft Office 2000 Premium, rewriting all files:

```
msiexec /fa {00000409-78E1-11D2-B60F-006097C998E7}
```

The /f switch can take either a package name or a product code. It also requires you to supply one or more options directly after the /f. I'll discuss the available repair options in a later section.

/ju, /jm, /t and /g

You can also advertise a package without installing it. There are three possible forms to do this using the /j switch, which I'll show schematically:

```
msiexec /j[u|m] <package_name>
msiexec /j[u|m] <package_name> /t <transform>
msiexec /j[u|m] <package_name> /g <language_id>
```

In this case, the brackets mean to choose one of the items separated by vertical bars.

You use /ju to advertise a package to a single user, or you can use /jm to advertise it to every user on the machine. The /t switch can be used to specify a transform to apply before advertising (see Chapter 11, "Merges and Transforms," for more information on transforms). The /g switch supplies a language ID for the advertisement. So, you could advertise the hypothetical Test1.msi to all users with this command line:

```
msiexec /jm e:\Test1.msi
```

/l

The /l switch can be used to create a log file from the Installer's actions. It takes two parameters: a list of options and the name of the log file. For example, this command line logs status and error messages to a file in the c:\temp folder:

```
msiexec /i e:\Test1.msi /lie c:\temp\Test1.log
```

Logging can be very useful if you're having problems with the installed application and want to know exactly what the Windows Installer is doing. I'll discuss both the available logging switches and reading log files later in this chapter.

/m

If your network uses SMS, you may want to specify the /m switch. This switch tells the Installer to generate an SMS-format .mif file while it's acting. You need to specify the filename, as in this example:

```
msiexec /I e:\Test1.msi /m c:\Test1.mif
```

Note that /m is different from the /jm combination used to advertise a product on a per-machine basis.

/p

To install a patch package, you specify the /p switch rather than the /i switch like so:

```
msiexec /p e:\Test1_patch.msi
```

I'll discuss patch packages in Chapter 10, "Creating and Using Patch Packages."

/q

The /q option is used to set the user interface level. There are six possible values for this switch:

/q ROM /qn   Specifies a "silent" installation, without any user interface.

/qn+   Displays only a modal dialog box at the end of the installation.

/qb   Displays the basic user interface, which includes only progress and error messages.

/qb-   Displays the basic interface without a modal dialog box at the end of the installation.

/qr   Displays the reduced user interface, which is a subset of the dialog boxes used in the installation plus a modal dialog box at the end of installation.

/qf   Displays the full user interface (see Chapter 5, "The Installer User Interface," for details on creating a user interface).

/y

The /y switch is used to self-register a Windows library at the end of the installation. For example, this command line would call the DLLRegisterServer entry point in MyServer.dll:

```
msiexec /y c:\Program Files\MyApp\MyServer.dll
```

/z

The /z switch is exactly the reverse of the /y switch. That is, it calls the DLLUnRegisterServer entry point. So for the previous case, the corresponding command line for uninstall might be as follows:

```
msiexec /z MyServer.dll
```

<table>
<tr><td>**WARNING**</td><td>Generally speaking, you should not use the /y or /z command-line options. It's preferable to deal with registering and unregistering servers using the Registry tables within the Installer package itself.</td></tr>
</table>

Using Multiple Command-Line Options

Of course, not every one of these command-line switches can be used together.

- /i, /x, /f, /j, /a, /p, /y, and /z should not be used together.
- The exception to the first rule is that /p and /a can be used together to patch an existing administrative installation.
- /t and /g can only be used with /j.

Table 2.1 summarizes the command-line switches for msiexec.exe.

T A B L E   2 . 1 :   Windows Installer Command-Line Switches

Switch	Meaning
/a <msifile>	Create an administrative install point from the specified Installer package.
/i <msifile>	Install application from the specified Installer package.
/qn	Don't display any user interface.
/qb	Display only progress and error messages.
/qr	Display "reduced" user interface, without collecting user information.
/qf	Display the full setup user interface.
/qn+	Display only a modal dialog box at the end of the setup
/qb+	Display progress and error messages, and a modal dialog box at the end of the setup.
/j[u|m] <package> /t <transform> /g <language ID>	Advertise the package without actually installing it.
/f<options>	Repair rather than install the program.
/x <msifile>	Uninstall the specified Installer package.
/l<actions> <logfile>	Log the specified actions to the specified log file.
/p <patch>	Apply a patch package.
/m <file>	Create an SMS .mif file.

Repair Options

When you invoke `msiexec` with the /f switch to repair an application, you need to supply a set of options to tell the Windows Installer what repairs to make. These options are specified with the letters listed in Table 2.2.

T A B L E 2 . 2 : Windows Installer Repair Options

Option	Meaning
a	Reinstall all files, regardless of checksum or version. The Installer database can store checksums that can be used to quickly check whether a file has been corrupted.
c	Reinstall if a file is missing or corrupt. This switch only operates on files with a checksum stored in the installation databases's File table.
d	Reinstall if a file is missing, or a different version is installed.
e	Reinstall if a file is missing, or an earlier or equal version is installed.
m	Recreate all Registry keys that go to the HKEY_LOCAL_MACHINE or HKEY_CLASSES_ROOT Registry keys. Also rewrite all information from the Class, Verb, PublishComponent, ProgID, MIME, Icon, Extension, and AppID tables. Reinstall all qualified components.
o	Reinstall if a file is missing, or an earlier version is installed.
p	Reinstall if a file is missing, or verify it against the source if it is present.
s	Reinstall all shortcuts and icons, replacing any that are present or cached.
u	Recreate all Registry keys that go to the HKEY_CURRENT_USER or HKEY_USERS Registry keys.
v	Force use of the package on the source media rather than any locally cached copy.

If you're writing your own interface for the repair functionality, you may wish to group multiple options together. For example, Figure 2.3 shows the dialog box that Microsoft Office 2000 Premium presents when you invoke the repair functionality of the Windows Installer.

This user interface interacts with the repair options this way:

- If the user selects Reinstall Office, the Windows Installer is called with the options /fecums.
- If the user selects Repair Errors but does not check Restore Shortcuts, the Windows Installer is called with the options /focum.
- If the user selects Repair Errors and checks Restore Shortcuts, the Windows Installer is called with the options /focums.

You'll see how to use the MsiReinstallFeature and MsiReinstallProduct API calls to perform repair operations without directly invoking `msiexec` in Chapter 8, "Using the Installer API."

FIGURE 2.3
Repair options in Microsoft Office 2000

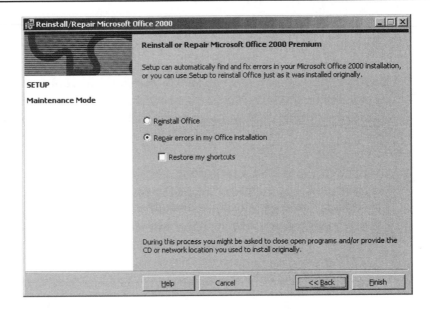

Setting Public Properties

During its operation, the Windows Installer uses global variables called *properties*. The Windows Installer supports two classes of properties:

Private properties   Have their value supplied from within the Installer database, and cannot be modified directly by the user.

Public properties   Have their default value supplied from within the Installer database, but this value can be changed by the user.

Some public properties are changed as the user interacts with the user interface during program installation. But there's another way to change public properties. You can also supply a value for public properties on the command line when you invoke the `msiexec` program. For example, this command line installs `Test1.msi` and sets the value of the public property OPTIONS equal to "Full":

```
msiexec /i e:\Test1.msi OPTIONS="Full"
```

The value to be assigned to the public property must be included between quote marks as shown. You can also clear the value of a public property by setting it equal to an empty string on the command line:

```
msiexec /i e:\Test1.msi OPTIONS=""
```

To include embedded quotes in a property value, double the quote marks:

```
msiexec /i e:\Test1.msi OPTIONS="String ""With"" Quotes"
```

The Windows Installer employs a convention to distinguish public properties from private properties. Public property names can only contain uppercase letters and numbers. Private property names can contain upper- and lowercase letters and numbers, and must contain at least one lowercase letter. So, if you see a lowercase letter in a property name, it's a private property. Otherwise, it's a public property.

Reading Installer Logs

When you use the /l switch to force the creation of a log file, you need to supply additional options to tell the Installer what it should log. Table 2.3 lists the possible logging options.

TABLE 2.3:   Command-Line Logging Options

Option	Meaning
a	Log start of actions.
c	Log initial user interface parameters.
e	Log error messages.
i	Log status messages.
m	Log out-of-memory and fatal exit messages
o	Log out-of-disk-space messages.
p	Log properties.
r	Log action-specific records.
u	Log user requests.
v	Log verbose output.
w	Log non-fatal warnings.
!	Flush each line to the log as it's written.
*	Log everything in non-verbose format.

To log all messages in verbose format, use the command-line option /l*v.

Logs can grow quite large, particularly if you're using the verbose format. To take an extreme example, a full verbose log for a Microsoft Office 2000 Premium installation can easily be 3MB or more.

WARNING   Log files are written to the user's temp folder and are *not* removed when the Installer is finished. If you've run the Installer multiple times, you may want to clean out your temp folder to reclaim space.

In the remainder of this section, I'll show some typical messages from the Windows Installer log (in this case, from an installation of Microsoft Office 2000 Premium). Not surprisingly, there's a lot of information buried in the large amount of data provided by verbose logging.

Somewhere near the top of the log file you'll find two lines resembling these:

```
MSI (c) (85:3D): Original package ==> \\BIGREDBARN\SHARED\O2K\data1.msi
MSI (c) (85:3D): Package we're running from ==> C:\WINDOWS\TEMP\44ca2a2.msi
```

These lines list the Installer package that was invoked from the command line; they also list the Installer package that's actually being run. The Installer always makes a copy to work with. This provides a copy that can be modified (for example, if a transform is applied to the installation) and also ensures that the Installer database will be present later if functionality such as install-on-demand is invoked.

You'll also find lines such as this in the log file:

```
MSI (c) (85:3D): Note: 1: 2262 2: AdminProperties 3: -2147287038
```

Such lines are Windows Installer messages. To interpret them, you'll need a copy of the help file msi.chm from the Windows Installer SDK. The number following the 1: is the error number (in this case, 2262) and the remaining items are numbered arguments that fill in the error message. You need to do this parsing yourself. For example, if you look up the Windows Installer Error Messages in the Appendix of the msi.chm help file, you'll find that 2262 translates as "Stream does not exist: [2]. System error: [3]." So, in this case, the expanded error message is "Stream does not exist: AdminProperties. System error –2147287038."

Custom actions lead to log sections like this:

```
MSI (c) (85:3D): Doing action: IsArabicOSAction
Action start 16:08:35: IsArabicOSAction.
MSI (c) (85:3D): Creating MSIHANDLE (4) of type 790542 for thread -451011
Action ended 16:08:35: IsArabicOSAction. Return value 1.
```

This shows that a custom action named IsArabicOSAction was invoked, required the creation of an MSIHANDLE object, and returned a value of 1. As a developer, knowing the actual return values from custom actions can greatly assist in debugging. This is especially valuable because there's no way to single-step through the installation process; all you can do is run it and see what happens. You'll learn more about custom actions in Chapter 6.

Sometimes you'll see error messages without the parameters:

```
Internal Error 2898: Please contact product support for assistance.
Internal Error 2826: Please contact product support for assistance.
```

Generally, this means that there was an error in the format of the Installer package itself. You're supposed to catch such errors with validation before you ship your product, but particularly in the early months of the Windows Installer, it's not unusual for shipping Installer packages to have problems. You'll learn more about validation in Chapter 13, "Validating Installer Databases."

When the Installer assigns a value to a variable, that information is also written to the log. For example, take a look at the following:

```
MSI (c) (85:3D): SOURCEDIR ==> \\BIGREDBARN\SHARED\O2K\
```

Another chunk of the log file will show you, on a feature-by-feature basis, what the Installer intends to do. For example, here's a line from a log:

```
MSI (c) (85:3D): Feature: EXCELFiles; ↵
Installed: Absent;   Request: Local;   Action: Local
```

This line says that the feature named ExcelFiles has been determined to be absent (because its keyfile wasn't found on the target machine), that the user has requested this component to be installed locally, and that, therefore, it will be installed locally. A *keyfile* is a file that the Installer checks to determine the status of a feature or component. You'll learn more about keyfiles in Chapter 3, "Basic Installer Concepts." The log file also contains similar information for components.

If you're generating a verbose log, every single file copy and Registry operation will also be logged. For example, look at this:

```
InstallFiles: Copying file: MSCAL.OCX (106496bytes) ↵
  to C:\Program Files\Microsoft Office\Office\
```

If things are ending up in unexpected places, this section of the log will help you figure out what went wrong.

Just before any reboot, the Installer writes the current values of all properties out to the log file. Here's a small portion of this section from a Microsoft Office 2000 Premium installation:

```
Property(C): Manufacturer = Microsoft Corporation
Property(C): ProductCode = {00000409-78E1-11D2-B60F-006097C998E7}
Property(C): ProductName = Microsoft Office 2000 Premium↵
Property(C): ProductVersion = 9.00.2720
```

Once again, having this information can help immensely if you're trying to debug a failed installation at a user's office.

NOTE   In addition to the Installer log, the Windows Installer writes a message to the Windows NT event log whenever an installation is completed. If there is no event log (which will be the case for software installed on Windows 9x), then the Installer writes to a file named `msievent.log` in the user's temp folder instead.

chapter 3

Basic Installer Concepts

- Products, Packages, and Databases

- Features and Components

- Using Cabinet Files

- File Versioning Rules

- Qualified Components

- Transitive Components

- The Summary Information Stream

Now that you've seen how to invoke the Windows Installer, it's time to look a bit further inside its operations. In this chapter, I'll introduce you to the way the Installer keeps track of things. This involves understanding the distinctions between packages and databases, and between components and features. First, I'll show you how to identify components, and then I will talk about other information that the Installer stores in the summary information stream of packages.

Understanding packages, databases, components, and features is the first step to preparing your own application for distribution via the Windows Installer. When you've just finished developing a product, it may seem like a single seamless whole to you. But part of the power of the Windows Installer lies in its ability to install only the parts of an application that a user needs. By learning the rules for breaking up an application, you'll be able to make use of this power.

Products, Packages, and Databases

At the very top level, the Windows Installer distinguishes between products, packages, and databases. In general, a product comes in a package, and a package contains a database. In the Windows Installer world, you need to start thinking of "product," "package," and "database" as specific technical terms. For example, if you happen to have a copy of Microsoft Office 2000 handy, the terms would apply this way:

- The *product* is the particular piece of software. In this case, that might be the U.S. English version of Microsoft Office 2000 Professional.
- The *package* is everything that the Installer needs to do its job of installing the software. In this case, that would be the contents of the CD-ROMs inside the Office box.
- The *database* is a particular file that contains instructions for the Installer. For Office 2000, that's a file named DATA1.MSI.

In the next few pages, I'll look at these three ideas in a bit more detail. You'll see how all three pieces fit together to help the Installer in its job of setting up an application on the user's computer.

Products

A product is anything that the Windows Installer can install. If you've worked in the software industry for a while, you might have run across the concept of *a stock-keeping unit (SKU)*. A SKU (generally pronounced "skew") is a particular box that might be on the shelf of your local computer store—for example, Microsoft Office 2000 Professional in English. One way to think of a Windows Installer product is as a unique SKU, as something that can be packaged in a box and put on the shelf.

Products are identified to the Windows Installer by unique product codes. A *product code* (like many other identifiers in the Windows Installer world) is a Globally Unique Identifier, or GUID. I'll show you how to generate GUIDs in a few pages.

If you ship multiple distinct versions of your product, you need to assign different product codes to each version. So, again taking an example from the Microsoft world, the English and Japanese versions of Microsoft Office 2000 Professional have different product codes.

You're not required to change the product code every time the product changes, though. If relatively minor changes are made to the product, you can keep the same product code. What's a minor change? Anything that you'd identify by only changing the minor version number of a product is probably minor enough that you can keep the same product code.

When in doubt, update the product code when you change a product. It can't hurt, and there are so many possible GUIDs that we won't run out even if you use up a few unnecessarily.

Packages

A package is a set of files that contains instructions for the Windows Installer. The file in a package that the Installer can read is distinguished by the file extension .msi. Like products, packages are identified by unique package codes. Package codes are also GUIDs. However, any change to a package, no matter how minor, requires generating a new package code. If you fail to follow this rule, the Windows Installer might use an old cached copy of your package instead of the new changed one, and you'll be left wondering why upgraded components weren't installed.

A single Installer package can contain the information for multiple products. For example, if you create an Installer package that installs either the English or the French version of your product, depending on the choices the user makes on the user interface of the installation program, you'd have a single package code but two product codes.

The .msi file in a package is a COM structured storage file. That is, it can contain multiple streams of information. These streams can include the following:

- An Installer database
- A summary information stream
- .cab files containing components to install
- Source files for the installation
- Transforms

If you like, you can put everything needed for an installation in the .msi file, and have a package consisting of a single file. On the other extreme, the .msi file can contain only the Installer database and the summary information stream, with the other package components stored in external files.

Sometimes the .msi file itself is referred to as an Installer package. While technically the package also includes any external files that go with the .msi file, this usually doesn't cause any confusion.

Databases

The Windows Installer is almost completely data driven. The information used to create setup dialogs, to choose which files and Registry keys to write, to know what actions to take in what order, and so on, is all stored in tables in a relational database. This database is called the Installer database, and it's one of the streams inside the .msi file contained in the Installer package.

Figure 3.1 shows a part of an Installer database using a tool called Microsoft Orca. Orca is a simple tool included in the Windows Installer SDK that is used for editing Installer databases. You'll learn more about Orca and alternative database editing tools in Chapter 12, "Installer Editing Tools." I'll use Orca for many of the screen shots in this book because it's readily available and sports a simple interface.

FIGURE 3.1
A view of an Installer database

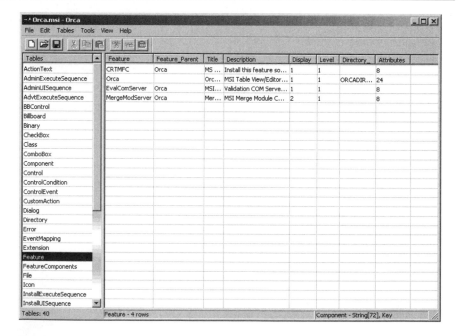

In this particular case, Orca is displaying its own Installer database. The left-hand side of the window shows all of the tables in the Installer database, and the right-hand side shows the rows in the currently selected table (here, the list of features for Orca).

You'll learn more about the structure of the Installer database in Chapter 4, "A Guide to the Installer Database."

Generating GUIDs

Product codes and package codes are two of the types of GUIDs that are used by the Windows Installer, but there are others. When you're working with the Installer, you'll find that you have a need to generate GUIDs.

GUIDs are generated from a formula that uses the current date and time, a record of how many GUIDs have already been generated on the computer, and the network card address (or other hardware-related information if the computer doesn't have a network card). GUIDs are 128-bit integers, and you can assume that they really are unique.

The most obvious way to generate GUIDs is with the GUIDGEN utility that ships as part of Visual Studio. If you've got Visual Basic 6.0, you'll find this utility in the Tools\IDGen folder on your CD-ROM. If you've got the entire Visual Studio 6.0 set, it's on CD 3 in the Common\Tools\VB\IDGen folder, or on Disk 1 in the \Common\Tools folder. Figure 3.2 shows GUIDGEN in action.

FIGURE 3.2
Generating GUIDs with
GUIDGEN

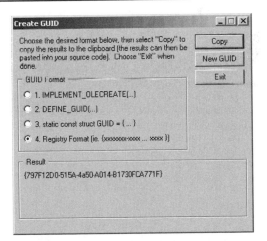

The Windows Installer uses GUIDs in what GUIDGEN calls "Registry Format," a string of 32 hexadecimal digits hyphenated in a standardized way. But the Windows Installer requires that all of the letters in a GUID (hex digits A through F) be capitalized, while GUIDGEN delivers these letters in lower case. So, if you use GUIDGEN to generate GUIDs for the Windows Installer, you'll need to do some editing.

If you're going to be generating a lot of GUIDs, it's simple to write a tool to provide them in whatever format you desire. The frmGUID form in the BasicConcepts.vbp sample project demonstrates how you can do this using two Windows API calls:

CoCreateGuid   The API call that creates GUIDs. This is the same API call that's used by programs such as GUIDGEN.

StringFromGUID2   The API call to convert a binary GUID to the Registry format.

When you click the Create button on frmGUID, it calls code to create a GUID. The only tricky part is that StringFromGUID2 returns a Unicode string, and of course, the Visual Basic user interface is relentlessly ANSI. But that's easily handled with the built-in StrConv function. Of course, you can use the Ucase function to convert any lowercase characters to uppercase. Listing 3.1 shows the code necessary to generate a GUID in the correct format for the Windows Installer.

Listing 3.1: Generating a GUID and Formatting It for the Windows Installer

```
' Binary storage used by a GUID
Private Type GUID
    Data1 As Long
    Data2 As Integer
    Data3 As Integer
    Data4(7) As Byte
End Type

' The CoCreateGuid API call generates binary GUIDs
Private Declare Function CoCreateGuid Lib "OLE32.dll" _
 (pGuid As GUID) As Long

' StringFromGUID2 prettifies GUIDs for human beings
Private Declare Function StringFromGUID2 _
 Lib "OLE32.dll" (ByRef rguid As GUID, _
 ByVal lpsz As String, _
 ByVal cbMax As Long) As Long

Private Sub cmdCreate_Click()
    ' Generate a fresh GUID in the format that
    ' the Windows Installer uses

    Dim tGUID As GUID
    Dim lngRet As Long
    Dim strGUID As String
    Dim lngChars As Long
```

```
' Generate a GUID in binary format
lngRet = CoCreateGuid(tGUID)
' If lngRet is nonzero, something
' serious went wrong
If lngRet <> 0 Then
    txtGUID = "#ERROR"
Else
    ' Initialize string storage
    strGUID = Space(255)
    ' Convert the binary GUID to a string
    lngChars = StringFromGUID2(tGUID, _
     strGUID, Len(strGUID))
    ' Convert the unicode string to ANSI
    strGUID = StrConv(strGUID, vbFromUnicode)
    ' Chop it off at the first null
    strGUID = Left(strGUID, lngChars - 1)
    ' Upper case it and place it on the form
    txtGUID = UCase(strGUID)
End If

End Sub
```

Features and Components

One of the key distinctions made by the Windows Installer is the distinction made between features and components. When you view an application from the point of view of the user and divide it into sensible chunks, you're specifying features. When you view that same application from the point of view of the developer and divide it into sensible chunks, you're specifying components.

A concrete example will make the distinction more clear. Suppose you've created a Visual Basic application that is designed to serve up random quotes from a database. You've implemented an ActiveX server that can retrieve a quote from the database and make it available as an object. You've also built two ActiveX clients for these objects. One inserts the quote as the tagline for an e-mail message, and the other displays it on screen in a "quote of the day" dialog box. You want to allow users to install either or both of these clients to use the application. Of course, being a good developer, you've also written a help file.

A reasonable set of features for this application would be as follows:

- E-Mail Taglines
- Quote of the Day
- Online Help

In contrast, a set of components for this same application could look like this:

- Database
- QuoteServer
- EmailClient
- QOTDClient
- Help File

Within the Installer database, there's a table of features and a table of components. There's also a table called FeatureComponents that provides a many-to-many mapping between features and components. It is this table that allows the Installer to determine which components to install based on which features the user chooses to install. Table 3.1 shows what the FeatureComponents table would look like for the hypothetical quote application.

T A B L E 3 . 1 : Sample FeatureComponents Table

Feature	Component
E-Mail Taglines	Database
E-Mail Taglines	QuoteServer
E-Mail Taglines	EmailClient
Quote of the Day	Database
Quote of the Day	QuoteServer
Quote of the Day	QOTDClient
Online Help	Help File

Note that some components are shared by more than one feature. In fact, it's even possible for components to be shared by features in more than one product.

Feature Hierarchies

The Windows Installer also introduces the concept of a feature parent. Each feature may be associated with another feature, its feature parent. Thus features can be arranged into a hierarchy. For example, suppose we wanted to make it easy to install both user interface components of the quote sample application. One way to do this would be to define a new feature named User Interface Components, and make that the feature parent of both the E-Mail Taglines and Quote of the Day components.

The user interface supported by the Windows Installer includes a control named the SelectionTree that can use this hierarchical information to automatically display features in a tree. You'll learn more about this and other user interface components in Chapter 5, "The Installer User Interface."

Generally, when a user uninstalls feature 'X', the Windows Installer automatically uninstalls all features that have feature 'X' as a feature parent. . However, such child features might not be entirely uninstalled if they include components that are also used by other features. This helps prevent uninstallation from accidentally breaking other applications.

Rules for Components

Like products and packages, components are identified by GUIDs; in this case, they are called component codes. For the Windows Installer to deliver the benefits promised in Chapter 1, it's important that the component identified by a GUID never change. If {564A5487-C378-4DA1-BFF2-A05C4E463413} identifies a particular version of the QuoteServer component, for example, than that GUID must always identify *exactly* that version of the QuoteServer component.

The Windows Installer determines whether a component is already present on a computer by using the key path of that component. A *key path* is a unique identifier for the component. It can be a file, a folder, a Registry key, or an ODBC data source. No two components can have exactly the same key path.

The Windows Installer enforces a number of rules on components:

- No applications that share a component can require different versions of any of the resources (files, Registry keys, and so on) included in that component. This is another way of saying that components are invariant.
- All files in a component must be installed to a single folder. Files can't be installed to subfolders without being contained in separate components.
- A component can include at most one COM server. If a component includes a COM server, that file must be the key path for the component.
- A component can include at most one file that is the target for a Start Menu or Desktop shortcut.
- No file can ever be included in more than one component. This rule applies not only across components in a single Installer database, but across products, versions, and even manufacturers. If you must include a file in a different component than it's already included in, you must change the name of the file. The same rule applies to Registry entries, shortcuts, and other resources.
- If a component is not 100 percent backwards compatible with a previous version, it must be assigned a new component code. If backwards compatibility hasn't been completely tested, you must assign a new component code.

- Because changing a component code amounts to defining a new component, when you change the component code, you must change the name of every file, Registry key, shortcut, and other resource in the component.

- Similarly, if you change the name of a file, you must change the component code for the component that contains that file, and then change the name of every other file and resource in that component.

- The version of a component is determined entirely by the version of the key path file. If the computer already contains a newer version of the key path file, the component will not be installed. The version of non–key path files in the component won't even be checked by the Installer.

Identifying Components

With all those rules, determining what should be a component can be a bit tricky. The Windows Installer team has recommended this process for identifying components:

1. List every file, folder, Registry key, and other resource required by the product.

2. Identify files, folders, Registry keys, and other resources that are shared across products and available in merge modules. You must not include any of these resources in the components that you author. Rather, you must merge the appropriate merge modules into your Installer package. You'll learn about merge modules in Chapter 11, "Merges and Transforms."

3. Define a new component for each .exe, .dll, and .ocx file in your application. Designate these files as the key path files for their components. Generate a component code for each of these components.

4. Define a new component for each .hlp or .chm file in your application. Designate these files as the key path files for their components. Generate a component code for each of these components. Add the associated .cnt or .chi files to these components.

5. Define a new component for every remaining file that serves as the target of a shortcut. Designate these files as the key path files for their components. Generate a component code for each of these components.

6. Group the remaining resources by the folder they're installed to. If there's a chance that files may ship separately in the future, put them in separate folders. Create one component for each folder. Designate any file in the folder as the key path file. Generate a component code for each of these components.

7. Add Registry keys to the components that contain the files those keys are used by.

There's a trade-off in creating components. The fewer components you create, the better the performance of the Installer. The more components you create, the more thoroughly the Installer will check file versions.

If you need to have the version of every file installed checked, you must define an individual component for each file.

Using Cabinet Files

The files that the Windows Installer works with can either be uncompressed or compressed. Uncompressed files are stored on the source media in exactly the same format that will be used on the target media when the files are installed. Compressed files are stored in cabinet files, which can contain many files in a compact format. By default, a cabinet file has the extension `.cab`. In this section, you'll learn how to work with cabinet files.

NOTE   Cabinet files are similar to other archive formats such as `.zip`, `.arc`, or `.lha`. The major difference appears to be that Microsoft invented cabinet files and therefore controls their format.

Creating Cabinet Files

If you're going to work with cabinet files, you should obtain a copy of the Microsoft Cabinet Software Development Kit (SDK). This SDK contains all of the tools and documentation necessary for the cabinet file developer, and can be obtained online from the MSDN Online Web Workshop at `msdn.microsoft.com/workshop/management/cab/cabdl.asp`.

The basic tool for creating cabinet files is `makecab.exe`. Because the Visual Basic Package and Deployment Wizard uses this tool, it's included in a complete installation of Visual Basic 6.0. You'll find it at `Microsoft Visual Studio\VB98\Wizards\PDWizard\makecab.exe`. Although `makecab.exe` ships with Visual Basic, its documentation does not. To get the full documentation for `makecab.exe`, you'll need to download the Cabinet SDK.

Creating a cabinet file using `makecab.exe` is a two-step process. In the first step, you create a `.ddf` file. DDF stands for "Diamond Directive File," Diamond being the original code name for the Microsoft cabinet technology. In its simplest form, a `.ddf` file is just a list of filenames. For example, you might create a file named `test.ddf`:

```
MyServer.dll
MyClient.exe
MyClient.hlp
```

To turn this list of files into a cabinet file, you invoke `makecab.exe` from the command line:

```
makecab /V /f test.ddf
```

The /V switch specifies verbose output, which is useful when you're trying to understand what `makecab.exe` is doing. You can also include directives in the `.ddf` file to control the type of compression, the distribution of the files among cabinet files, and so on. By default, a cabinet file named `1.cab` will be created in a folder named Disk1.

Viewing the Contents of a Cabinet File

If you're working in Windows 2000 or Windows 98, viewing the contents of a cabinet file is easy: just double-click the file in Windows Explorer. It's this easy because these versions of Windows have built-in knowledge of the cabinet file format. Windows 2000 even integrates cabinet files into the Explorer tree. Figure 3.3 shows a cabinet file open in Windows 2000 Explorer.

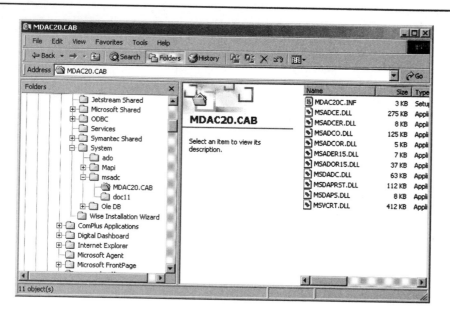

FIGURE 3.3
Browsing a cabinet file with
Windows 2000

For older Windows operating systems, Microsoft has released several graphical cabinet viewers over the years. The Cabinet SDK also includes a utility named `cabarc.exe` that can list the files within a cabinet file. However, I find that the shareware utility Win-Zip is more convenient than any of these alternatives. Starting with version 7.0, WinZip can display the contents of cabinet files. Figure 3.4 shows a cabinet file open in the Win-Zip interface.

FIGURE 3.4
Browsing a cabinet file with
WinZip

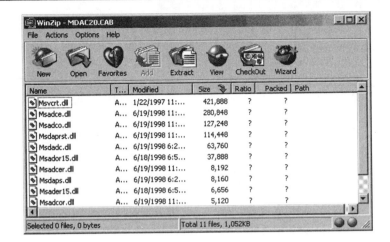

You can download a copy of the latest version of WinZip from www.winzip.com. If you use the shareware version, remember to send the registration fee to the shareware author.

Including a Cabinet File in a Package

The Windows Installer can use cabinet files in two ways. First, it can retrieve files from within a cabinet file that's located on the source media in the root of the source tree. You place such an external cabinet file on the source media just like any other file.

The second way you can use cabinet file is by including it as a separate stream within the .msi file that holds the Installer database. This is an internal cabinet file. Using an internal cabinet file makes particular sense when you're designing a setup to be downloaded from the Internet. By compressing all of the source files into a single cabinet file and then including that cabinet file as a stream within the .msi file, you can deliver your entire setup as one (probably large) file. This makes downloading simpler for the end user.

To insert a cabinet file as a stream in an .msi file, you can use the msidb tool. You'll learn more about msidb, which is part of the Installer SDK, in Chapter 12. Alternatively, you can use Installer API calls to create a new stream in the .msi file and read in the data from a cabinet file to that stream. I'll cover this technique in Chapter 8.

File Versioning Rules

Suppose your installation source contains a file named newstuff.dll, and the Installer finds a copy of newstuff.dll already on the user's hard drive. How would you decide whether to overwrite the existing copy on the hard drive with a new copy from the source media? Your first idea might be to compare file dates; you would then overwrite if the copy in the source media was newer. A more sophisticated version of this technique is to look at the internal file version information, and overwrite if the copy in the source media has a higher version.

The Windows Installer uses an even more complex algorithm when deciding whether to keep an existing file or install a new copy. It takes into account not just the file dates and the version, but the languages involved as well. Here's the set of rules the Windows Installer follows:

Highest version wins.   All other things being equal, the file with the highest version number wins, whether that's the file on the hard drive or the file in the source media.

Any version is higher than no version at all.   If the copy in the source media contains version information, and the copy on the hard drive has no version information, Windows Installer chooses the one with the version information.

Favor the new language.   All other things being equal, if the file being installed is localized for a different language than the file on the computer, Windows Installer uses the copy with the language that matches the product being installed.

Meet the product's needs for multiple languages.   If both copies support multiple languages, Windows Installer ignores the common languages and uses the copy that supports the most languages out of the set of languages that the product uses.

Keep the maximum number of languages.   If the copies differ in the number of languages they support and both support all the languages that the product needs, Windows Installer keeps the copy that supports the most languages.

Treat non-versioned files as user data.   If there is no version information for either copy, Windows Installer compares the file creation date and the last modification date for the file on the computer. If the modification date is later than the creation date, Windows Installer assumes this file has been customized by the user and does not overwrite it. Otherwise, it installs a new copy.

Companion files go along with the versioned file.   It's possible to mark a file within the Installer database that does not include version information as a companion file to a file that does include version information. In this case, the companion file is installed if the other file is installed. There is one exception to this rule, though. If the companion file is not present on the target machine, it's installed even if the versioned file is not installed.

It's a good thing that these rules match the way most developers would like installations to behave because there's no way for you to change them. Of course, you can pervert their intention if you feel you must. One way to guarantee that a file from the source media is installed is to set its version string in the File table to 65535.65535.65535.65535, which is the maximum version number that the Windows Installer accommodates. Beware, though: if you do this, you'll never be able to use the Windows Installer to replace that copy of the file with a new version.

> **WARNING**   Although the version information for existing files is read directly from those files, the version information for files in your installation is read from the Version column in the File table of the Installer database. If you update your Installer package to contain a new version of a file, you must remember to update the Version column to avoid unexpected behavior. The Installer will not automatically perform this update for you!

Qualified Components

Qualified components are a concept that the Windows Installer SDK makes a good deal more opaque than necessary. In the `msi.chm` help file, they're described as "a method of single-level indirection, similar to a pointer." That's true, but it doesn't give you much of a hint about why you'd like to use qualified components.

The easiest way to understand qualified components is to consider some of the problems of localized software. Suppose you've created a program that uses a file named `tips.txt` to hold "tip of the day" information that the user can choose to display. Being a developer of software for the global market, you've had `tips.txt` translated into five different languages. And being a good user of the Windows Installer, you've chosen to advertise this component, rather than install it, so that it doesn't take up disk space unless the user chooses to view tips.

Now, think about the code within your product at the time when the user chooses to turn on the tips and you need to install the advertised file. The Windows Installer provides an API call named MsiProvideComponent that, given a component code (the GUID for a component), will install that component.

If this was your only choice for installing components, the logic of your code might look like this (of course, this is pseudocode, not actual Visual Basic code):

```
If Language = English Then
    Call MsiProvideComponent(EnglishGUID)
ElseIf Language = French Then
    Call MsiProvideComponent(FrenchGUID)
```

```
ElseIf Language = German Then
    Call MsiProvideComponent(GermanGUID)
ElseIf Language = Japanese Then
    Call MsiProvideComponent(JapaneseGUID)
ElseIf Language = Spanish Then
    Call MsiProviderComponent(SpanishGUID)
```

Code based on this pseudocode would get the job done, but there's a better alternative, and that's where qualified components come in. The Windows Installer provides another API call named MsiProvideQualifiedComponent. This API call takes a component category code (another GUID) and a text qualifier and uses them to find the actual component to install. Using MsiProvideQualifiedComponent would reduce the pseudocode to the following line:

```
Call MsiProvideQualifiedComponent(CategoryGUID, Language)
```

That's much simpler, of course, and it also won't need to be modified if you add a sixth language, so long as you put the new language's tips files into the Installer database.

MsiProvideQualifiedComponent works by using three columns in the Publish-Component table:

The ComponentID column   Contains a component category code. Note that this is *not* a component code.

The Qualifier column   Contains a string that's the qualifier.

The Component_ column   Contains the actual component code to be returned when you use that combination of ComponentID and Qualifier.

I'll show you an actual example of using MsiProvideQualifiedComponent when I discuss the Installer API in Chapter 8.

Transitive Components

Transitive components are regular components that are arranged in mutually exclusive groups. The simplest example of a transitive component is a library that has different versions for Windows 95 and Windows NT. When you install the product, it installs either the Windows 95 or the Windows NT version, depending on the current operating system, but not both.

What happens if the user upgrades from Windows 95 to Windows NT after installing the product? Well, in the old days (pre-Windows Installer), the answer was simple: the product stops working, because the wrong library is installed. With the Windows Installer, you can invoke msiexec with the /fm switch, and it will fix the problems.

The Component table inside the Installer database lists all of the components and their component codes. It also has two other columns that are important for transitive components: Attributes and Condition. The Attributes column is made up of a series of bits, one of which identifies transitive components. The Condition column provides a Boolean condition that the Installer evaluates, installing the component only if the condition is true.

When a component is marked as transitive, the Windows Installer re-evaluates the Condition column on a reinstall. If the Condition is true, the Installer installs the component. If the Condition is false, the Installer removes the component, even if other products use that component (that way, the first product to be reinstalled gets fixed even if other products aren't reinstalled).

If a component isn't marked as transitive, reinstalls restore the component to whatever state is was left in at the end of the original installation. That is, the Condition column is not re-evaluated.

In addition to operating system changes, you can use transitive components to handle other machine upgrades, such as installation of a better video card or more memory, if your application contains components that can take better advantage of the new hardware.

The Summary Information Stream

As I mentioned earlier, .msi files are a type of file known as COM structured storage, which can include multiple streams of information within a single file. COM defines a standard stream named the summary information stream. The Windows Installer uses this stream to hold summary information about the application that is being installed.

The summary information stream includes 17 standard properties. For some of these, the Installer fills in an obvious value. For others, the standard from the Installer is less obvious. Table 3.2 lists these standard properties and their contents in an .msi file.

TABLE 3.2: Summary Information Stream Properties

Property	Value
Title	The literal string "Installation Database".
Subject	Set to the value of the ProductName property.
Author	Set to the value of the Manufacturer property.
Keywords	Free-form list of keywords.

TABLE 3.2:   Summary Information Stream Properties *(continued)*

Property	Value
Comments	The literal string "This Installer database contains the logic and data required to install <ProductName property>".
Template	Platform(s) and language(s) supported. For example, the Template property might be set to "Intel;Alpha;1033" for a program that supports both the US English Intel platform and the US English Alpha platform.
Last Saved By	Set to the value of the USERNAME property.
Revision Number	Set to the value of the package code for the package.
Last Printed	Date and time the Installer file was printed.
Create Time/Date	Date and time the Installer file was created.
Last Saved Time/Date	Date and time the Installer file was last saved.
Page Count	Minimum version of the Installer required, multiplied by 100 (so 100, for example, indicates that version 1.0 or higher of the Windows Installer Service is required to use this package).
Word Count	Indicates the type of the source file image. Values are a bit field, with bit 0 set to 1 for short file names and 0 for long file names; bit 1 set to 0 for uncompressed and 1 for compressed files; and bit 2 set to 0 on the original media and 4 on the results of an administrative installation.
Character Count	NULL
Creating Application	Software package used to build this package.
Security	Set to 2, which means that read-only is recommended.
Codepage	The number of the codepage used to display the summary information.

Tools that can edit .msi files will let you set these properties. Figure 3.5, for example, shows the summary properties of an .msi file open in the Orca editor. You can also read the summary information using the Windows Installer API calls MsiGetSummary-Information and MsiSummaryInfoGetProperty.

FIGURE 3.5

Editing summary informa-
tion for an .msi file

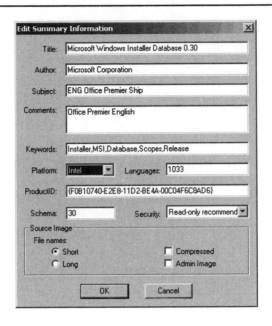

chapter 4

A Guide to the Installer Database

- Data Types

- Core Tables

- File Tables

- Registry Tables

- ODBC Tables

- Service Tables

- Locator Tables

- Program Information Tables

- Installation Procedure Tables

- User Interface Tables

- System Tables

- Patching Tables

As I've already mentioned, the Windows Installer is completely data-driven. The .msi file in an Installer package contains an Installer database, a relational database with a set of tables that dictate both the interface and functionality used for this particular installation.

In this chapter, I'll describe the structure of the Installer database. This database is quite complex and contains many interrelated tables. I'll try to give you a sense of what's in each table, as well as what related tables contain complementary information. For more details, you'll also want to refer to the Windows Installer SDK help file, msi.chm.

NOTE The Installer database uses a database engine designed expressly for the Windows Installer Service. You can't interact with this database from standard database engines such as Microsoft Jet or Microsoft SQL Server. You'll learn about some tools for manipulating Installer databases in Chapter 12, "Installer Editing Tools."

Data Types

One reason that the Windows Installer uses its own database engine is that it uses a wide variety of specialized data types. In fact, there are 25 data types that are used in an Installer database:

- Text
- UpperCase
- LowerCase
- Integer
- DoubleInteger
- Time/Date
- Identifier
- Property
- Filename
- WildCardFilename
- Path
- Paths
- AnyPath
- DefaultDir
- Formatted
- RegPath

- Template
- Condition
- GUID
- Version
- Language
- Binary
- CustomSource
- Cabinet
- Shortcut

Some of these data types (for example, Path and Paths) are quite similar to each other. By using this assortment of data types, though, the Windows Installer is able to impose quite a bit of "sanity checking" on the information entered in its tables. Before looking at the tables where these data types are used, I'll take a few pages to explain each one in detail.

Text

The Text data type is just what it sounds like—a string of characters. The Windows Installer supports Unicode text, so you can use any character you like in a Text column. Each Text column in an Installer database has a maximum length specification.

UpperCase

The UpperCase data type is the same as the Text data type, except that it's constrained to contain only uppercase characters.

LowerCase

The LowerCase data type is the same as the Text data type, except that it's constrained to contain only lowercase characters.

Integer

The Integer data type is a two-byte integer value. Normally it ranges from –32,767 to 32,767, although some Integer columns may be constrained to smaller ranges.

DoubleInteger

The DoubleInteger data type is a four-byte integer value. Normally it ranges from –2,147,483,647 to 2,147,483,647, although some DoubleInteger columns may be constrained to smaller ranges.

Time/Date

The Time/Date data type uses four bytes to store both time and date. Time is stored as hours, minutes, and 2-second intervals, while date is stored as month, day, and year. In the encoding used by the Installer, the year is an integer from 0 to 119, with 1980 being represented as year zero. Thus, the Installer can hold dates from January 1, 1980 to December 31, 2099.

Identifier

The Identifier data type is a constrained Text data type. An Identifier column may contain letters, digits, underscores, and periods. It must begin with either a letter or an underscore.

Property

The Property data type is an Identifer data type with an additional valid syntax. Besides the entire range of Identifiers, a column with the Property data type may contain values such as %Temp, which is interpreted as the value of an environment variable named Temp.

Filename

The Filename data type is used to contain filenames. These filenames cannot have path information associated with them; they are strictly the names of files. You must provide a short filename (the old 8+3 syntax) for any file. You may optionally provide a long filename by separating it from the short filename with a vertical bar. For example, all of these are valid in a column with the Filename data type:

```
Sugar.jpg
Sugarb~1.jpg
Sugarb~1.jpg|Sugar Bowl.jpg
```

WildCardFilename

The WildCardFilename data type is identical to the FileName data type, except that it may also contain the ? and * special characters, with ? matching exactly one character, and * representing zero or more characters.

Path

A column with the Path data type can contain either a UNC or a local path name, without any trailing slash. You may also enclose the name of an Installer property in square brackets as one portion of the path, and the Installer will make the appropriate substitution at runtime. Folder names within a path can conform to either the short or long naming convention. For example, any of these is a valid value for a column with the Path data type:

```
C:\Temp
C:\Program Files\My Company
\\MyServer\MyShare
C:\Program Files\[username]
```

Paths

A column with the Paths data type can hold one or more path names (conforming to the syntax of the Path data type), separated by semicolons.

AnyPath

A column with the AnyPath data type can hold anything that a column with the Path data type can. In addition, an AnyPath column can use a relative subpath. So, in addition to the examples shown under Path, these are valid for an AnyPath column:

```
\Temp
\Temp\Install
```

DefaultDir

The DefaultDir data type is used only in the Directory table (see the section on the core tables group later in this chapter). It can hold either a Filename or an Identifier.

Formatted

The Formatted data type is similar to the Text data type in that it can contain arbitrary strings of Unicode text. However, the Windows Installer performs a number of substitutions on special substrings of a Formatted column at runtime. This makes the Formatted data type a powerful way to adjust your installation to conform to different environments or user choices.

Here are the rules for the Formatted data type:

- Unmatched square brackets or curly braces are left unchanged.
- Substrings enclosed in square brackets are evaluated as property names. For example, if a Formatted column contains the text "[Property1]", then that portion of the text is replaced with the value of Property1 at runtime.
- Property evaluation is recursive. For example, suppose the value of the property named Property1 is "Property2". In this case, if a Formatted column contains the text "[[Property1]]", then that portion of the text is replaced with the value of Property2 at runtime (that is, the value of the value of Property1).

- Substrings enclosed in square brackets that are not property names are left unchanged.
- Substrings of the form [%variablename] are evaluated as environment variables at runtime.
- Substrings of the form [\x] are replaced with "x" at runtime. This provides a mechanism for quoting characters that would otherwise be treated as special characters.
- A substring enclosed in curly braces that does not contain any property names in square brackets is left unchanged at runtime.
- A substring enclosed in curly braces that contains property names in square brackets is replaced by the text with resolved substitutions and without the curly braces at runtime, if all of the square bracketed values can be resolved as actual property names. For example, if the value of Property1 is "dog" and the value of Property2 is "cat", then the string "{The [Property1] chased the [Property2]}" would be replaced by "The dog chased the cat" at runtime. If either Property1 or Property2 did not exist, the string would be left unchanged.
- The substring "[~]" is replaced by a null character at runtime. This is primarily useful for creating Registry keys in the REG_MULTI_SZ format, which requires embedded nulls.
- A substring of the form [#filekey] is used as a key into the File table. The filekey value is matched with the File column in that table, and the substring is replaced with the full path and filename of the file as installed.
- A substring of the form [!filekey] is also used as a key into the File table. The filekey value is matched with the File column in that table, and the substring is replaced with the full path and filename of the file, in short filename (8+3) format. This format is only valid in the Registry and IniFile tables.
- A substring of the form [$componentkey] is used as a key into the Component table. The componentkey value is matched with the Component column in that table, and the substring is replaced with the installation directory of that component. If the component is being installed locally, the target directory is used; if the component is selected to run from source, the source directory is used. If the component isn't installed at all, the substring is replaced by an empty string.

RegPath

A column with the RegPath data type contains Registry paths. These paths may not begin or end with a backslash. The RegPath data type performs property, file key, and component key substitution using the rules for the Formatted data type.

Template

The Template data type is used for columns that interpret Installer messages. It uses the full Formatted data type syntax. In addition, it can contain numbers in square brackets, which are replaced by parameters supplied by the Installer. For example, when binding executables, the Installer passes back the name of each file as parameter 1. In this case, you might fill in the Template column in the ActionText table to contain the following:

```
Binding file [1]
```

Condition

A column with the Condition data type is used to hold Boolean conditions that can be evaluated as either True or False. Conditions can check literal text enclosed in quotes, integer numbers, or variables. Variables include the following:

Property names   Return the value of the property.

Environment variables in the format %variablename   Return the value of the environment variable.

Component table keys in the format $componentname   Return the action state of the component.

Component table keys in the format ?componentname   Return the install state of the component.

Feature table keys in the format &featurename   Return the action state of the feature.

Feature table keys in the format !featurename   Return the install state of the feature.

You can use a variety of operators in conditional expressions, including the following.

Logical operators   Not, And, Or, Xor, Eqv, Imp.

Comparison operators   =, <>, >, >=, <, <=.

Substring operators   These include ><, which is True if the left string includes the right string; <<, which is True if the left string starts with the right string; and >>, which is True if the left string ends with the right string.

Bitwise operators   These include ><, which is True if the two integers have any bits in common; <<, which is True if the high 16 bits of the left integer are equal to the right integer; and >>, which is True if the low 16 bits of the left integer are equal to the right integer.

Feature and component states can take on these values:

INSTALLSTATE_UNKNOWN (-1)   Meaning no action is being taken.

INSTALLSTATE_ADVERTISED (1)   Meaning the feature is advertised (not available for components).

INSTALLSTATE_ABSENT (2)   Meaning the feature or component is absent.

INSTALLSTATE_LOCAL (3)   Meaning the feature or component is installed locally.

INSTALLSTATE_SOURCE (4)   Meaning the feature or component is installed to run from the source media.

GUID

A column with the GUID data type is used to hold Globally Unique Identifiers. These must be stored in the canonical Registry format, {XXXXXXXX-XXXX-XXXX-XXXX-XXXXXXXXXXXX}, where each X represents a hexadecimal digit. The data must include the curly braces, and all of the letters must be uppercase.

NOTE	For a discussion of creating GUIDs in the correct format see Chapter 3, "Basic Installer Concepts."

Version

The Version data type is used to hold version strings. These consist of one through four non-negative integers separated by periods. Each integer can have a maximum value of 65535. Some examples of valid version strings:

```
3
3.5
3.5.0.2908
65535.65535.65535.65535
```

Language

The Language data type is used to hold language IDs. These are represented in decimal format (for example, US English is 1033). If there are multiple language IDs, they are separated by semicolons. A neutral language file is indicated by storing zero in the Language data type.

NOTE   Microsoft Windows supports roughly 150 languages. For a complete list of Language IDs, see the Platform SDK topic `Base Services\International Features\National Language Support\National Language Support Reference\Language Identifiers`.

Binary

A column with the Binary data type can hold any binary data stream. Typically this is used for storing such things as icons or libraries containing custom actions.

CustomSource

The CustomSource data type is used in the CustomAction table. Depending on the type of custom action, this can be an identifier or a foreign key into the Binary, File, Directory, or Property tables.

For more information on custom actions, see Chapter 6, "Installer Actions."

Cabinet

The Cabinet data type is used in the Media table. If a value in this column is prefaced by the # sign, then the cabinet file is contained within the Installer package, and the rest of the value is the identifier for the stream containing the cabinet. Otherwise, the value is the short filename of the cabinet file itself, which must be stored at the root of the source tree for the package.

Shortcut

If a column with the Shortcut data type contains square brackets, it's interpreted using the rules for the Formatted data type. If the column doesn't contain square brackets, then it must contain a text value that can be used as a key into the Feature table. This data type is only used in the Shortcut table.

Core Tables

It's convenient to consider the tables in an Installer database in groups. For the first group, let's look at the core tables. These are the tables most directly related to the Installer's job of placing features and components on the user's computer. The following tables are included in this category:

- Feature
- Component
- FeatureComponents

- PublishComponent
- Condition
- Directory
- Complus
- IsolatedComponent

As I start to describe the tables in the Installer database, you'll see that they are all interrelated. Grasping the structure of this database is the toughest task you'll have in trying to understand how to program the Installer. Don't be afraid to skip around in this chapter and refer back to it later when you need to dig up the details on a particular corner of the database. You may also find it useful to open up an Installer database in an editor and actually look at some of these tables while you're reading this chapter. You'll find more information on editors in Chapter 12.

The Feature Table

The Feature table lists all of the features in the product. Additionally, it defines the tree structure that will be used to display these features, and it contains information on their preferred installation state. As you learn more about the tables in the Installer database, you'll see that this multiple use is not uncommon.

NOTE   In the listings of columns in this table, each column is followed by its data type in parentheses. If the data type is followed by the letter K, the column is part of the primary key of the table. If the data type is followed by the letter N, the column allows nulls. Key fields in most tables do not allow nulls. The exceptions to this rule are the ControlEvent and Upgrade tables, which contain key fields that allow nulls. Columns that do not allow nulls must have an actual value in the column.

The Feature table contains these columns:

Feature (Identifier, K)   The name of the feature.

Feature_Parent (Identifier, N)   This is the name of the parent of this feature. Root features have a null in this column. A feature can't have itself as a parent.

Title (Text, N)   This is the title to display for this feature on the user interface.

Description (Text, N)   This is a longer description of the feature that can also be used on the user interface.

Display (Integer, N)   Features are displayed on the user interface in order of this column; that is, a feature with a Display of 5 is above a feature with a Display of 12 in the selection tree. Features with a Display of zero or null are never displayed in the selection tree. If a feature has an odd Display, the node for that feature is initially expanded in the selection tree. If it has an even Display, the node is initially collapsed.

Level (Integer)   This is the initial install level of the feature. I'll talk about install levels later in this section.

Directory_ (Identifier, N)   If there's an entry in this column, it's a foreign key into the Directory table and represents a directory that can be edited by the end user.

Attributes (Integer)   This is a bit field containing a combination of the flags listed in Table 4.1.

T A B L E   4 . 1 :   Flags for the Attributes Column in the Feature Table

Flag	Value	Explanation
msidbFeatureAttributesFavorLocal	0	Feature is installed locally by default.
msidbFeatureAttributesFavorSource	1	Feature is installed to run from source by default.
msidbFeatureAttributesFollowParent	2	The feature's state is the same as the state of its parent. You can't set this bit for a feature that is a parent itself.
msidbFeatureAttributesFavorAdvertise	4	The feature is advertised.
msidbFeatureAttributesDisallowAdvertise	8	The feature can't be advertised.
msidbFeatureAttributesUIDisallowAbsent	16	The user interface won't let the user make this feature completely absent.
msidbFeatureAttributesNoUnsupportedAdvertise	32	Disables the choice to install on demand if the operating system doesn't support this feature.

Both installations and features have an install level. The initial install level of the installation itself is determined by the InstallLevel property in the property table. As you'll see later, it's quite possible to change property values "on the fly" from the user interface, so this might change before the installation is actually performed. In particular, you could use a change of install level to move from a "typical" to a "complete" installation.

A feature is installed only if its install level (initially determined by the InstallLevel column in the feature table) is less than or equal to the install level of the installation as a whole. There is one exception to this rule: a feature with an install level of zero is never installed.

The Component Table

The Component table, as you would expect, lists the components in an installation. It has these columns:

Component (Identifier, K)   The name of the component.

ComponentID (GUID, N)   This is the unique identifier of this particular component. This can be null, oddly enough, if the component is not to be registered.

Directory_ (Identifier)   This is a foreign key into the Directory table that identifies the path where this component should be installed.

Attributes (Integer)   This is a bit field containing a combination of the flags listed in Table 4.2.

Condition (Condition, N)   This column can be used to hold a conditional statement controlling whether or not a component should be installed. The condition is only evaluated on the initial installation unless the Attributes column indicates that this is a transitive component.

KeyPath (Identifier, N)   The KeyPath identifies the file or folder that the Installer uses to tell whether this component is already installed on the machine. If the KeyPath is null, the folder specified by the Directory_ column is used as the key path that is checked to determine whether the Component is already installedOtherwise, the Key-Path may be a foreign key into the Registry, ODBCDataSource, or File table, depending on the Attributes column. To install a component consisting of an empty folder, you must use the CreateFolder table instead of the Component table.

TABLE 4.2:   Flags for the Attributes Column in the Component Table

Flag	Value	Explanation
msidbComponentAttributesLocalOnly	0	Component cannot be run from source.
msidbComponentAttributesSourceOnly	1	Component can only be run from source.
msidbComponentAttributesOptional	2	Component can run locally or from source.
msidbComponentAttributesRegistryKeyPath	4	The value in the KeyPath column is a foreign key into the Registry table. This bit should always be set for Registry entries in the HKEY_CURRENT_USER hive to ensure proper functioning when there are multiple users on the same computer.
msidbComponentAttributesSharedDllRefCount	8	The Installer will increment the shared DLL RefCount value in the Registry for this component.
msidbComponentAttributesPermanent	16	The Installer will not remove this component if the product is uninstalled.
msidbComponentAttributesODBCDataSource	32	The value in the KeyPath column is a foreign key into the ODBCDataSource table.

TABLE 4.2: Flags for the Attributes Column in the Component Table *(continued)*

Flag	Value	Explanation
msidbComponentAttributesTransitive	64	The component is a transitive component. See Chapter 3 for an explanation of transitive components.
msidbComponentAttributesNeverOverwrite	128	Prevents the Installer from overwriting the key path file or Registry entry if it already exists.

The Installer keeps track of the number of times it has installed a particular component, whether that component is being tracked by a SharedDLL entry in the Registry or not. If there's already a Registry reference count for a component, the Installer will increment that count on installation and decrement it on uninstallation. If there's not already a Registry reference count, the Installer will create one only if the msidbComponentAttributesSharedDllRefCount bit is set in the Flags column.

In almost all cases, you'll want to fill in a GUID in the ComponentID column for every component in your installation. The exception is for "helper" components that aren't needed after the installation is complete. For example, your installation might include a program that converts data files in an old format to a new format. You might install this component, use it (via a custom action) to convert data files, and then want the Installer to remove the component when the installation is finished. In this case, you should leave the ComponentID column set to null.

The FeatureComponents Table

The FeatureComponents table is used to define the relationship between features and components. It only has two columns:

Feature_ (Identifier, K)   This column is a foreign key back to the Feature table.

Component_ (Identifier, K)   This column is a foreign key back to the Component table.

> **NOTE**   The Windows Installer uses the same concept of foreign keys as any other relational database. A foreign key column is constrained to contain only values that also appear in the primary key column of the related table.

Database designers will recognize this as a classic "linking table" in a many-to-many relationship, and indeed, that's what it is. One component can be installed by many features, and one feature can require many components. This provides the designer with a good deal of flexibility in terms of just what components to install.

If you're using Windows 9*x*, one feature can reference a maximum of 800 components. Under Windows NT or Windows 2000, one feature can reference a maximum of 1600 components.

The PublishComponent Table

The PublishComponent table is used to define qualified features, which I discussed in Chapter 3. It has these columns:

ComponentID (GUID, K)   This is a unique identifier for a category of components. Note that despite the name of this column, it is *not* a foreign key into the Component table.

Qualifier (Text, K)   This column is the identifier for a particular member of the category.

Component_ (Identifier, K)   This column is the foreign key into the Component table; it identifies the qualified component that's returned for the specified combination of ComponentID and Qualifier.

AppData (Text, N)   This is an optional text string describing the component. This can be displayed to the user to help choose which of a selection of qualified components they want to install.

Feature_ (Identifier)   This column is a foreign key into the Feature table; it identifies the feature that uses this particular qualified component.

This table does not have anything to do with advertising features. That's done by setting appropriate values into the Attributes columns in the Feature and Components table. This table is used strictly for resolving qualified components so that the right version of a particular file (for example, one that's supplied in several languages) is installed.

The Condition Table

The Condition table allows you to conditionally control the installation of features. It includes these columns:

Feature_ (Identifier, K)   This is a foreign key to the Feature table.

Level (Integer, K)   This is the install level to be set for the specified feature.

Condition (Condition, N)   This is a conditional expression to be evaluated.

When the Windows Installer reaches the CostFinalize action in its setup process (see Chapter 6 for a discussion of actions), it evaluates all of the conditions in this table. If any condition evaluates to True, then the corresponding feature has its install level altered to the Level specified in this table.

Typically, you use the Condition table to prevent the installation of features on inappropriate platforms. For example, you might reference a feature and set its level to 0 with a condition of "VersionNT>=500" to prevent this feature from being installed on Windows 2000.

NOTE   To conditionally control the installation of entire components, you use the Condition column in the Components table.

The Directory Table

The Directory table specifies the file layout of your installation. This layout must be the same in both the source tree (the media you deliver) and the target tree (the installation on the user's system). This table has these columns:

Directory (Identifier, K)   This column contains a unique identifier for the directory.

Directory_Parent (Identifier, N)   This is a foreign key back into the Directory table itself, representing the parent directory of the current row.

DefaultDir (DefaultDir)   This column contains the directory's name underneath the parent directory (in other words, the actual directory name to use on the hard drive). Directory names in this column may use the ShortName | LongName syntax.

The Directory column can contain the name of a property. In this case, the property specifies the path to the target directory.

If the Directory_Parent column is null or equal to the value of the Directory column, this is the root directory of the installation. Only one root directory is allowed per installation.

The Directory column in the row for the root directory must be set equal to the installation's TARGETDIR property. The DefaultDir column for the root directory must be set equal to the installation's SOURCEDIR property.

Typically, the root entry in the Directory table will have the Directory column equal to TARGETDIR, the Directory_Parent column set to null, and the DefaultDir column equal to SOURCEDIR. Then, for example, a directory named Foo directly under this would have the Directory column equal to an identifier such as FooDir, the Directory_Parent column equal to TARGETDIR, and the DefaultDir column equal to Foo.

The Complus Table

The Complus table contains information used to install COM+ applications. COM+ applications make use of the latest version of the Windows component services available on Windows 2000. This table has these columns:

Component_ (Identifier, K)   A foreign key back to the Component table; it identifies the component that contains the COM+ application.

ExpType (Integer, N)   This column contains the export flags generated when the .msi file for the COM+ application was created.

You shouldn't need to create or edit the Complus table in your own Installer databases. This table is automatically generated by the Component Services administrative tool when it creates an installation package for a COM+ application or application proxy.

The IsolatedComponent Table

The IsolatedComponent table enables the installation of "side-by-side" DLLs. A side-by-side DLL is one that is contained in the same folder as the application that uses the library. Windows has the ability to load multiple versions of side-by-side DLLs for different applications, even if they have the same name. Thus, side-by-side DLLs can provide a solution to DLL conflict problems. This table contains these columns:

Component_Shared (Identifier, K)   Foreign key back to the Component table. This column identifies the component that contains the library to be loaded as a side-by-side DLL.

Component_Application (Identifier, K)   Foreign key back to the Component table. This column identifies the component that will load the side-by-side DLL.

The Component_Shared and Component_Application columns must point to two different components. You should consider creating an IsolatedComponent table if you're shipping a new version of an existing DLL and are worried about possible side effects from using this new version with previous applications.

File Tables

The tables in the File Tables group include tables that specify the files to be used in the installation. This includes files to be installed, moved, or duplicated, as well as to be self-registered. This group includes these tables:

- File
- RemoveFile
- MoveFile

- DuplicateFile
- IniFile
- RemoveIniFile
- Font
- SelfReg
- Media
- BindImage
- Environment
- Icon
- CreateFolder

The File Table

The File table is the most important of this set of tables. It contains a complete list of the files that will be installed by the Installer. The following columns appear in this table:

File (Identifier, K)   This is a unique identifier for the file. In many cases, it can be the filename, but it doesn't have to be. If you're using qualified components, for example, you might have several entries for files named intl.dll in the File table. In this case you might use identifiers such as intl.dll_001, intl.dll_002, and so on.

Component_ (Identifier)   This is a foreign key into the Component table. It identifies the component that installs this file.

Filename (Filename)   This is the filename to be used for the installed file. Although Windows itself is not case-sensitive, you need to remember that your installation might be downloaded across the Internet, and some Web servers are case-sensitive. So, the filename should match that of the actual file completely, including case.

Filesize (DoubleInteger)   The actual size of the file in bytes. The Installer uses this to calculate the progress bar.

Version (Version, N)   This is the version string for the file. It can also be left null in the case of unversioned files. Or, you can set it equal to the File column for another file in the same installation, resulting in a companion file. See Chapter 3 for a discussion of versions and companion files.

Language (Language, N)   This is a comma delimited list of decimal language IDs for this file.

Attributes (Integer, N)   This is a bit field containing a combination of the flags listed in Table 4.3.

Sequence (Integer)   Each file is assigned an integer sequence number. This number is used to identify which of several source disks a file might be on, by consulting the Media table. In the case of compressed source files, the Sequence numbering in the File table must match the sequence of files in the cabinet. Sequence numbers are not necessarily unique. If all files are uncompressed and there's only one source disk, you could give every file the same sequence number. Note that in this case, you can't predict the order that the Installer will choose to install the files.

TABLE 4.3:   Flags for the Attributes Column in the File Table

Flag	Value	Explanation
msidbFileAttributesReadOnly	1	Install the file as read-only.
msidbFileAttributesHidden	2	Install the file hidden.
msidbFileAttributesSystem	4	Install the file as a system file.
msidbFileAttributesVital	512	This file is vital for the component to operate properly.
msidbFileAttributesChecksum	1024	The file contains a valid checksum. Executable files generally contain a checksum.
msidbFileAttributesPatchAdded	4096	This indicates that this particular file is installed by a patch rather than by a full Installer database.
msidbFileAttributesNoncompressed	8192	The file is uncompressed on the source.
msidbFileAttributesCompressed	16384	The file is compressed on the source.

The RemoveFile Table

The RemoveFile table lists files that the Installer should remove. Here are the columns in this table:

FileKey (Identifier, K)   This is an arbitrary key to identify this entry in the table. It can be the same as the filename, but that's not a requirement.

Component_ (Identifier)   This is a foreign key into the Component table. The file removal action is tied to this component.

FileName (WildCardFilename, N)   This column holds the name of the file to be removed. You can use wildcards in the name, in which case, all matching files are removed. If the FileName is null, the entire folder is removed instead, but only if it is empty.

DirProperty (Identifier)   This column holds the name of a property that resolves to a full path and directory. This may be a foreign key into the Directory table, but it doesn't have to be.

InstallMode (Integer)   This value controls what the Installer will actually do. It can be set to msidbRemoveFileInstallModeOnInstall to remove the file when the associated component is being installed, to msidbRemoveFileInstallModeOnRemove to remove the file when the associated component is being removed, or to msidbRemoveFileInstallModeOnBoth to remove the file when the associated component is being either installed or removed.

The RemoveFile table is processed during the RemoveFiles action.

The MoveFile Table

The MoveFile table lists files that the Installer should move or copy during the installation. It contains these columns:

FileKey (Identifier, K)   This is an arbitrary key to identify this row of the table. You can use the filename if you like, but that's not required.

Component_ (Identifier)   This is a foreign key into the Component table that identifies the component that this move or copy action is tied to.

SourceName (WildCardFilename, N)   This column holds the name of the file to act on. It can contain wildcards, in which case, all the specified files are moved or copied. It can also contain null; if it does, the SourceFolder column must completely specify the name of the file.

DestName (Filename, N)   This column contains the name to be given to the file after it's moved or copied. If it's blank, the source name is used.

SourceFolder (Identifier, N)   This column contains a property that resolves to either a path (if the SourceName column has a value) or a full path and filename (if the SourceName column is null).

DestFolder (Identifier)   This column contains a property that resolves to a full path to the destination folder.

Options (Integer)   This column can be either zero, to copy the file, or 1, to move the file.

File copy and move operations are performed by the MoveFiles action.

The DuplicateFile Table

Despite the name, the DuplicateFile table has nothing to do with locating or dealing with duplicate files. Rather, this table contains a list of files that need to be duplicated to multiple locations when the product is installed. This table contains these columns:

FileKey (Identifier, K)   This is a unique identifier for the row in the table. You can use the filename or any other identifier here.

Component_ (Identifier)   This is a foreign key to the Component table. If the component this key points to isn't installed, then this duplicate file action isn't carried out.

File_ (Identifier)   This is a foreign key into the file table. This key identifies the file that is to be duplicated.

DestName (Filename, N)   This is the name to be given to the duplicate file. If this column contains a null, then the duplicate copy will have the same name as the original.

DestFolder (Identifier, N)   This is a property that resolves to the full path where the duplicate should be located.

If DestFolder is null but DestName has a filename, then the duplicate will be located in the same folder as the original copy. If both DestFolder and DestName are null, no action will be taken by the Installer.

This table is used by both the DuplicateFiles action and the RemoveDuplicateFiles action. If a row in this table references a component that's being uninstalled, then the duplicate file is removed as well as the original.

WARNING   Files that are duplicated must be those installed by the Installer itself. You can't use this table to make copies of existing files.

The IniFile Table

The IniFile table contains information that needs to be written to .ini files during an installation. This table contains these columns:

IniFile (Identifier, K)   This is a unique identifier for this table. This can be the name of the .ini file or any other string that makes sense to you.

FileName (Text)   This is the actual name of the .ini file to be modified.

DirProperty (Identifier, N)   This is a property that resolves to the name of the directory that contains the desired .ini file. If this column contains a null, then the value of the built-in WindowsFolder property is used.

Section (Formatted)   This is the .ini file section to modify.

Key (Formatted)   This is the key in the specified section to modify.

Value (Formatted)   This is the value to use for this key.

Action (Integer)   This is a code indicating the action to be taken. Valid choices here are 0, to create or update an entry; 1, to create an entry only if the specified key doesn't already exist; and 3, which creates a new entry if one doesn't exist or appends a comma-separated value if the entry already exists.

Component_ (Identifier)   A foreign key into the Component table that identifies the component that this action is tied to.

.ini file information is only written when a component is selected to be installed locally or to be run from source. This table is processed during the WriteIniValues and RemoveIniValues actions.

The RemoveIniFile Table

The RemoveIniFile table contains information that the Installer should delete from existing .ini files (it does not remove .ini files themselves). It contains these columns:

RemoveIniFile (Identifier, K)   This is an arbitrary key for this table.

FileName (Text)   This is the actual name of the .ini file to be modified.

DirProperty (Identifier, N)   This is a property that resolves to the name of the directory that contains the desired .ini file. If this column contains a null, then the value of the built-in WindowsFolder property is used.

Section (Formatted)   This is the .ini file section to modify.

Key (Formatted)   This is the key in the specified section to modify.

Value (Formatted, N)   This is the value to be deleted from this key. A value is required when the Action column is 4, optional otherwise.

Action (Integer)   This is a code indicating the action to be taken. Valid choices here are 2, to delete the entire key, or 4, to delete a specified value from a list of values in the key.

Component_ (Identifier)   This is a foreign key into the Component table that identifies the component that this action is tied to.

If you remove the last key from a section, the Installer will automatically delete the section. There's no way to delete a section without individually deleting the keys in that section.

This table is processed during the RemoveIniValues action.

The Font Table

The Font table is used to list fonts that the Installer should register on the user's system. This is one of the simplest tables in the Installer database:

File_ (Identifier, K)   This is both the unique identifier for a row in this table and a foreign key to the File table. It identifies the file that contains the font to be registered.

FontTitle (Text, N)   If specified, this is the title to use when registering the font. If this column is left null, the Installer uses the font title that's embedded within the font file itself.

The Font table is used during the RegisterFonts and UnregisterFonts actions.

The SelfReg Table

The SelfReg table lists libraries that should be self-registered by calling their DllRegister-Server entry point. This table has these columns:

File_ (Identifier, K)   This functions as both the unique identifier for a row in this table and a foreign key to the File table. It identifies the file that should be self-registered.

Cost (Integer, N)   If supplied, this must be a positive number. It's used to calculate how far the progress bar should move when this self-registration action is performed. The measure of cost is bytes, because most of the progress bar is determined by copying files.

If it was up to the Windows Installer team, there probably wouldn't even be a SelfReg table. There are many reasons why self-registration doesn't fit well into the Installer worldview:

- DllRegisterServer can't be safely rolled back if an installation fails because there's no way to tell whether Registry keys are shared by other applications.
- The information the Installer needs to advertise components isn't exposed.
- DllRegisterServer doesn't support the notion of per-user information in the HKEY_CLASSSES_ROOT Registry hive.
- Self-registering DLLs may fail in a "run from source" network installation.

For these reasons, the Installer team strongly recommends that you use the other tables in the Installer database (see the section on the Registry tables below) to hold information that would have been placed in the DllRegisterServer routine in the past. Nevertheless, sometimes you just won't have a choice. For example, Office 2000 uses this table to register 72 files. But if you do have an option, you should try to minimize your use of self-registration and avoid it entirely in newly-developed components.

The Media Table

The Media table holds information on the disks that are the source media for the installation. There will always be at least one row in this table. If your installation is distributed across multiple diskettes or CDs, there will be one row for each piece of physical medium. This table contains these columns:

DiskId (Integer, K)   This must be a positive integer. This column determines the order that the media are processed in.

LastSequence (Integer)   This is the file sequence number (corresponding to the Sequence column of the File table) for the last file on this particular piece of media. A disk contains all files between the LastSequence number for the previous disk and the LastSequence number for itself.

DiskPrompt (Text, N)   This is the name that the Installer will use to prompt the user for this particular disk.

Cabinet (Cabinet, N)   This is the name of the cabinet file on the disk, if any of the files on the disk are compressed into a cabinet file. If there is no cabinet file on the disk, this column should be null.

VolumeLabel (Text, N)   This is the physical volume name of the disk. The Installer uses this to verify that the correct disk is in the drive.

Source (Property, N)   This column is only used by patch files, and only if a cabinet file with the patch files is located somewhere other than the original media. For normal installations this column should be left null.

If the source files are contained within the Installer package itself, in a cabinet file stored in a stream, you still need to make an entry in the Media table. In this case, though, you must prepend a pound sign (#) to the cabinet filename.

The BindImage Table

The BindImage table specifies files that should be processed by the BindImage action. It contains two columns:

File_ (Identifier, K)   This is both the unique identifier for a row in this table and a foreign key to the File table. It identifies the file that should be self registered.

Path (Paths, N)   If present, this column specifies a list of paths to search for imports to the specified file.

The BindImage action fixes up the import address table of the specified file to make the libraries it calls load faster. Generally, you should put executable and library files that import objects from other libraries into this table to optimize the installed application.

The Environment Table

The Environment table contains information on environment variables that the Installer should set or remove. It has these columns:

Environment (Identifier, K)   This is an arbitrary identifier for this particular environment action.

Name (Text)   The Name column contains a prefix and the name of the environment variable. The prefix indicates what action the Installer should take. Valid prefixes are listed in Table 4.4.

Value (Formatted, N)   This is the value that is to be set for the variable, or set to null if the variable is to be removed. You can also use a special notation to modify an existing environment variable. If you set the Value column to "[~];NewValue" (without the quotes), then NewValue is appended to the existing value, along with a semicolon. If you set the Value column to "NewValue;[~]" (without the quotes), then NewValue is prepended to the existing value, along with a semicolon.

Component_ (Identifier)   This is a foreign key to the Component table, indicating the component that's associated with this setting.

TABLE 4.4:   Prefixes for the Name Column in the Environment Table

Prefix	Meaning
=	Set the environment variable during installation.
+	Create the variable if it doesn't exist, and set it during installation.
-	Remove the environment variable when the component is being installed.
*	Under Windows NT or Windows 2000, this puts the environment variable in the system environment; otherwise, it is placed in the user environment.
=-	Set the variable on install and remove it on uninstall.
!-	Remove the environment variable whether the component is being installed or uninstalled.

This table is processed during the WriteEnvironmentStrings and RemoveEnvironment-Strings actions.

The Icon Table

The Icon table contains information necessary to create desktop icons. This table contains these columns:

Name (Identifier, K)   This is the name to use for the icon file.

Data (Binary)   This is the actual icon data, in .exe, .dll, or .ico format.

You might think that the Installer could just create icons from the actual executable files it's installing. But this scheme wouldn't work for advertised products, where the icon needs to be present on the user's desktop without the product being installed. So this table provides alternative files that have the icons for advertised products.

Generally, you should make entries in this table for each shortcut, file extension, and CLSID registered with the Installer.

The CreateFolder Table

The CreateFolder table contains information about folders that the Installer should create explicitly. This table has these columns:

Directory_ (Identifier, K) This is a foreign key into the Directory table, which identifies the folder to be created.

Component_ (Identifier, K) This is a foreign key into the Component table, which identifies the component that requires this folder.

Note that the Installer implicitly creates folders that files are installed into, so you don't need to include those files into this table. This table is intended primarily for the creation of empty folders since empty folders are otherwise removed by the Installer.

Registry Tables

The Registry tables are one of the more complex areas of the Windows Installer database. As I mentioned above, the Installer developers discourage the use of self-registration. Instead, Registry entries should be made through these tables. While there is one table that simply writes Registry keys (the Registry table), there are others that are more specialized. These specialized tables enable the Installer to make full use of COM, support advertising of COM components, and uninstall such components completely.

The Registry tables group includes these tables:

- Extension
- Verb
- TypeLib
- MIME
- Class
- ProgId
- AppId
- Registry
- RemoveRegistry

NOTE   Populating the Registry tables by hand can be an immense amount of work because you need to include every key that self-registration would create. The major editors for Installer databases offer automated help for this process.

The Extension Table

The Extension table contains the information necessary to register file extensions with the operating system. This information allows the Installer to support common operations, such as opening files directly from a mail message, or providing a context menu to them in Windows Explorer. This table has these columns:

Extension (Text, K)   This is the actual file extension to be registered. Do not put a period in front of the extension. The maximum length for this column is 255 characters.

Component_ (Identifier, K)   This column is a foreign key to the Component table. It identifies the component that controls the registration of this extension.

ProgId_ (Text, N)   This is a foreign key to the ProgId table. It identifies the ProgId (if any) that should be associated with this extension.

MIME_ (Text, N)   This is a foreign key to the MIME table. It identifies the MIME (Multipurpose Internet Mail Extension) type (if any) that should be associated with this extension.

Feature_ (Identifier)   This column is a foreign key into the feature table. It identifies the feature that provides the server application for this extension.

This table is processed by the RegisterExtensionInfo and UnregisterExtensionInfo actions.

The Verb Table

The Verb table contains the information that's used to create command-verb information associated with file types (for example, the "Open" or "Print" commands on a Windows Explorer shortcut menu). It includes these columns:

Extension_ (Text, K)   This column is a foreign key that refers back to a row in the Extension table, specifying the file extension that's being used.

Verb (Text, K)   This is the verb for the command, just as it should be displayed.

Sequence (Integer, N)   If there are multiple verbs for an extension, you can use this column to specify the order in which they should be displayed. The verb with the lowest number becomes the default action for the file type.

Command (Formatted, N)   This is the text to display on the context menu. This can include a shortcut character, for example, you could use "&Edit" to display Edit with the E underlined. If this column is null, then the value from the Verb column is used.

Argument (Formatted, N)   Command-line arguments that should be passed to the server when this verb is invoked.

This table is processed by the RegisterExtensionInfo and UnregisterExtensionInfo actions.

The TypeLib Table

The TypeLib table is used to register type library information. This table includes these columns:

LibID (GUID, K)   This is the GUID identifying the type library. Note that unlike most of the GUIDs used in the Installer database, this one isn't arbitrary; it's the GUID from the type library itself.

Language (Integer, K)   This column specifies the language ID of the type library.

Component_ (Identifier, K)   This column is a foreign key into the Component table. It identifies the component whose key file is the type library being registered.

Version (Integer, N)   This integer encodes the version of the type library. The major version is in the upper eight bits, and the minor version in the lower eight bits. So, for example, a Version of 513 translates to a type library version of 2.1.

Description (Text, N)   This is a description of the type library. This is the string shown, for example, in the Visual Basic References dialog box.

Directory_ (Identifier, N)   This column is a foreign key into the Directory table. It specifies the path to the help files for the type library. If the column is null, the help files are assumed to be in the same folder as the type library itself.

Feature_ (Identifier)   This column is a foreign key into the Feature table. It specifies a feature that must be installed or advertised for this type library to be registered.

Cost (DoubleInteger, N)   This column can be used to specify a cost for registering the type library to be used when the Installer updates the progress bar. Like other costs, this is measured in the equivalent of installed bytes.

This table is used by the RegisterTypeLibraries and UnregisterTypeLibraries actions.

The MIME Table

The MIME table contains the information needed to register MIME file types. This table includes these columns:

ContentType (Text, K)   This is the MIME identifier to be registered.

Extension_ (Text)   This column is a foreign key into the Extension table. It indicates the file type that will use this MIME identifier.

CLSID (GUID, N)   If filled in, this is the CLSID of the COM server that will handle this MIME file type. This can be any CLSID, whether the corresponding server is installed by the current Installer package or not. If this column is null, the information from the Extension table is used to determine the responsible server.

The MIME table is used by the RegisterMIMEInfo and UnregisterMIMEInfo actions.

The Class Table

The Class table contains the information needed to register COM classes supported by servers in the current installation. This table has one of the more complex structures in the Registry group:

CLSID (GUID, K)   This is the class identifier to be registered. This isn't an arbitrary GUID; it's a part of the COM server's description in its type library.

Context (Identifier, K)   This is the server context to be registered. This must be one of the following: LocalServer, LocalServer32, InprocServer, InprocServer32.

Component_ (Identifier, K)   This column is a foreign key into the Component table, and it indicates the component that contains the COM server for this class.

ProgId_Default (Text, N)   This is the default Program ID associated with this Class ID.

Description (Text, N)   This is the description for this class. This description is localized.

AppId_ (GUID, N)   This column is a foreign key into the AppId table, and it contains information for DCOM registration. This column isn't used by version 1 of the Installer.

FileTypeMask (Text, N)   This column contains file type information for the class. Most classes won't use this column.

Icon_ (Identifier, N)   This column has a foreign key into the Icon table, which specifies the icon to use for this class. If this column is null, the icon from the COM server is used. Note that you must use an icon in the Icon table for advertisement to supply the icon.

IconIndex (Integer, N)   This is the index into the specified icon file or into the server's list of icons.

DefInprocHandler (Filename, N)   For local servers, this column contains information on which inproc server should be the default.

Argument (Formatted, N)   This column shows the Argument used by COM for invoking the server.

Feature_ (Identifier)   This is a foreign key into the Feature table, which specifies the feature that provides the COM server for this class.

Attributes (Integer, N)   This column was added to the Installer database schema in version 1.1, so you won't find it in older databases. If you set this column to 1, then this class can be provided by a side-by-side DLL listed in the IsolatedComponent table.

This table is used by the RegisterClassInfo and UnregisterClassInfo actions. It's very unlikely that you'll make entries to this table by hand; instead, you should plan on using one of the automated tools for creating Installer tables from type library information.

The ProgId Table

The ProgId table includes the information that the Installer uses to advertise COM servers and to register their Program IDs. This information is presented in the following columns:

ProgId (Text, K)   This is the program ID or version-independent program ID to register.

ProgId_Parent (Text, N)   This column is only used for version-independent program IDs. If you're defining a version-independent program ID, this column holds the corresponding program ID for the current version.

Class_ (GUID, N)   This is a foreign key into the Class table. This column must be null for version-independent program IDs.

Description (Text, N)   This is the localizable description for this program ID.

Icon_ (Identifier, N)   If provided, this is a foreign key into the Icon table, specifying the icon to use for this program.

IconIndex (Integer, N)   This is the index to the icon in the icon file to be used.

The AppId Table

The AppId table is intended to help the Installer advertise distributed server information under COM+. It includes these columns:

AppId (GUID, K)   This is the GUID assigned to this AppId entry in the Registry.

RemoteServerName (Formatted, N)   This column contains the value that will be written to the RemoteServerName value.

LocalService (Text, N)   This column contains the value that will be written to the LocalService value.

ServiceParameters (Text, N)   This column contains the value that will be written to the ServiceParameters value.

DllSurrogate (Text, N)   This column contains the value that will be written to the DllSurrogate value.

ActivateAtStorage (Integer, N)   This column contains the value that will be written to the ActivateAtStorage value.

RunAsInteractiveUser (Integer, N)   This column contains the value that will be written to the RunAsInteractiveUser value.

The Registry Table

The Registry table holds all the miscellaneous (that is, not directly related to COM or COM+) information that the Installer needs to write to the Registry to install your application. It includes these columns:

Registry (Identifier, K)   This column is an arbitrary key for the table. You might consider using strings that describe the keys you're creating.

Root (Integer)   This column indicates the Registry hive to be written to. It must have one of the values shown in Table 4.5.

Key (RegPath)   The Registry key to be written.

Name (Formatted, N)   This column contains the name of the Registry value being written. If the column is null, then the value is written to the default for the Registry key. If the Value column is null, then this column should contain one of the special characters + (to create the key when the component is installed), - (to delete the key when the component is uninstalled) or * (to create the key on installation and delete it on uninstallation).

Value (Formatted, N)   This is the actual data to write to the Registry value.

Component_ (Identifier)   This is a foreign key to the Component table that identifies the component controlling this Registry operation.

TABLE 4.5:   Values for the Root Column of the Registry and RemoveRegistry Tables

Constant	Value	Explanation
none	-1	For a per-user installation, write to HKEY_CURRENT_USER. For a per-machine installation, write to HKEY_LOCAL_MACHINE.
msidbRegistryRootClassesRoot	0	HKEY_CLASSES_ROOT.

TABLE 4.5: Values for the Root Column of the Registry and RemoveRegistry Tables *(continued)*

Constant	Value	Explanation
msidbRegistryRootCurrentUser	1	HKEY_CURRENT_USER.
msidbRegistryRootLocalMachine	2	HKEY_LOCAL_MACHINE.
msidbRegistryRootUsers	3	HKEY_USERS.

Some special characters have meaning in the Value column. The rules for interpreting this column are as follows:

- If the value starts with #x, it's stored as a hexadecimal value.
- If the value starts with #%, it's stored as an expandable string.
- If the value starts with #, it's stored as an integer.
- The special string [~] is stored as a null. If this string occurs, the value is stored as a list of strings.
- If the string starts with [~], the value is appended to any existing value.
- If the string ends with [~], the value is prepended to any existing value.
- If the value starts with ##, it's stored as a string starting with a single # sign.

The Registry table is used by the WriteRegistryValues action.

The RemoveRegistry Table

The RemoveRegistry table lists information that the Installer should delete from existing Registry keys when a product is installed. It has these columns:

RemoveRegistry (Identifier, K) This is an arbitrary key for the row of the table.

Root (Integer) This column identifies the Registry hive that is to be edited. The RemoveRegistry table uses the same constants here that the Registry table uses; see Table 4.5 for a complete list.

Key (RegPath) This is the Registry key to be edited.

Name (Formatted, N) This is the Registry value to be deleted. You can use the special value "-" (without the quotes) to delete the entire key including any subkeys.

Component_ (Identifier) This is a foreign key to the Component table, indicating the component whose installation triggers the removal of the keys.

This table is used by the RemoveRegistryValues action.

ODBC Tables

The Open Database Connectivity (ODBC) tables group consists of five tables that allow the Installer to install ODBC drivers and data sources:

- ODBCDataSource
- ODBCDriver
- ODBCTranslator
- ODBCAttribute
- ODBCSourceAttribute

The ODBCDataSource Table

The ODBCDataSource table lists the ODBC data sources in the installation. This table has these columns:

DataSource (Identifier, K)   This is an arbitrary string identifying the data source to the Installer.

Component_ (Identifier)   This column is a foreign key into the Component table. The data source is installed as part of the referenced component.

Description (Text)   This is the description that should be shown to the user when they browse to the data source on their machine.

DriverDescription (Text)   This is the driver name to be used for this data source. This might be a driver in the ODBCDriver table, or it might be a driver that's already on the user's computer.

Registration (Integer)   This column can contain either 0, to register the data source per machine, or 1, to register the data source per user.

The ODBCDriver Table

The ODBCDriver table contains the information needed to install ODBC drivers. This includes the following:

Driver (Identifier, K)   This is an arbitrary key for this table.

Component_ (Identifier)   This column is a foreign key into the Component table; it indicates the component that includes this driver.

Description (Text)   This is the non-localizable ODBC key for the driver.

File_ (Identifier)   This column is a foreign key into the File table. It must point to the DLL that contains the ODBC driver.

File_Setup (Identifier, N)   This column is also a foreign key into the File table. It can be used to indicate a DLL that is called to do the setup of the listed ODBC driver. If this column is null, then the file listed in the File_ column is assumed to handle its own setup duties.

The ODBCTranslator Table

It should come as no surprise that the ODBCTranslator table is used to install ODBC translation DLLs. This table includes these columns:

Translator (Identifier, K)   This is an arbitrary key for the table.

Component_ (Identifier)   This column is a foreign key into the Component table; it indicates the component that includes this translator.

Description (Text)   This is the non-localizable description of this translator.

File_ (Identifier)   This column is a foreign key into the File table. It must point to the DLL that contains the ODBC translator.

File_Setup (Identifier, N)   This column is also a foreign key into the File table. It can be used to indicate a DLL that is called to do the setup of the listed ODBC translator. If this column is null, then the file listed in the File_ column is assumed to handle its own setup duties.

The ODBCAttribute Table

The ODBCAttribute table contains attributes for ODBC drivers that need to be registered when the drivers are installed. This table includes these columns:

Driver_ (Identifier, K)   This column is a foreign key into the ODBCDriver table; it indicates the driver that requires this attribute.

Attribute (Text, K)   This column holds the name of the attribute.

Value (Text, N)   This column contains the value to be registered for the attribute, if any.

The ODBCSourceAttribute Table

The ODBCSourceAttribute table contains attributes for ODBC data sources that need to be registered when the data sources are installed. This table includes these columns:

DataSource_ (Identifier, K)   This column is a foreign key into the ODBCDataSource table, it indicates the data source that requires this attribute.

Attribute (Text, K)   This column holds the name of the attribute.

Value (Text, N)   This column contains the value to be registered for the attribute, if any.

Service Tables

The Service Tables group includes two tables that are used to handle Windows NT and Windows 2000 services:

- ServiceInstall
- ServiceControl

The ServiceInstall Table

The ServiceInstall table lets the Installer add a new service to the user's computer. This table contains these columns:

ServiceInstall (Identifier, K)   This is an arbitrary key for this table.

Name (Formatted)   This column contains the name of the service—that is, the name you'd see in the Services applet under Windows NT.

DisplayName (Formatted, N)   This is an alternative, user-friendly name for the service that can be retrieved from the user interface.

ServiceType (DoubleInteger)   This column can be either SERVICE_WIN32_OWN_PROCESS (0x10) for a service that runs in its own process; SERVICE_WIN32_SHARE_PROCESS (0x20), for a service that shares a process; or SERVICE_INTERACTIVE_PROCESS (0x100), for a service that can interact with the desktop. The latter value must be added to one of the other two, so the valid values for this column are 0x10, 0x20, 0x110, and 0x120. The Windows Installer doesn't support installing kernel drivers or file system drivers.

StartType (DoubleInteger)   This column can be either SERVICE_AUTO_START (0x2), for a service that automatically starts when the system is started; SERVICE_DEMAND_START (0x3), for a service that is started manually; SERVICE_DISABLED (0x4), for a disabled service; SERVICE_BOOT_START (0x0), for a boot driver; or SERVICE_SYSTEM_START (0x1,) for a driver that's started during system startup.

ErrorControl (DoubleInteger)   This column specifies the behavior if the service fails to start. It can be set to SERVICE_ERROR_IGNORE (0) to just log any error, SERVICE_ERROR_NORMAL (1) to log the error and display a message, or SERVICE_ERROR_CRITICAL (3) to restart the system using the Last Known Good configuration.

LoadOrderGroup (Formatted, N)   If this service is part of a load ordering group, then this column contains the group name.

Dependencies (Formatted, N)   This column lists any services that must be started before this service, separated by null characters, which you can represent with the [~] shortcut. The list must end with an extra null character. If there are no dependencies, you must explicitly put a null character into this column.

StartName (Formatted, N)   This column specifies the account name, if any, that the service should log on as. Leave this column blank to use the default LocalSystem account.

Password (Formatted, N)   This column specifies the password to use if an account name is supplied in the StartName column.

Arguments (Formatted, N)   This column contains any command-line arguments used to start the service.

Component_ (Identifier)   This column is a foreign key to the Component table, it specifies the component to which the service belongs.

Description (Formatted, N)   This column contains the localizable description of the service. This column was not present in Windows Installer 1.0 databases. If the column is missing or null, an empty string is used for the description.

WARNING   In almost all circumstances you should use the default LocalSystem account rather than supplying a StartName and Password for services. Services installed with a StartName and Password may not be successfully removed by rollback.

The ServiceControl Table

The ServiceControl table allows the Installer to start and stop services. These can be services that were already present on the user's computer, or services listed in the ServiceInstall table. This table has these columns:

ServiceControl (Identifier, K)   This is an arbitrary primary key for this table.

Name (Formatted)   This column holds the name of the service to be controlled since it's registered with Windows.

Event (Integer)   This column contains a combination of the flags shown in Table 4.6 to control the effects of this entry.

Arguments (Formatted, N)   This is a null-separated list of arguments to use when starting the service.

Wait (Integer, N)   This column can be set to 0, to wait until the service is in a pending state, or to 1, to wait until the service is completely started.

Component_ (Identifier)   This is a foreign key into the Component table. It identifies the component that needs to perform this service operation.

TABLE 4.6: Values for the Event Column of the ServiceControl Table

Constant	Value	Description
msidbServiceControlEventStart	1	Starts the service during the StartServices action
msidbServiceControlEventStop	2	Stops the service during the StopServices action
msidbServiceControlEventDelete	8	Deletes the service during the DeleteServices action
msidbServiceControlEventUninstallStart	16	Starts the service during the StartServices action when an uninstall is being performed
msidbServiceControlEventUninstallStop	32	Stops the service during the StopServices action when an uninstall is being performed
msidbServiceControlEventUninstallDelete	128	Deletes the service during the DeleteServices action when an uninstall is being performed

Locator Tables

The Locator Tables group contains a set of tables that can be used to search for applications and files on the user's computer before the new software is installed. The primary uses for this set of tables are to find old versions of components being upgraded or to check to make sure the user has installed software prerequisites. The tables in this group are as follows:

- Signature
- RegLocator
- IniLocator
- CompLocator
- DrLocator
- AppSearch
- CCPSearch

The Signature Table

The Signature table holds information that the Installer uses to check whether a file it has found is the one that the developer has in mind. This table includes these columns:

Signature (Identifier, K)   This column is an arbitrary primary key for the table.

FileName (Text)   This is the name of the file being checked.

MinVersion (Text, N)   If this column is non-null, the Installer checks the version of the file and only accepts the file as identical if the file version is greater than or equal to this version.

MaxVersion (Text, N)   If this column is non-null, the Installer checks the version of the file and only accepts the file as identical if the file version is less than or equal to this version.

MinSize (DoubleInteger, N)   If this column is non-null, the Installer checks the size of the file and only accepts the file as identical if the file size is greater than or equal to this size.

MaxSize (DoubleInteger, N)   If this column is non-null, the Installer checks the size of the file and only accepts the file as identical if the file size is less than or equal to this size.

MinDate (DoubleInteger, N)   If this column is non-null, the Installer checks the creation date of the file and only accepts the file as identical if the file creation date is greater than or equal to this date.

MaxDate (DoubleInteger, N)   If this column is non-null, the Installer checks the creation date of the file and only accepts the file as identical if the file creation date is less than or equal to this date.

Languages (Text, N)   If this column is non-null, the Installer checks the languages supported by the file and only accepts the file as identical if all of the languages on this list are supported by the file.

NOTE   If you need to check for a single file in multiple languages, you should add multiple rows to this table.

The RegLocator Table

The RegLocator table is used to locate files that are referred to in the Registry. It contains these columns:

Signature_ (Identifier, K)   This column can be either a foreign key into the Signature table, or a unique identifier that occurs only in this table. In the latter case, you're assumed to be searching for a directory rather than a file.

Root (Integer)   This is a constant that indicates which Registry hive to search: 0 for HKEY_CLASSES_ROOT, 1 for HKEY_CURRENT_USER, 2 for HKEY_LOCAL_MACHINE, 3 for HKEY_USERS.

Key (RegPath)   This is the key for the Registry value to evaluate.

Name (Formatted, N)   This is the name of the Registry value to evaluate.

Type (Integer, N)   If zero, the key path is a directory. If 1 or missing, it's a file. If 2, it's a Registry value.

The IniLocator Table

The IniLocator table is used to locate files and directories referred to in `.ini` files. It has these columns:

Signature_ (Identifier, K)   This column can be either a foreign key into the Signature table, or a unique identifier that occurs only in this table. In the latter case, you're assumed to be searching for a directory rather than a file.

Filename (Text)   This is the `.ini` filename.

Section (Text)   This is the section within the `.ini` file.

Key (Text)   This is the key within the section.

Field (Integer, N)   The field in the `.ini` line to read, starting with 1 as the first field. If zero or null, the entire line is read.

Type (Integer, N)   If zero, the key path is a directory. If 1 or missing, it's a file.

The CompLocator Table

The CompLocator table takes advantage of the Installer's own configuration information to find files. This table contains three columns:

Signature_ (Identifier, K)   This column can be either a foreign key into the Signature table, or a unique identifier that occurs only in this table. In the latter case, you're assumed to be searching for a directory rather than a file.

ComponentID (GUID)   This is the Installer component ID of the component whose keyfile you're searching for. This need not be a component installed by the current Installer package.

Type (Integer, N)   If zero, the key path is a directory. If 1 or missing, it's a file.

The DrLocator Table

The DrLocator table contains information used to locate files by searching on the user's hard drive. This table contains these columns:

Signature_ (Identifier, K)   This column can be either a foreign key into the Signature table, or a unique identifier that occurs only in this table. In the latter case, you're assumed to be searching for a directory rather than a file.

Parent (Identifier, KN)   This column holds the signature of the parent directory of the file in the Signature_ column. If this field is null, and the Path column doesn't evaluate to a full path, then all the fixed drives in the user's system are searched.

Path (AnyPath, KN)   This is the path or subpath on the user's system to search.

Depth (Integer, N)   This is the number of levels of subdirectories to recursively search. If zero or null, then no subdirectories are searched.

The AppSearch Table

The AppSearch table contains a list of properties to be set by the AppSearch action. It contains two columns:

Property (Identifier, K)   This is the name of a property. It should be a public property (all capital letters).

Signature_ (Identifier, K)   This column is a foreign key into the Signature, RegLocator, IniLocator, CompLocator or DrLocator tables.

When the AppSearch action is executed, it looks for the files referred to by the Signature_ column, and if they're found, it sets their names into the corresponding properties in the Property column.

The CCPSearch Table

The CCPSearch table contains a list of signatures that should be used with the Compliance Checking Program (CCP). It has a single column:

Signature_ (Identifier, K)   This column is a foreign key into the Signature, RegLocator, IniLocator, CompLocator or DrLocator tables.

This table is used by the CCPSearch and RMCCPSearch actions.

Program Information Tables

The Program Information tables group contains tables with information that's used for the Installer's internal operations. This group includes these tables:

- Property
- Binary
- Error
- Shortcut
- ReserveCost

The Property Table

The Property table contains all of the properties that are present in this installation. It includes two columns:

Property (Identifier, K)   This is the name of the property. Public properties are identified by being in entirely uppercase letters.

Value (Text)   This is the value of the property.

Note that you can't store a property with a null value in this table. Also, you can't use this table to set one property to another property. To set a property equal to another property, use a custom action of type 51 (see Chapter 5, "The Installer User Interface").

The Binary Table

The Binary table holds binary data (such as images and icons) used by other parts of the Installer, chiefly on the user interface. This table has these two columns:

Name (Identifier, K)   This column uniquely identifies this row of the table.

Data (Binary)   This is unformatted binary data.

The Error Table

The Error table is used by the Installer to convert error numbers and associated data into meaningful messages. It contains these columns:

Error (Integer, K)   This is the error number.

Message (Template, N)   This is the template used to display this message.

Error numbers from 25000 to 30000 are reserved for custom actions.

The Shortcut Table

The Shortcut table contains information used to create shortcuts on the user's computer. This table contains these columns:

Shortcut (Identifier, K)   This is the name of the shortcut.

Directory_ (Identifier)   This is a foreign key into the Directory table, which specifies the directory where this shortcut will be created.

Name (Filename)   This is the name of the shortcut file to create.

Component_ (Identifier)   This column is a foreign key to the Component table; it specifies the component that owns this shortcut.

Target (Shortcut)   If the shortcut is advertised, the column is a foreign key to the Feature table. If the shortcut is non-advertised, this is a property whose value supplies the target for the shortcut.

Arguments (Formatted, N)   This column shows any command-line arguments to be used with this shortcut.

Description (Text, N)   This is the description to be used for this shortcut.

Hotkey (Integer, N)   This is the hotkey for this shortcut, if there are any. Since it's not possible for you to know what hotkeys the user has already assigned, you should normally leave this column null.

Icon_ (Identifier, N)   This is a foreign key to the Icon table. If this is null, the icon in the target file is used.

IconIndex (Integer, N)   This is the index of the icon to use from the icon file.

ShowCmd (Integer, N)   This is the style that the shortcut should use to launch the application. Valid values are 0 (normal), 3 (maximized) and 7 (minimized and inactive).

WkDir (Identifier, N)   This is the working directory for the shortcut. This will normally be a property name.

Advertising a feature will only create an advertised shortcut on Windows 2000 and Windows 98, or older systems running Internet Explorer 4.01 or higher.

This table is used by the CreateShortcuts and RemoveShortcuts actions.

The ReserveCost Table

The ReserveCost table is used to set aside free space on the user's hard drive as part of the minimum requirements for an installation. This table includes these columns:

ReserveKey (Identifier, K)   This is an arbitrary primary key for the table.

Component_ (Identifier)   This column is a foreign key into the Component table. It identifies the component that needs to reserve the space.

ReserveFolder (Identifier, N)   This is a property that evaluates to the name of a directory where the space should be reserved.

ReserveLocal (DoubleInteger)   This is the number of bytes to reserve if the indicated component is installed locally.

ReserveSource (DoubleInteger)   This is the number of bytes to reserve if the indicated component is installed to run from source.

You can use the ReserveCost table to make sure that there's enough space left for user files after the installation is complete. You can also use it to set aside space for files that are installed as a part of custom actions. If you don't set the space aside, those files won't be taken into account by the Installer when it considers free disk space.

Installation Procedure Tables

The Installation Procedures Tables group includes tables that control the sequence of actions during an installation. This group includes these tables:

- InstallUISequence
- InstallExecuteSequence
- AdminUISequence
- AdminExecuteSequence
- AdvtUISequence
- AdvtExecuteSequence
- CustomAction
- LaunchCondition
- LockPermissions
- Upgrade

The InstallUISequence Table

This table includes three columns:

Action (Identifier, K)   This is the name of the action to execute. It can be a built-in action, a custom action, or the name of a dialog box from the Dialog table.

Condition (Condition, N)   If present, this condition is evaluated before the action is executed. If it evaluates to False, the action is skipped.

Sequence (Integer, N)   The actions are run in increasing sequence order. There are exceptions to this rule. Table 4.7 lists the special numbers you can use in this column.

TABLE 4.7:   Values for the Sequence Column of Sequence Tables

Value	Meaning
Positive number	Run the action in this sequence.
Zero	Don't run this action.
Null	Don't run this action.
-1	Run this action when an installation is successfully completed.
-2	Run this action when the user cancels during an installation.
-3	Run this action in case of a fatal error.

TABLE 4.7: Values for the Sequence Column of Sequence Tables *(continued)*

Value	Meaning
-4	Run this action when the installation is suspended.
Other negative numbers	Don't run this action.

This InstallUISequence table is one of half a dozen sequence tables in the Installer database. The actions in this table are executed when the top-level INSTALL action is executed and the user interface level is set to the full UI or reduced UI. If the user interface level is set to basic UI or no UI, the actions in this table are skipped.

NOTE   You'll learn more about sequence tables in Chapter 6.

The InstallExecuteSequence Table

The InstallExecuteSequence table has the same structure as the InstallUISequence table. The actions in this table are executed when the top-level INSTALL action is executed and the Installer is done processing the actions in the InstallUISequence table. If the user interface level is set to basic UI or no UI, then this table is the only one that is executed.

The AdminUISequence Table

The AdminUISequence table has the same structure as the InstallUISequence table. The actions in this table are executed when the top-level ADMIN action is executed and the user interface level is set to the full UI or reduced UI. If the user interface level is set to basic UI or no UI, the actions in this table are skipped.

The AdminExecuteSequence Table

The AdminExecuteSequence table has the same structure as the InstallUISequence table. The actions in this table are executed when the top-level ADMIN action is executed and the Installer is done processing the actions in the AdminUISequence table. If the user interface level is set to basic UI or no UI, then this table is the only one that is executed.

The AdvtUISequence Table

The AdvtUISequence table has the same structure as the InstallUISequence table. The actions in this table are executed when the top-level ADVERTISE action is executed and the user interface level is set to the full UI or reduced UI. If the user interface level is set to basic UI or no UI, the actions in this table are skipped.

The AdvtExecuteSequence Table

The AdvtExecuteSequence table has the same structure as the InstallUISequence table. The actions in this table are executed when the top-level ADVERTISE action is executed and the Installer is done processing the actions in the AdvtUISequence table. If the user interface level is set to basic UI or no UI, then this table is the only one that is executed.

The CustomAction Table

The CustomAction table includes the basic information necessary to enable the Installer to run custom actions. Custom actions are bits of code that are called from external DLLs and other locations that are not part of the Installer proper. I'll cover them in detail in Chapter 7, "Putting the Pieces Together." This table includes these columns:

Action (Identifier, K)   This is the name that the custom action is known as in the sequence tables.

Type (Integer)   This column indicates the custom action type and additional details about how it should be run. See Table 4.8 for further details.

Source (CustomSource, N)   The meaning of this column depends on the type of the custom action.

Target (Formatted, N)   The meaning of this column depends on the type of the custom action.

T A B L E 4 . 8 :   Flags for the Type Column of the CustomAction Table

Value	Meaning
1, 2, 5, 6, 7, 17, 18, 19, 21, 22, 23, 34, 35, 37, 38, 39, 50, 51, 53, 54	These are the basic types of custom actions. They may be modified by adding the other values in this table.
+64	Synchronous execution, ignoring the exit code from the action.
+128	Asynchronous execution, but waits for the exit code at the sequence end.
+192	Asynchronous execution, with no wait for the exit code. Execution can continue after the Installer exits.

TABLE 4.8: Flags for the Type Column of the CustomAction Table *(continued)*

Value	Meaning
+256	Action may be included in both the UI and Execute tables and it will only execute once, even if both tables are evaluated.
+512	Action may be included in both the UI and Execute tables and it will only execute once per process.
+768	Action will only be executed during the Execute sequence if it was already executed in the UI sequence.
+1024	Execute as deferred action.
+1280	Execute only on rollback.
+1536	Execute only on commit.
+3072	Execute in system context instead of user context.

For more details on the Source and Target columns see Chapter 6.

The LaunchCondition Table

The LaunchCondition table contains conditions that can prevent the Installer from continuing with this installation. It contains these two columns:

Condition (Condition, K)   This column holds a condition to evaluate before the installation begins.

Description (Text)   This is an error message to be displayed to the user if the Condition evaluates to false.

If any entry in the LaunchCondition table evaluates to False, the software can't be installed.

The LockPermissions Table

The LockPermissions table can be used to secure installed objects under Windows NT or Windows 2000. It includes these columns:

LockObject (Identifier, K)   This column specifies the object to be secured. It is a foreign key into another table. The other table is determined by the value of the Table column.

Table (Text, K)   One of literal values "File," "Registry," or "CreateFolder" indicating the table that the LockObject column is a foreign key into.

Domain (Formatted, KN)   This is the name of the domain which contains the user whose permissions are to be adjusted.

User (Formatted, K)   This is the name of the user whose permissions are to be adjusted.

Permission (DoubleInteger, Y)   This is the Windows NT permission to be applied. In most cases, you won't need to make any entries into this table.

The Upgrade Table

The Upgrade table contains information that's used when an Installer database is used to make a major upgrade to an existing product. This table contains these columns:

UpgradeCode (GUID, K)   This column matches the UpgradeCode property of any products that are to be upgraded by this database. Unlike the ProductCode, different products may share the same UpgradeCode.

VersionMin (Version, KN)   This column specifies the minimum version to be upgraded. A null value means there is no lower bound on the version to be upgraded.

VersionMax (Version, KN)   This column specifies the maximum version to be upgraded. A null value means there is no upper bound on the version to be upgraded.

Language (Text, KN)   This column contains the languages to be upgraded, separated by semicolons. A null value means that any language can be upgraded. The meaning of this column can be reversed by adding 1024 to the Attributes column.

Attributes (Integer, K)   This column can contain any combination of these bit flags: 1 to enable the MigrateFeatureStates action, 2 to detect but not change previous versions, 4 to install the new version even if the old version can't be removed, 256 to include VersionMin in the versions upgraded, 512 to include VersionMax in the version to be upgraded, and 1024 to upgrade all languages except those listed in the Language column.

Remove (Formatted, N)   This column contains a comma-delimited set of names of existing features to be removed.

ActionProperty (Identifier, N)   This column contains the name of a public property in the Property table that will be set to a semicolon-delimited list of product codes of products to be upgraded by the FindRelatedProducts action.

You should include an Upgrade table in any Installer database. You don't need to put any records in this table if this is the first version of a product. If it's not the first version, you can use the Upgrade table to specify features to be removed or migrated when the new version is installed.

Any Installer database should have an Upgrade property assigned to it so that future upgrades using this table will be possible.

User Interface Tables

Like everything else about the Installer, the user interface is contained in a set of tables. If you're used to working with visual design tools like Visual Basic, this can be confusing. Perhaps the easiest way to think about it is that the Installer stores all the properties needed to create dialogs and controls without providing any visual designer for those objects.

The User Interface Tables group contains these tables:

- Dialog
- Control
- ControlCondition
- ControlEvent
- EventMapping
- TextStyle
- UIText
- ActionText
- Billboard
- BBControl
- Checkbox
- ComboBox
- ListBox
- ListView
- RadioButton

The Dialog Table

The Dialog table has one row for each dialog box that can be displayed by the Installer. It includes these columns:

Dialog (Identifier, K)   This is the name of the dialog box.

HCentering (Integer)   This is the column that specifies the position of the left side of the dialog box, on a scale of 0, at the left edge of the screen, to 100, at the right edge of the screen.

VCentering (Integer)   This is the column that specifies the position of the top of the dialog box, on a scale of 0, at the top edge of the screen, to 100, at the bottom edge of the screen.

Width (Integer)   This column specifies the width of the dialog box, including the borders. This is measured in *Installer units*. An Installer unit is one-twelfth the height of the system font.

Height (Integer)   This column controls the height of the dialog box, including the borders. This is measured in Installer units.

Attributes (DoubleInteger, N)   This is a set of attributes for the dialog box. The values for this column are listed in Table 4.9.

Title (Formatted, N)   This is the caption to use for the dialog box.

Control_First (Identifier)   This is a foreign key into the Control table, which identifies the control that receives the focus when the dialog box is first displayed.

Control_Default (Identifier, N)   This is a foreign key into the Control table, which identifies the default control for the dialog box.

Control_Cancel (Identifier, N)   This is a foreign key into the Control table, which identifies the cancel control for the dialog box.

TABLE 4.9:   Values for Attributes Column in the Dialog Table

Name	Value	Meaning
Visible	1	Dialog box is visible.
Modal	2	Dialog box is modal.
Minimize	4	Dialog box can be minimized.
SysModal	8	Dialog box is system modal.
KeepModeless	16	Keep other dialog boxes when this dialog box is created.
TrackDiskSpace	32	This dialog box dynamically keeps track of free disk space.
UseCustomPalette	64	Use the palette of the first control for this dialog box.
RTLRO	128	The dialog uses right-to-left reading order.
RightAligned	256	Text is right-aligned in this dialog box.
LeftScroll	512	Scroll bar is located at the left side of this dialog box.
BiDI	896	A combination of RTLRO, RightAligned and LeftScroll. Appropriate for languages that read right-to-left.
Error	65536	This dialog is used to display error messages.

The Control Table

The Control table includes detailed information on each control on every dialog box displayed by the Installer. This table contains these columns:

Dialog_ (Identifier, K)   This column is a foreign key to the Dialog table; it indicates the dialog box where this control appears.

Control (Identifier, K)   This is the name of the control. This must be unique within any given dialog. Controls on different dialog boxes can have the same name.

Type (Identifier)   This is the type of the control. This must be one of these values: Billboard, Bitmap, Checkbox, ComboBox, DirectoryCombo, DirectoryList, Edit, GroupBox, Icon, Line, ListBox, ListView, MaskedEdit, PathEdit, ProgressBar, PushButton, RadioButtonGroup, ScrollableText, SelectionTree, Text, VolumeCostList, or VolumeSelectCombo. It can also be the name of a custom control. You'll learn more about each of these control types in Chapter 5.

X (Integer)   This is the horizontal coordinate of the left edge of the control measured in Installer units.

Y (Integer)   This is the vertical coordinate of the upper edge of the control measured in Installer units.

Width (Integer)   This is the width of the control measured in Installer units.

Height (Integer)   This is the height of the control measured in Installer units.

Attributes (DoubleInteger, N)   This is a set of attributes for the control. The values for this column are listed in Table 4.10.

Property (Identifier, N)   This is the name of a property whose value is tied to this control.

Text (Formatted, N)   This is the initial text of the control. That might be the caption of a Text control or the initial text displayed in an Edit control, for example.

Control_Next (Identifier, N)   This is the name of the next control in the tab order of this dialog box.

Help (Text, N)   This is an optional string for use as help. It consists of two parts separated by a | character. The first part is used as a tooltip for the control; the second part is used for context-sensitive help. Note that context-sensitive help is not yet supported by the Windows Installer Service as of version 1.1.

TABLE 4.10: Values for Attributes Column in the Control Table

Name	Control Type	Value	Meaning
Visible	All	1	Control is visible.
Enabled	All	2	Control is enabled.

TABLE 4.10: Values for Attributes Column in the Control Table *(continued)*

Name	Control Type	Value	Meaning
Sunken	All	4	Control is displayed with a sunken visual effect.
Indirect	All	8	If set, the control's property specifies the identifier for the actual property to change.
IntegerControl	All	16	Any associated property is an integer. Otherwise it is a string.
RTLRO	All	32	Right-to-Left Reading Order.
RightAligned	All	64	Text in the control is right-aligned.
LeftScroll	All	128	Any scroll bar for the control is displayed on the left.
BiDi	All	224	Same as BiDi for the Dialog table.
FormatSize	Text	524288	Format numbers displayed in the control with KB, MB, or GB as appropriate.
Transparent	Text	65536	The control has a transparent background.
NoPrefix	Text	131072	Do not convert & to shortcut keys.
NoWrap	Text	262144	Text in the control does not wrap.
Password	Text	2097152	Characters typed in control display as "*" no matter what character was typed.
UsersLanguage	Text	1048576	Use the user's code page rather than the default code page.
Progress95	ProgressBar	65536	Draw the progress bar as a series of rectangles rather than a smooth bar.
RemovableVolume	Volume and Directory controls	65536	Show removable volumes.
FixedVolume	Volume and Directory controls	131072	Show fixed volumes.
RemoteVolume	Volume and Directory controls	262144	Show remote volumes.
CDROMVolume	Volume and Directory controls	524288	Show CD-ROMs.
RAMDiskVolume	Volume and Directory controls	1048576	Show RAM disks.
FloppyVolume	Volume and Directory controls	2097152	Show floppy drives.
Sorted	List, ListView, and Combo box	65536	Entries are sorted.
ComboList	ComboBox	131072	Limits selections to entries already in the list.

T A B L E 4 . 1 0 :   Values for Attributes Column in the Control Table *(continued)*

Name	Control Type	Value	Meaning
MultiLine	Edit	65536	The control will have a vertical scroll bar and allow multiple lines of text.
ImageHandle	Picture buttons	65536	Handle to a dynamic image (set at runtime).
PushLike	Picture buttons	131072	The control is drawn as a pushbutton.
Bitmap	Picture buttons	262144	The control displays a bitmap rather than text.
Icon	Picture buttons	524288	The control displays an icon from the Icon table.
FixedSize	Picture buttons	1048576	The image is cropped to fit the control.
IconSize16	Picture buttons	2097152	Display a 16x16 icon image.
IconSize32	Picture buttons	4194304	Display a 32x32 image.
IconSize48	Picture buttons	6291456	Display a 64x64 image.
HasBorder	RadioButton	16777216	Display a border around radio button groups.
ControlShow-RollbackCost	VolumeCostList	4194304	Include rollback files in the displayed space requirements.

The ControlCondition Table

The ControlCondition table allows you to make some changes to controls based on conditional logic. It contains these columns:

Dialog_ (Identifier, K)   This is a foreign key to the Dialog table, which indicates the dialog box that contains the control that you wish to modify.

Control_ (Identifier, K)   This is a foreign key to the Control table, which indicates the control that you wish to modify.

Action (Text, K)   This column holds one of the following values: "Default" (set the control as the default for the dialog), "Disable" (disable the control), "Enable" (enable the control), "Hide" (make the control invisible), or "Show" (make the control visible).

Condition (Condition, K)   This column houses the condition to be evaluated. If the condition is true, the action specified in the Action column is carried out.

The ControlEvent Table

You can think of the ControlEvent table as the Windows Installer equivalent of writing event procedures in Visual Basic. This table specifies the events that happen when the user interacts with controls. This table contains these columns:

Dialog_ (Identifier, K)   This is a foreign key to the Dialog table, which indicates the dialog box that contains the control that you wish to register an event for.

Control_ (Identifier, K)   This is a foreign key to the Control table, which indicates the control for which you wish to register an event.

Event (Formatted, K)   This is the type of event that should take place when the user works with the control. For a complete list of possible events, see Chapter 5.

Argument (Formatted, K)   This column shows additional information required by the particular event.

Condition (Condition, KN)   This is a conditional statement. The Installer evaluates this statement and only triggers the event if the statement evaluates to True. If you wish an event to take place unconditionally, enter a 1 in this column.

Ordering (Integer, N)   If you have several events tied to the same control, you can enter positive integers in this column to control the order of execution of the events.

The EventMapping Table

In addition to handling events from controls, the Installer also generates some events that controls can subscribe to. For example, there's a TimeRemaining event that the Installer uses to tell the user interface how long is left in a particular installation. You use the EventMapping table to set the controls that respond to a particular Installer event. This table contains these columns:

Dialog_ (Identifier, K)   This is a foreign key to the Dialog table, which indicates the dialog box that contains the control that you wish to subscribe to an event.

Control_ (Identifier, K)   This is a foreign key to the Control table, which indicates the control that you wish to subscribe to an event.

Event (Identifier, K)   This is the event that you want to subscribe to. See Chapter 5 for a complete list of events.

Attribute (Identifier)   This is the name of the control attribute that should be set by the event.

The TextStyle Table

The TextStyle table lists the fonts that can be used on controls. This table has these columns:

TextStyle (Identifier, K)   This is a name for the text style.

FaceName (Text)   This is the font name to use for this text style.

Size (Integer)   This is the size of the font to use for this text style, specified in Installer units.

Color (DoubleInteger, N)   This column is only used if the text style is used in a text control. All other controls use the system default text color. This value is computed by combining the red, green, and blue values with the formula (65536 * blue) + (256 * green) +red.

StyleBits (Integer, N)   This column can contain a combination of any of these constants: 1 for bold, 2 for italic, 4 for underline, and 8 for strikethrough.

The UIText Table

The UIText table is used to hold localizable strings that don't belong elsewhere. This table has two columns:

Key (Identifier, K)   This is an identifier for the string.

Text (Text, N)   This is the text for the string.

The ActionText Table

The ActionText table contains the information that is displayed in the Installer progress dialog box and written to the log. It has these columns:

Action (Identifier, K)   This is the name of the action.

Description (Text, N)   This is the description to be displayed or written to the log.

Template (Template, N)   This is a template used to format the data from the action.

You should have an entry in the Action table for each action in the sequence tables. In addition, you should have entries for the actions "Rollback", "RollbackCleanup", and "GenerateScript", which are internal actions that the Installer automatically performs.

The Billboard Table

Billboards are dialogs that progress dynamically while an action is taking place. Typically they're used to entertain the user or provide information while files are being installed. The Billboard table lists all of the billboards in the installation using these columns:

Billboard (Text, K)   This is an identifier for the billboard.

Feature_ (Identifier)   This column is a foreign key to the Feature table. The billboard is displayed when this feature is being installed.

Action (Identifier, N)   The name of the action during which this billboard should be displayed.

Ordering (Integer, N)   If there are multiple billboards for a single action, you can use positive integers in this column to specify the display order.

The BBControl Table

The BBControl table lists the controls to be displayed on billboards. This table has these columns:

Billboard_ (Identifier, K)   This column is a foreign key to the Billboard table, which indicates the billboard where this control appears.

BBControl (Identifier, K)   This is the name of the control. This must be unique within any given billboard. Controls on different billboards can have the same name.

Type (Identifier)   This is the type of the control. Only static controls (Text, Bitmap, Icon or static custom controls) can be placed on billboards.

X (Integer)   This is the horizontal coordinate of the left edge of the control measured in Installer units.

Y (Integer)   This is the vertical coordinate of the upper edge of the control measured in Installer units.

Width (Integer)   This is the width of the control measured in Installer units.

Height (Integer)   This is the height of the control measured in Installer units.

Attributes (DoubleInteger, N)   This is a set of attributes for the control. The values for this column are listed in Table 4.10.

Text (Text, N)   This is the initial text to be displayed in the control.

The Checkbox Table

The Checkbox table lists properties that are set by checkbox controls. This table has these two columns:

Property (Identifier, K)   This is the name of a property set from a checkbox.

Value (Formatted, N)   This is the value that the property is set to when the associated checkbox is checked.

The ComboBox Table

The ComboBox table lists the text and values for the lists displayed by combo boxes. This table contains these columns:

Property (Identifier, K)   This is the name of a property set from a combo box.

Order (Integer, K)   The items in a combo box are ordered according to the values in this column. All items with the same value in the Property column are shown in the same drop-down list.

Value (Formatted)   This is the value that the property is set to when this item is selected from the combo box.

Text (Text, N)   This is the text to display in the combo box. If this column contains a null, then the Value is used as the display text.

The ListBox Table

The ListBox table lists the text and values for the lists displayed by list boxes. This table contains these columns:

Property (Identifier, K)   This is the name of a property set from a list box.

Order (Integer, K)   The items in a list box are ordered according to the values in this column. All items with the same value in the Property column are shown in the same list box.

Value (Formatted)   This is the value that the property is set to when this item is selected from the list box.

Text (Formatted, N)   This is the text to display in the list box. If this column contains a null, then the Value is used as the display text.

The ListView Table

The ListView table lists the text and values for the lists displayed by listview controls. This table contains these columns:

Property (Identifier, K)   This is the name of a property set from a listview.

Order (Integer, K)   The items in a listview are ordered according to the values in this column. All items with the same value in the Property column are shown in the same listview.

Value (Formatted)   This is the value that the property is set to when this item is selected from the listview.

Text (Formatted, N)   This is the text to display in the listview. If this column contains a null, then the Value is used as the display text.

Binary_ (Identifier, N)   This column contains a foreign key to the Binary table. It's used to specify an icon to display with the item in the listview.

The RadioButton Table

The RadioButton table contains information for radio buttons displayed in option groups. This table contains these columns:

Property (Identifier, K)   This column contains the name of a property set from a RadioButton group box.

Order (Integer, K)   This column displays an ordering for the buttons within a group box. All of the buttons with the same Property value are displayed in the same RadioButton group box.

Value (Formatted)   This is the value that the property is set to when this radio button is selected.

X (Integer)   This is the horizontal position of this radio button within the bounding group box measured in Installer units.

Y (Integer)   This is the vertical position of this radio button within the bounding group box measured in Installer units.

Width (Integer)   This is the width of the text for this radio button measured in Installer units.

Height (Integer)   This is the height of the text for this radio button measured in Installer units.

Text (Formatted N)   This is the text to display with the Radio button. If the button displays a picture, this column is a foreign key to the Binary table.

Help (Text, N)   This is an optional string for use as help. It consists of two parts separated by a | character. The first part is used as a tooltip for the control; the second part is used for context-sensitive help. Note that the Installer Service does not yet support context-sensitive help.

System Tables

The System tables contain the metadata for the Installer database—that is, they are the tables that describe the tables in the database. There are five system tables:

- _Tables
- _Columns
- _Streams
- _Storages
- _Validation

NOTE   You're unlikely to need to modify the system tables or even to work directly with them, unless you're writing some kind of tool that manipulates Installer databases. Because it's possible for developers to add their own tables to an Installer database, you may occasionally need to query these tables to see what's in a particular Installer database.

The _Tables Table

The _Tables table lists all of the tables in the Installer database. It has one column:

Name (Text, K)   This column displays the name of the table.

The _Columns Table

The _Columns table describes all of the columns in all of the tables in the Installer database. This table has these columns:

Table (Text, K)   This column is a foreign key to the _Tables table, and it names the table that contains the column that this row of the Columns table describes.

Number (Integer, K)   This is the order in which the column appears within the table.

Name (Text)   This is the name of the column.

The _Streams Table

The _Streams table lists embedded OLE data streams in the Installer database. This table contains these columns:

Name (Text, K)   This column contains the name of the stream.

Data (Binary, N)   This is the raw binary data for the stream.

This table is only created when it's referenced by a SQL statement.

The _Storages Table

The _Storages table lists embedded OLE data storages in the Installer database. This table contains these columns:

Name (Text, K)   This column displays the name of the storage.

Data (Binary, N)   This is the raw binary data for the storage.

The _Validation Table

The _Validation table contains information on the acceptable range for columns in the Installer database. This table has these columns:

Table (Identifier, K)   This column contains a foreign key into the _Table table; it identifies the table being validated.

Column (Identifier, K)   This is a foreign key into the _Column table; this column identifies the column being validated.

Nullable (Text)   This column identifies whether the target column is nullable. The value may be Y if the column allows nulls, N if it does not allow nulls, or @ if it's part of a multicolumn key but still allows nulls.

MinValue (DoubleInteger, N)   This column shows the minimum permissible value for a date, numeric, or version column.

MaxValue (DoubleInteger, N)   This column shows the maximum permissible value for a date, numeric, or version column.

KeyTable (Identifier, N)   If this column is non-null, the target column is a foreign key into the table identified here.

KeyColumn (Integer, N)   If this column is non-null, the target column is a foreign key to the column number in the KeyTable identified here.

Category (Text, N)   This column specifies the data type of the target column.

Set (Text, N)   If present, this is a semicolon-delimited list of acceptable values for the column.

Description (Text, N)   This is a description of the data stored in the target column.

Patching Tables

The Patching Tables group contains tables that are added to the Installer database by a patch package. As such, you won't find them in most Installer databases, nor will you normally write to them. But you may find these tables in an Installer database for a product on your hard drive:

- PatchPackage
- Patch

For more information on patch packages, see Chapter 10, "Creating and Using Patch Packages."

The PatchPackage Table

The PatchPackage table describes all of the patch packages that have been applied to a particular installation. It includes these columns:

PatchId (GUID, K)   This is a unique identifier for the patch package.

Media_ (Integer)   This column is a foreign key to the Media table and refers to the disk that contained the patch package.

The Patch Table

The Patch table lists patches that have been applied to particular tables. This table contains these columns:

File_ (Identifier, K)   This column is a foreign key into the File table. It specifies the file that has been patched.

Sequence (Integer, K)   This is the sequence number of this particular patch on the media specified by the Media_ field within the PatchPackage table.

PatchSize (DoubleInteger)   This is the size of the patch in bytes.

Attributes (Integer)   This can be zero (failure to apply this patch is a fatal error) or 1 (failure to apply this patch is not a fatal error).

Header (Binary)   This is a binary header used for patch validation.

This table is processed by the PatchFiles action when a patch is applied to a product.

chapter 5

The Installer User Interface

- Overview of the User Interface

- Reserved Dialog Boxes

- Dialog Box Style Bits

- Controls

- Events

Now that you've seen the internals of the Installer database, it's time to look at the face that the Installer presents to the world. In this chapter, I'll explore the user interface provided by the Installer. As you'll see, you get some user interface behavior automatically, but the Windows Installer also provides extensive customization facilities to let you create your own interface.

Overview of the User Interface

Creating a user interface for the Installer, like most other Installer operations, means adding entries to the Installer database. These entries define the dialog boxes and controls that your users will see when they install your program; they also define the events that these controls will generate. Depending on the user interface level that the installation is being run with, the user may see all, some, or none of the dialog boxes in the Installer database.

User Interface Levels

The Windows Installer supports four different levels of user interface; None, Basic, Reduced, and Full. In Chapter 2, "Running the Installer," I discussed the use of command-line switches to choose the level of interface you'd like to use. You'll also see in Chapter 8, "Using the Installer API," that you can use the MsiSetInternalUI to set the level of user interface when you're interacting with the Installer programmatically.

From the least to the most user interface elements, these levels are as follows:

None   Performs a silent installation.

Basic   Displays only progress messages to the user.

Reduced   Displays essential dialog boxes and progress messages.

Full   Displays an entire wizard interface.

I'll concentrate on the full user interface, because it provides the most flexibility and the best installation experience for your users. If you author a full user interface into your Installer database, you can always choose to display the reduced or basic interface, or not use any user interface at all (None) in special circumstances.

NOTE   The Installer also supports the MsiSetExternalUI API, which allows you to create a user interface in a completely external program that communicates with the Installer via callback functions. I won't cover the use of external user interfaces in this book.

Dialog Boxes

The Installer divides dialog boxes into two types:

- Reserved dialog boxes
- Custom dialog boxes

For the Installer to function, the Installer database must contain the reserved dialog boxes. For example, there's a reserved dialog box named Error. You must provide a dialog box with this name in the database, to be used by the Installer when it detects an error. You can't use this dialog box for any other reason. Later in the chapter, I'll list all of the reserved dialog boxes and explain what they're used for.

You can also create custom dialog boxes. These dialog boxes can be used to display or prompt for just about anything you can dream of. Generally, you'll display custom dialog boxes in response to control events. For example, you might want to create a dialog box that displays important information for upgrading users. You might also want to place a button on your initial dialog box that displays this dialog box when the button is pressed.

WARNING   Although the Installer reserves names for some dialog boxes, it does not create these dialog boxes for you. To create these reserved dialog boxes, you must add entries to the User Interface tables listed in Chapter 4, "A Guide to the Installer Database," just as you would for custom dialog boxes. One good starting point is the `UISample.msi` file that's shipped as part of the Installer SDK. This file contains samples for all of the reserved dialog boxes that you can copy to your own Installer database.

Controls

The Installer supports a wide variety of native controls that you can use to build your user interface. These include standard controls such as labels, text boxes, and buttons. There are also some specialized controls that you're unlikely to encounter in other contexts. For example, the Installer ProgressBar control is specially designed to keep your users informed of the progress of an installation; it's not a general-purpose progress bar.

I'll discuss the available native controls and show you examples of their use later in this chapter.

NOTE   The Windows Installer also allows you to use custom controls on dialog boxes. I won't be covering custom controls in this book.

You can make your dialog boxes more flexible by using the various tables in the User Interface Tables group together with controls. For example, take a look at the following:

- You can use the ControlCondition table to hide, show, enable or disable controls based on a conditional statement. Among other things, this allows your user interface to vary in different versions of Windows.
- You can tie a control to a particular property in the Installer database so that changes to the control change the property. Properties tied to controls in this fashion must be public properties (that is, their names must consist entirely of capital letters).
- You can use the TextStyle table to create predefined font styles for controls. For example, you might define a style named "Bold" in the TextStyle table that uses boldface text. Any control whose Text property then starts with {\Bold} will use this TextStyle for its display.

Events

The Installer supports control events using a publish-and-subscribe metaphor. The Installer publishes some events itself, and individual controls are free to publish their own events as well. Multiple controls can subscribe to a single event. Each subscribing control will be notified when that event happens.

The ControlEvent table is used to publish events, and the EventMapping table is used to subscribe to events.

I'll discuss events, with an emphasis on those events provided by the Installer, later in the chapter. Because the Installer supports event-driven programming, VB developers should find it relatively easy to create workable user interfaces for the Installer.

Reserved Dialog Boxes

The Installer supports eleven reserved dialog boxes that fall into three general categories. First, there are four dialog boxes that are required in all installations:

- Error
- Exit
- FatalError
- UserExit

The second group of reserved dialog boxes is optional, but if any member of this grouping is present, the Installer will use it:

- FilesInUse
- FirstRun

The final group contains five dialog boxes that aren't actually reserved at all, except by convention. The Installer doesn't explicitly search for these names, but most Installer databases will treat these as standard dialog boxes nonetheless:

- Browse
- Cancel
- DiskCost
- LicenseAgreement
- Selection

Each of these dialog boxes is described in the following pages.

Error

The Error dialog box is a modal dialog box that the Installer uses to display error messages. To tell the Installer which dialog box it should use as the error dialog box, you must make an entry in the Property table. The property name is ErrorDialog and the property value is the name of the dialog box that you want to use to display errors. If, for some reason, this property is missing, or it doesn't point to a valid dialog box, errors will only be recorded in the installation log. You also need to set the error dialog box style bit in the Dialog table for this dialog box (see below for more information on dialog box style bits).

Table 5.1 shows the controls that this dialog must contain to be used by the Installer.

TABLE 5.1: Standard Controls for the Error Dialog Box

Name	Type	Comments
A	PushButton	The Abort button
C	PushButton	The Cancel button
I	PushButton	The Ignore button
N	PushButton	The No button
O	PushButton	The OK button
R	PushButton	The Retry button
Y	PushButton	The Yes button
ErrorText	Text	Used to display the error message

In the ControlEvent table, all of the PushButton controls should publish an EndDialog event. You can use the Argument column of these table entries to distinguish one button from another in cases where you need to tell which button the user pressed at runtime.

When the Installer has an error message to display, it opens the Error dialog box to do so. Depending on the parameters of the message, it will hide some of the PushButton controls, showing only the ones that apply to the current message. It will also rearrange the visible PushButton controls so that they are evenly spread across the dialog box. Because of this arrangement, you should avoid having any other controls in the same horizontal area as the PushButton controls on this dialog box.

Figure 5.1 shows a sample Error dialog box, from the UISample.msi file supplied with the Installer SDK. In this particular screenshot, the dialog box has been shown using the dialog preview capabilities of the Orca editor. The reason that it seems to only have a single button is that all seven buttons are stacked in one place. This doesn't really matter because the Installer will just move them around anyhow.

FIGURE 5.1

A sample Error dialog box

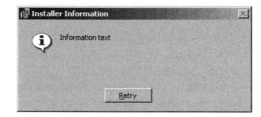

To display dialog boxes using Orca, follow these steps:

1. Open Orca and load the .msi file that contains the dialog boxes.

2. Choose Tools ➢ Dialog Preview....

3. Click the dialog box you want to see, and then click Preview.

4. When you're finished, click Done on the Dialog Preview dialog box. The controls on the dialog box being previewed won't be active, so don't bother clicking on any of them.

Exit

The Exit dialog box is used as the final dialog box when the installation is over. In the simplest case, this dialog box might just have some text such as "Installation is completed" and an OK button. If you're using a wizard-style interface, you'll want something a bit dressier, but the essentials are the same. Figure 5.2 shows the sample Exit dialog box from UISample.msi.

FIGURE 5.2

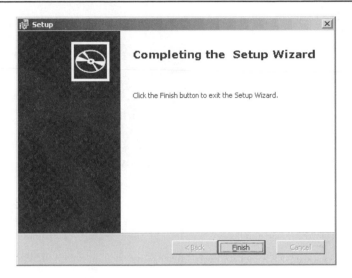

To tell the Installer that a particular dialog box is the Exit dialog box, you need to make entries in the InstallUISequence and AdminUISequence tables. In each case, the entry should have these values:

Action   The name of the dialog box from the Dialog table

Condition   Null

Sequence   -1

FatalError

Of course, no matter how bulletproof using the Windows Installer makes your setup program seem, things can still go wrong. If something goes so drastically wrong that the Installer can't recover, it will roll back the installation and then display the FatalError dialog box.

In the simplest case, this dialog box might just have some text such as "Installation failed" and an OK button. If you're using a wizard-style interface, you'll want something a bit dressier, so that it is obvious that the wizard is notifying the user of a problem. Figure 5.3 shows the sample FatalError dialog box from UISample.msi.

To tell the Installer that a particular dialog box is the FatalError dialog box, you need to make entries in the InstallUISequence and AdminUISequence tables. In each case, the entry should have these values:

Action   The name of the dialog box from the Dialog table

Condition   Null

Sequence   -3

FIGURE 5.3
A FatalError dialog box

UserExit

In addition to completing successfully or failing disastrously, an installation can also end if the user clicks a Cancel button while it's in progress. In this case, the Installer displays the UserExit dialog box when it's ready to shut down. Like the Exit and Fatal-Error dialog box, this might be a simple message or a wizard screen. Figure 5.4 shows the sample UserExit dialog box from UISample.msi.

FIGURE 5.4
A UserExit dialog box

To tell the Installer that a particular dialog box is the UserExit dialog box, you need to make entries in the InstallUISequence and AdminUISequence tables. In each case, the entry should have these values:

Action   The name of the dialog box from the Dialog table

Condition   Null

Sequence   -2

FilesInUse

The FilesInUse dialog box is used by the Installer to display a list of other applications that ought to be closed before the installation proceeds. Note that the installation won't necessarily fail if these applications aren't closed. Instead, an additional reboot might be required. Figure 5.5 shows the sample FilesInUse dialog box from the UISample.msi Installer database.

FIGURE 5.5

A FilesInUse dialog box

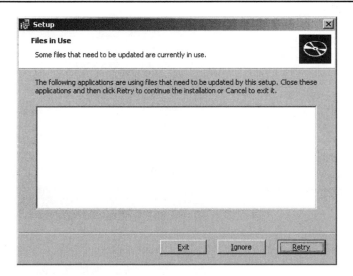

The FilesInUse dialog box must include a ListBox control in which the Property column is set to the value FileInUseProcess. When the Installer executes the InstallValidate action, it checks the current state of every file that will be overwritten or deleted by the installation. If any of these files are in use by a currently-executing process, the Installer adds a record to the ListBox table, with these values:

Property   FileInUseProcess

Value   The name of the process

Text   The caption of the main window of the process

Once this table has been built, the Installer calls the FilesInUse dialog box. It knows which dialog box to call because of the reserved name FilesInUse. The list box will automatically display the processes that are causing problems.

NOTE For more details on how the InstallValidate action responds to user choices in this dialog box, see Chapter 6, "Installer Actions."

FirstRun

The FirstRun dialog box is designed to collect information from the user. The Installer identifies this dialog box by its name. Normally, it will look something like the dialog box in Figure 5.6. In this case, the caption of the dialog box is "Setup" and the most prominent text is "Customer Information," but the dialog box is still named FirstRun in the Installer database.

FIGURE 5.6
A sample FirstRun dialog box

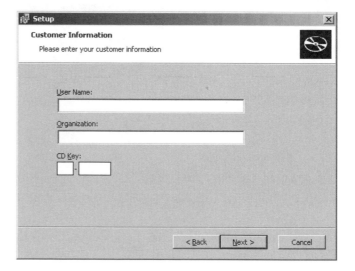

Controls on this dialog box should be tied to the public USERNAME and COMPANY-NAME properties to ensure that the Installer uses the correct values for these properties. If you're performing product validation, you'll also need a control for the PIDKEY property. In that case, you should also call the ValidateProductId control event (discussed later in this chapter) when the user leaves this dialog box.

DiskCost

The DiskCost dialog box is displayed when the Installer decides there is insufficient space for an installation. It determines whether to display this dialog box by checking for a dialog box with this exact name. In most cases, you'll want to include a Volume-CostList control and an OK button so that the user can see which drive is out of space, correct the problem, and then click OK. Figure 5.7 shows a sample DiskCost dialog box from the UISample.msi sample project.

FIGURE 5.7
A sample DiskCost
dialog box

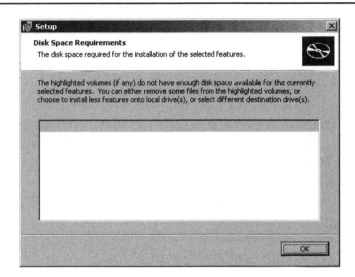

Browse

Assuming that you want to allow the user to choose where to install your product, you'll need to provide a Browse dialog box. This is not a reserved dialog box in the sense that the Installer will automatically use it. However, by convention, Browse is the name used for this dialog box. Typically, you'd want to open this dialog box only if the user chooses "Customize" in the main logic of the installation.

Figure 5.8 shows a sample Browse dialog box from the UISample.msi Installer database.

FIGURE 5.8
A sample Browse
dialog box

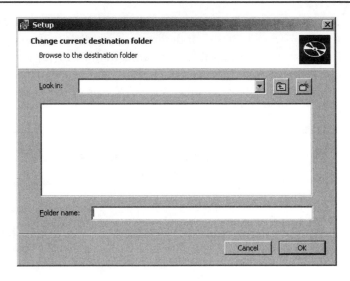

Typically, a Browse dialog box will contain these controls:

DirectoryCombo control   Shows the part of the selected path that currently exists on the user's computer.

DirectoryList control   Shows the subdirectories of the current path.

PathEdit control   Lets the user edit the full path directly.

Pushbutton   Moves up one folder in the tree.

Pushbutton   Creates a new folder.

Normally, the DirectoryCombo, DirectoryList, and PathEdit control will all be set to the same property so that they stay synchronized. Later, that property can be used to determine where to actually install files.

Cancel

In order to avoid unpleasant user experiences caused by accidentally clicking Cancel, it's advisable to provide an "Are you sure?" dialog box to be called when the user does click Cancel. By convention, this dialog box is named Cancel. Figure 5.9 shows a sample Cancel dialog box from the UISample.msi Installer database.

FIGURE 5.9
A sample Cancel dialog box

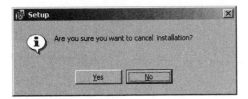

Here the dialog box consists of an icon, a message, and two PushButton controls. The No button calls the EndDialog event with the Return action, which causes the Installer to just go back to the dialog box that displayed this dialog box. The Yes button calls the EndDialog event with the Exit action, which causes the Installer to display the UserExit dialog box, rollback, and end the installation.

LicenseAgreement

A LicenseAgreement dialog box is used to display text that a user must agree to in order to proceed. Figure 5.10 shows one example of a LicenseAgreement dialog box, this one from the UISample.msi Installer database.

FIGURE 5.10
A sample License-Agreement dialog box

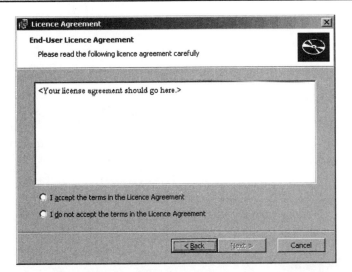

Note that the LicenseAgreement dialog box uses a ScrollableText control rather than a simple Text control to display the agreement. This allows the user to scroll up and down to see the entire agreement. Also note that neither of the radio buttons is selected by default. If the license agreement ever has to stand up in court, this may make a difference.

Selection

Finally, if your installation allows the user to choose which features to install, you should include a Selection dialog box in your Installer database. Figure 5.11 shows Microsoft Office 2000's Update Features dialog box, which is an example of a Selection dialog box.

FIGURE 5.11
A Selection dialog box

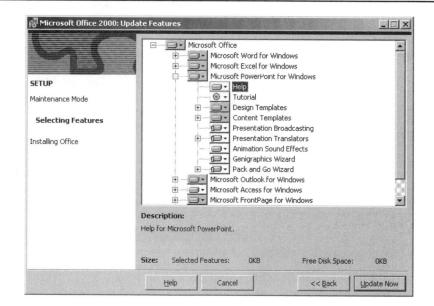

The heart of the Selection dialog box is the SelectionTree control that displays the hierarchy of features in the application. This control publishes an event that is subscribed to by the Text control. The Text control displays the description of the selected feature so that the description remains in sync with the tree.

This dialog box is not required by the Installer. If you don't show such a dialog box, then the set of features installed is dictated entirely by the entries you make in the Feature table and the InstallLevel you set from within your Installer database.

Dialog Box Style Bits

The Attributes column of the Dialog table is made up of a number of bit flags. Together, these specify the behavior of the dialog box defined by that particular row in the table. Table 5.2 shows these flags and the constants that are available for referring to them in code. (These are used, for example, when referring to the dialog box using the objects that I'll discuss in Chapter 9, "Using the Installer Automation Model.")

TABLE 5.2: Style Bits for Dialog Boxes

Name	Decimal	Hexidecimal	Constant
Visible	1	0x00000001	MsidbDialogAttributesVisible
Modal	2	0x00000002	msidbDialogAttributesModal
Minimize	4	0x00000004	msidbDialogAttributesMinimize
SysModal	8	0x00000008	msidbDialogAttributesSysModal
KeepModeless	16	0x00000010	msidbDialogAttributesKeepModeless
TrackDiskSpace	32	0x00000020	msidbDialogAttributesTrackDiskSpace
UseCustomPalette	64	0x00000040	msidbDialogAttributesUseCustomPalette
RTLRO	128	0x00000080	msidbDialogAttributesRTLRO
RightAligned	256	0x00000100	msidbDialogAttributesRightAligned
LeftScroll	512	0x00000200	msidbDialogAttributesLeftScroll
BiDi	896	0x00000380	msidbDialogAttributesBiDi
Error	65536	0x00010000	msidbDialogAttributesError

NOTE Each of these flags is represented by a single bit in the Attributes column except for the BiDi flag, which is a logical combination of the RTLRO, RightAligned, and LeftScroll flags.

If a dialog box has the Visible bit set, the dialog box is visible when it's first displayed. Otherwise, it's created hidden, and you need to modify the Attributes value later to make it visible. In most cases, you'll want to keep this bit set on all your dialog boxes.

Setting the Modal bit for a dialog box makes that dialog box modal. In other words, the processing stops while the user is dealing with the dialog box, and other dialog boxes cannot be displayed on top of it. Generally you'll want to make all of the dialog boxes in a wizard modal.

If you set the Minimize bit for a dialog box, that dialog box displays a Minimize button and can be minimized. By default, this behavior is off (that is, by default, dialog boxes cannot be minimized).

The SysModal bit sets a dialog box to be system modal. A system modal dialog box forces the user to deal only with it until it is dismissed. No other application on the system can take the focus while a system modal dialog box is displayed. Except for very exceptional circumstances, there's no reason to set this bit.

Normally, when the Installer displays one dialog box, it destroys any dialog box that's already displayed. This allows for a smooth progression between the various dialog boxes that make up a wizard-style interface. However, at times, you will want to display a dialog box while keeping the previous dialog box in existence. For example, if you're letting the user browse to set the installation location for a product, you might want both the Browse dialog box and the dialog box that spawned it to remain on screen. To enable this behavior, set the KeepModeless bit of the dialog box being spawned.

When you set the TrackDiskSpace bit on a dialog box, that dialog box receives periodic notification of the amount of free disk space that's projected to remain on the system when an installation is completed. This is useful for dialogs, such as the DiskCost dialog box, that need to keep track of this information.

The UseCustomPalette style bit instructs the system to use the color palette from the first control on the dialog box when displaying that dialog box. If you've got a picture that uses many colors, you may get a better display by setting this bit and making that picture the first control on the dialog box.

The RTLRO bit sets the dialog box and the controls on it to right-to-left reading order mode. This ensures that strings are displayed starting at the right-hand side of controls and grow to the left (the opposite of the way that text is displayed in English and other western languages).

The RightAligned style bit forces text on the dialog box to right-align. The default is left alignment. Unless you're working in a language with right-to-left reading order you should not set this bit.

The LeftScroll bit forces any vertical scroll bars in the dialog box to display on the left-hand side of the controls rather than the standard right-hand side.

The BiDi style "bit" is simply a convenience (and the only one of the group that isn't really a bit). It combines right-to-left reading, right alignment, and left scroll bars into a single setting. This makes it easier for developers of localization tools to handle what are usually called the bidi languages, such as Hebrew and Arabic, where the words are read from right to left.

The Error bit must be set for any dialog box that's identified in the Property table as an error dialog box. You can set this bit for more than one dialog box in your application if you'd like, and you can update the Property table to switch to the appropriate dialog box as your installation progresses.

Controls

The controls supported by the Windows Installer can be divided naturally into two groups. First, there are the controls that are not associated with a property in the Property table:

- Bitmap
- GroupBox
- Icon
- Line
- ProgressBar
- PushButton
- ScrollableText
- Text
- VolumeCostList

The other group of controls are those that are (or can be) associated with a property in the Property table. By associating a control with a property, you can allow the user's choices on the user interface to influence the installed features or components. For example, if your installation includes the Microsoft Data Access Components (MDAC), you could include a checkbox to allow the user to disable this part of the installation. The controls in this group include the following:

- CheckBox
- ComboBox
- DirectoryCombo
- DirectoryList
- Edit
- ListBox
- ListView
- MaskedEdit
- PathEdit
- RadioButtonGroup
- SelectionTree
- VolumeSelectCombo

NOTE   Any properties that are changed via the user interface in this fashion must be public properties. That is, their names must consist entirely of capital letters.

In this section, I'll take a quick look at the available native controls and discuss their use. If you're familiar with basic Windows user interface guidelines you'll see that the Installer includes all the controls necessary to build a standard user interface.

For information on control attributes, see the section on the Control table and its Attributes column in Chapter 4.

Bitmap

The Bitmap control is used to display a static bitmap on the user interface. Figure 5.12 shows a bitmap control on a dialog box (as well as a number of other static controls).

FIGURE 5.12
Installer static controls

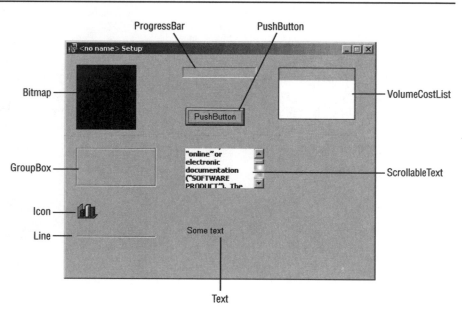

The source for the bitmap control's image depends on whether or not the Image-Handle flag is set in the control's Attributes column (see the section on the Control table in Chapter 4 for a discussion of the various flags that you can set in this column). If the ImageHandle flag is set, then the Text column for the control must contain the bitmap handle of a bitmap already in memory at the time the control is displayed. If the Image-Handle flag is not set, then the Text column contains the name of a bitmap stored in the

Binary table. Unless you need dynamic bitmaps for some reason, the second option is much easier to implement.

If the FixedSize flag is set in the Attributes column of the Control table, the bitmap is either centered or cropped in the control, depending on whether it is smaller or larger than the control. If this flag is not set, then the bitmap is stretched to fit the control.

GroupBox

The GroupBox control exists to visually group other controls. If you like, you can specify a caption for the GroupBox by filling in the Text column of the Control table.

WARNING	The GroupBox does not do any logical control grouping (unlike the similar GroupBox control in Visual Basic). To group, for example, radio buttons into one logical group you set their Property column to the same value in the RadioButton table.

Icon

The Icon control is similar to the Bitmap control, except that it displays an image from an icon file instead of a bitmap image. You can use the Attributed column of the Control table to specify which image to display in the case of a multiple-resolution icon file.

The source for the icon control's image depends on whether or not the ImageHandle flag is set in the control's Attributes column (see the section on the Control table in Chapter 4 for a discussion of the various flags that you can set in this column). If the ImageHandle flag is set, then the Text column for the control must contain the icon handle of an icon already in memory at the time the control is displayed. If the ImageHandle flag is not set, then the Text column contains the name of an icon stored in the Binary table. Unless you need dynamic icons the second option is much easier to implement.

Line

The Line control displays a horizontal line. This line is automatically set to the "etched" style to provide a three-dimensional effect.

NOTE	The Installer doesn't provide a native Vertical line control, but you can fake it with a GroupBox sized to have no width. For lines at any other angle, the best you can do is to use a Bitmap control.

ProgressBar

The ProgressBar control is designed to help the user keep track of the progress of an installation by displaying a horizontal bar graph showing the proportion of elapsed time to expected time. Depending on the Attributes you set for the control, this bar graph can be either continuous or made up of a series of small blocks.

When the user has finished selecting options and the Installer is generating an execution script, it keeps track of the actions to be performed and assigns a tick count to each of these actions. Then, while the installation is actually taking place, the Installer broadcasts a progress message at the end of each action. These progress messages include both the total number of ticks and the number of ticks elapsed.

Each of these messages generates a SetProgress control event. By subscribing the ProgressBar control to this event, you get a control that will automatically format a bar graph based on the tick count information.

The Installer also broadcasts a TimeRemaining control event on each progress message. This event attempts to estimate the amount of time remaining by using the information about time taken so far. For example, if 30 percent of the action ticks have passed, and that has taken three minutes, the Installer will estimate that seven minutes remain.

If you like, you can use a Text control to subscribe to the TimeRemaining event by setting its TimeRemaining control attribute. However, unless you do a perfect job of estimating how long each action will take, the time is likely to fluctuate up and down. I don't recommend displaying the time remaining information; it tends to just confuse the user.

PushButton

A PushButton control provides a simple way for the user to interact with the user interface. A PushButton control looks and acts very much like a Visual Basic command button. Typically, in a wizard-style interface, PushButton controls are used to move forward and back in the installation sequence. This is implemented by adding a NewDialog event to the ControlEvent table with the name of the dialog box to spawn. There are other events that will sometimes be called from PushButtons, but I'll discuss these later in the chapter.

PushButton controls can display text, a bitmap or an icon:

To display text   Put the text in the Text column of the Control table.

To display a bitmap   Set the Bitmap flag in the Attributes column of the Control table, and place the name of the bitmap from the Binary table in the Text column.

Alternatively, you can set the Bitmap flag and the ImageHandle flag, and then set the image handle of a bitmap into the Text column at runtime.

To display an icon Set the Icon flag in the Attributes column of the Control table, and place the name of the icon from the Binary table in the Text column. Alternatively, you can set the Icon flag and the ImageHandle flag, and then set the image handle of an icon into the Text column at runtime.

ScrollableText

A ScrollableText control is designed to display more text than can easily fit in a Text control. Typically, this control is used for longwinded legalese in the form of license agreements, in which the lawyers insist you put a lot of text on the user interface and there's obviously no room to do so.

The text for this control is entered in the Text column of the Control table. However, there are two special things you need to be aware of with this control as compared to other controls:

1. Embedded properties in the text are not resolved. If your text depends on embedded properties, you'll need to use a regular Text control.

2. The text must be specified as an RTF (Rich Text Format) string. If you just type the text in the Text column, nothing will be displayed because the text won't have the proper RTF headers.

NOTE Perhaps the easiest way to create the text for a ScrollableText control is to use an editor such as Word or WordPad that implements Save As RTF. You would then need to open the resulting file in Notepad, and cut and paste the RTF string to the Control table.

Text

The Text control is designed to display static text on the user interface. In this respect, it's very similar to the Visual Basic Label control. Like the Label control, you can change the Text control's text at runtime if you need to, but you should probably try to avoid this.

To set the font for a Text control, make an entry in the TextStyle table, and then prefix the Text column for the control with the name of the TextStyle in the format {\TextStyle-Name}. It's good practice to define a default text style in the TextStyle table and use it for every control, rather than depending on the Installer to pick a good default.

If you like, you can define a Text control that displays the remaining time in the installation. To do this, set the TimeRemaining flag in the control's Attributes column in the Control table. Then use the EventMapping table to subscribe this control to the TimeRemaining event. You also need to include a string in the UIText table named TimeRemaining. This string is used to format the display of remaining time, and should have placeholders for minutes and seconds.

VolumeCostList

The VolumeCostList control is specialized to deal with one of the common problems of software installations: displaying the free space on the drives in a system. Although there is a VolumeCostList control on Figure 5.12, it's hard to tell what it does because that figure is a preview from within the Installer. Figure 5.13 shows a VolumeCostList control in action. This control is the entire listview showing the disk volumes and sizes as well as the column headers.

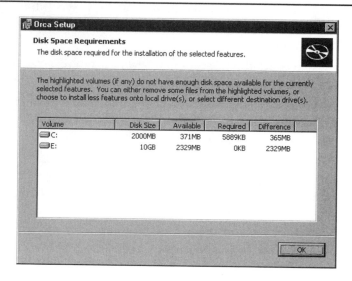

FIGURE 5.13
The VolumeCostList control in action

To use the VolumeCostList control, you need to put entries into the UIText table containing the strings that it will display. The column headers are specified as these strings:

- VolumeCostAvailable
- VolumeCostDifference
- VolumeCostSize
- VolumeCostRequired
- VolumeCostVolume

The Installer also expects to find strings that it can use when constructing drive sizes. These strings have these names:

- Bytes
- KB
- MB
- GB

It's possible to specify the font and column widths for the VolumeCostList control by making an entry in the Text column of the Control table entry for the control. Use the standard {\TextStyleName} format to set the font. To set the column widths, you can append up to five numbers in curly braces. {0} will hide the column; otherwise, the number gives the width of the column in pixels. Of course, the user can always resize columns at runtime, as well as click column headers to sort the list.

CheckBox

The CheckBox control provides a two-state (checked/unchecked) control. You can associate the control with a property by putting that property's name in the Property column of the Control table. Checking the box sets the property to the value listed in the Value column of the CheckBox table for the row where the Property column is the same as the name of the Checkbox. If there's no such row in the Checkbox table, then checking the box sets the property to the initial value for the property listed in the Property table.

ComboBox

The ComboBox control allows you to associate the value of a property with the user's choice from the drop-down list in the combo box. When you select a value in the ComboBox, the Installer looks through the ComboBox table to find a row that has the selected value in the Text column. It then sets the associated property to the value listed in the Value column of the same row in the table.

By default, the ComboBox allows the user to type in a value that's not in the drop-down list (to disable this behavior, set the ComboList flag in the Attributes column in the Control table). You can limit the number of characters that the user types by putting a number in braces after any font specification in the Text column of the Control table. For example, if you set the Text column to {\DefaultStyle}{100}, that combo box will use the TextStyle named DefaultStyle and allow a maximum of 100 characters.

DirectoryCombo, DirectoryList, and PathEdit

I'm covering these three controls together because they are almost always used together on a single dialog box for a single purpose: to allow the user to pick an installation directory. Figure 5.14 shows these controls in action.

FIGURE 5.14
Choosing an installation directory

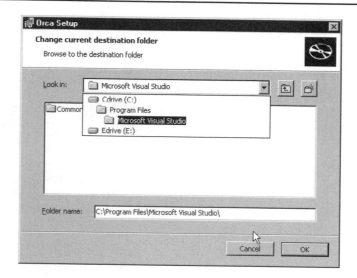

The DirectoryCombo control is the combo box control. In the figure, it is shown dropped down and it displays the path to the parent directory of the currently-chosen directory. Dropped down, it shows the path tree to that point, as well as the other drives that you can choose for the installation.

The DirectoryList control is the list box in the middle of the dialog box, shown partially obscured by the DirectoryCombo control's drop-down box in the figure. This control shows all of the existing subdirectories of the current directory.

The PathEdit control is the text box that's labeled "Folder Name:" in the figure. This control lets you edit the entire path for the installation, including adding new folders that don't yet exist.

Together, the DirectoryCombo and DirectoryList controls display the path shown in the PathEdit control.

You can determine whether the DirectoryCombo control will show removable drives, CD-ROM drives, and so on by setting appropriate flags in the Attributes column of the Control table.

All three of these controls should be associated with the same property. This property must be specified in the Property table with at least a volume name and a path (for example, C:\). Alternatively, it can be the name of a directory in the Directory table. As the user changes the controls, they are all kept synchronized and the property will be left with the value showing in the PathEdit control.

Typically, you'll use this set of three controls on a Browse dialog box.

Edit

The Edit control is the Installer analog of the Visual Basic TextBox control. The user can type text into the box and edit it until they move to another dialog box. Although you're not required to do so, you'll normally want to store the control's final value in a property. To do this, just put the name of the property in the Property column of the Control table.

You can limit the number of characters that the user types by putting a number in braces after any font specification in the Text column of the Control table. For example, if you set the Text column to "{\DefaultStyle}{100}Initial Value" that particular Edit control will use the TextStyle named DefaultStyle and allow a maximum of 100 characters. Its default value will be the string "Initial Value."

ListBox

The ListBox control allows you to associate the value of a property with the user's choice from a fixed list of values. You specify the property by putting the property's name in the Property column of the Control table. Selecting a line in the ListBox sets the property to the value listed in the Value column of the ListBox table for the row with the selected value in the Text column.

ListView

As implemented by the Installer user interface, the ListView control is really just a prettier ListBox control. As with the ListBox, the ListView control allows you to associate the value of a property with the user's choice from a fixed list of values. You specify the property by putting the property's name in the Property column of the Control table. Selecting a value sets the property to the value listed in the Value column of the List-View table for the row with the selected value in the Text column.

The only difference between the ListBox and the ListView controls is that the ListView table includes a Binary_ column. This column lets you specify an icon to be displayed alongside each item in the ListView control by pointing at an entry in the Binary table.

The Installer does not provide any facilities for customizing the columns in a ListView control.

MaskedEdit

The MaskedEdit control is a TextBox control that includes a mask (specified in the Text column of the Control table) that allows only certain characters to be entered by the user. In addition, it can include characters that can't be edited or seen by the user, which is useful for things like product IDs where part of the value should be kept secret (though not too secret; remember, there are utilities to view the data in an Installer database).

Table 5.3 shows the characters that you can use in the mask for a MaskedEdit control.

TABLE 5.3: Special Characters for the MaskedEdit Control

Character	Meaning
<	Start of the visible portion of the text. Everything to the left of and including this character is hidden from the user interface.
>	End of the visible portion of the text. Everything to the right of and including this character is hidden from the user interface.
#	Accepts a digit only.
%	Accepts a digit only. Custom actions can use the alternative representations to impose additional validation on certain characters.
@	A randomized digit generated by the Installer. This should only be used in the invisible portion of the mask.
_	Accepts any alphanumeric character.
^	Accepts any alphanumeric character.
?	Accepts any alphanumeric character.
'	Accepts any alphanumeric character.
=	Field terminator. Accepts one more character of the same type as the proceeding symbol and then inserts a dash in the generated string.

RadioButtonGroup

To the Installer, a RadioButtonGroup control is analogous to a ListBox control. It's used to choose one of a fixed number of alternatives. You can't address the individual radio buttons in any way (for example, you can't hide or disable individual radio buttons).

As with the ListBox, the RadioButtonGroup control allows you to associate the value of a property with the user's choice from a fixed list of values. You specify the property by putting the property's name in the Property column of the Control table. Selecting a

RadioButton sets the property to the value listed in the Value column of the Radio-Button table for the row with the selected value in the Text column.

The RadioButton table allows you to set the *x* and *y* coordinates of the individual buttons within the RadioButtonGroup.

SelectionTree

The SelectionTree control is at the heart of the Installer user interface (unless you're developing an installation that doesn't let the user select which features they'd like to install). This control automatically populates a TreeView from the Feature table, and it lets the user choose the installation state for each feature. Figure 5.15 shows a Selection-Tree control in action.

FIGURE 5.15
Choosing installation state with a SelectionTree control

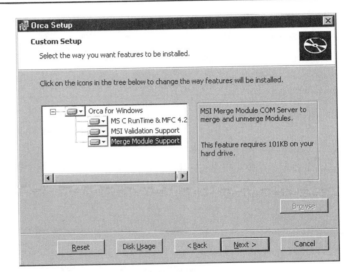

The SelectionTree control automatically publishes eight events. I've listed these in Table 5.4. Using these events, it's easy to synchronize other controls on the user interface so that they change as the user moves through the tree.

TABLE 5.4: Events Published by the SelectionTree Control

Event	Description
SelectionAction	Publishes the chosen state, using the appropriate string from the UIText table.
SelectionBrowse	Generated when the user clicks a Browse button on the same dialog box to select a location for a feature.

TABLE 5.4:   Events Published by the SelectionTree Control *(continued)*

Event	Description
SelectionDescription	Publishes the description of the highlighted item using the Title string from the Feature table.
SelectionIcon	Publishes the icon handle of the icon for the highlighted item.
SelectionNoItems	Published whenever the highlighted node has no children. Useful for disabling other controls.
SelectionPath	Publishes the path of the highlighted item.
SelectionPathOn	Publishes a boolean indicating whether there is a path associated with the highlighted item.
SelectionSize	Publishes the size of the highlighted item in bytes, KB, MB, or GB as appropriate.

This control depends on a number of strings in the UIText table to format the data it displays, either in its right-hand section or in the drop-down state-selection lists in the TreeView. These strings are listed in Table 5.5.

TABLE 5.5:   UIText Strings for the SelectionTree Control

String	Used For
AbsentPath	Path to display for a feature that will not be installed
Bytes	Size in bytes
GB	Size in gigabytes
KB	Size in kilobytes
MB	Size in megabytes
MenuAbsent	Drop-down selection for feature not to be installed
MenuAllCD	Drop-down selection for feature to be run from source together with all children
MenuAllLocal	Drop-down selection for feature to be installed locally together with all children
MenuAllNetwork	Drop-down selection for feature to be run from network together with all children
MenuCD	Drop-down selection for feature to be run from source
MenuLocal	Drop-down selection for feature to be installed locally
MenuNetwork	Drop-down selection for feature to run from network
SelAbsentAbsent	Absent feature that will remain absent
SelAbsentCD	Absent feature that will be run from CD
SelAbsentLocal	Absent feature that will be installed locally
SelAbsentNetwork	Absent feature that will run from network
SelCDAbsent	Run from CD feature that will be removed
SelCDCD	Run from CD feature that will remain run from CD

TABLE 5.5: UIText Strings for the SelectionTree Control *(continued)*

String	Used For
SelCDLocal	Run from CD feature that will be installed locally
SelChildCostPos	Leaf feature (with no children) that will take up space
SelChildCostNeg	Leaf feature (with no children) the will free space
SelLocalAbsent	Locally installed feature that will be removed
SelLocalCD	Locally installed feature that will be run from CD
SelLocalLocal	Locally installed feature that will remain locally installed
SelLocalNetwork	Locally installed feature that will run from network
SelNetworkAbsent	Run from network feature that will be removed
SelNetworkLocal	Run from network feature that will be installed locally
SelNetworkNetwork	Run from network feature that will remain run from network
SelParentCostNegNeg	Parent feature that will free space and that includes child features that will free space
SelParentCostNegPos	Parent feature that will free space and that includes child features that will take up space
SelParentCostPosNeg	Parent feature that will take up space and that includes child features that will free space
SelParentCostPosPos	Parent feature that will take up space and that includes child features that will take up space

The information used by the SelectionTree control is generated by the CostInitialize and CostFinalize actions, so you should not display a dialog box containing this control until those two actions have been executed.

VolumeSelectCombo

The VolumeSelectCombo control is a specialized combo box, designed to display a list of the drives on the user's system. Selecting a drive sets the name of the drive into the associated property for the control. Figure 5.16 shows one possible use for the VolumeSelectCombo.

FIGURE 5.16
The VolumeSelectCombo control

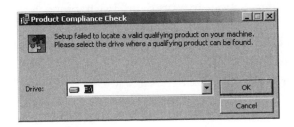

You can control the type of drives that are shown in the drop-down list (floppy, CD, hard drive, and so on) by setting the appropriate flags in the Attributes column of the Control table.

Events

The Windows Installer supports 35 different events for communication between different parts of the user interface, and for communication between the user interface and the rest of the installation process. In this section, I'll discuss the mechanics of events in the Installer; I'll then go through the individual events one by one.

Overview of Event Processing

If you're used to Visual Basic, you may find the Installer event model a bit confusing. Rather than each control having a fixed set of events, the Installer allows you to pick events that you'd like to publish from individual controls. In addition, the Installer itself publishes some events as it performs the various actions in the installation process. You can then decide which controls should subscribe to the published events. There are also events to which the Installer automatically subscribes.

To publish an event, you make an entry into the ControlEvent table, listing the control that will trigger the event and the event name.

To subscribe to an event, you make an entry into the EventMapping table, listing the control that will subscribe to the event and the event name. You can also cause an event to automatically change an attribute on the control (such as Visible or Enabled) by listing the attribute name in the Attribute column of the EventMapping table.

Controls may only subscribe to events that are published by the Installer itself or by other controls in the same dialog box. That's because usually there is only one dialog box displayed by the Installer at any given time.

ActionData

As the Installer goes about its work, it performs numerous actions. For example, it performs an InstallFiles action to copy files from the source media to the user's hard drive. I'll discuss actions in more detail in Chapter 6. For the moment, though, it's important to know that each action may generate one or more ActionData messages. For example, the InstallFiles action generates messages listing the name of each file, its size in bytes, and its target directory.

For each ActionData message, the Installer publishes an ActionData control event. You can use these messages to update a dialog box with progress information while the installation is proceeding. The simplest way to do this is to place a Text control on a dialog box, and then use the EventMapping table to subscribe the Text attribute of the control to the ActionData event. This will cause the Installer to update the control every time a new ActionData message is generated.

ActionText

The ActionText control event is very similar to the ActionData control event. Instead of receiving the detailed data from each action taken, though, subscribers to the ActionText event receive only the name of the action currently being executed. You might choose to display this above the detailed data on a progress dialog box, or you might want to use only the ActionText event if you don't want to overwhelm your users with too many messages.

AddLocal and AddSource

The AddLocal event sets a feature to be installed locally. The Argument column in the ControlEvent table must contain either the name of a feature from the Feature table or the string "ALL" to install all features locally. You might use this event if you have only a few features and don't want to present a SelectionTree control to your users. For example, if you only have three features in your application, you could create a dialog box with three CheckBox controls and have each of the three publish an AddLocal event for a particular feature.

The AddSource control event has the same syntax as the AddLocal control event. The only difference is that the specified feature is set to run from the source instead of to be installed locally.

CheckExistingTargetPath and CheckTargetPath

The CheckExistingTargetPath control event tells the Installer to inspect a particular property and determine whether it contains a writeable path. The property name is the argument to the event. If the property is not a writeable path, then further control events published by the same control are cancelled.

This event might be used on the Next button of a dialog box that allows the user to pick an install location, for example. You could tie two events to the Next button. The first would be a CheckExistingTargetPath event that used the property where the install location was stored as its argument. The second event would be a NewDialog event to open the next dialog box in your installation program. If the user can't install the software to the specified location, then the NewDialog event won't be executed, and the user will remain on the dialog box where the installation directory was selected.

The CheckTargetPath control event is similar to the CheckExistingTargetPath event. However the CheckTargetPath event only checks that the path is valid, not that it is writeable.

DirectoryListNew, DirectoryListOpen, and DirectoryListUp

The DirectoryListNew event notifies the DirectoryList control that it should create a new folder and select the name of the new folder for immediate editing.

The DirectoryListOpen event tells the DirectoryList control to open the currently selected folder and show its subfolders.

The DirectoryListUp event notifies the DirectoryList control to move to the parent of the current directory (or to do nothing, if the current directory is a root directory).

Any DirectoryList control automatically subscribes to these events if they're published by other controls on the same dialog box. Typically, you'll want to create New, Open, and Up PushButton controls on the dialog box and use the ControlEvent table to publish the DirectoryListNew, DirectoryListOpen, and DirectoryListUp events from them respectively. The Argument column is ignored for these events, so you can just enter a zero to provide the required data in that column.

DoAction

The DoAction control event executes a custom action. You'll learn more about custom actions in Chapter 6. Because the Installer can call a function from an external DLL as a custom action, a custom action can do pretty much anything. The Argument column of the ControlEvent column supplies the name of the custom action to execute.

WARNING   Custom actions offer problems for a clean installation. Notably, anything they do to the user's system can't be undone by a rollback or uninstall. Before you resort to a custom action, you should be absolutely sure that there's no way to accomplish your purpose with the Installer's native functionality.

EnableRollback

The EnableRollback control event can be used to enable or disable the Installer's built-in rollback capabilities. To enable rollback, pass True as the argument to this event; to disable rollback, pass False as the argument to this event.

Because rollback is enabled by default, you're more likely to use this control event to disable rollback. Figure 5.17 shows a dialog box from the Office 2000 installation that uses this event. This dialog box is called when the Installer detects that there's not enough disk space to store all of the rollback information. If the user clicks Yes, the EnableRollback event is called with an argument of False.

FIGURE 5.17
One reason to disable
rollback

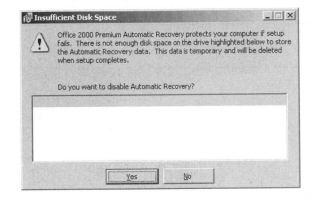

EnDialog

The EndDialog control event is used to destroy the current dialog box and return control to the Installer. Typically, you'll only want to call this when you want to get out of your dialog box sequence (see the NewDialog control event below for another option). The Argument column for this row in the ControlEvent table must be one of these four values:

Exit   Returns control to the Installer with the UserExit return value.

Retry   Returns control to the Installer with the Suspend return value.

Ignore   Returns control to the Installer with the Finished return value.

Return   Returns control to the parent of this dialog box with the Success return value.

You can use EndDialog with the Return argument to safely close a modal dialog box.

IgnoreChange

You probably won't need this event. I'm only including it for the sake of completeness. The IgnoreChange event is published by the DirectoryList control when the user highlights a directory but doesn't open it. It's subscribed to by the DirectoryCombo control on the same dialog box to ensure that the DirectoryList and DirectoryCombo controls remain in synchronization.

NewDialog, SpawnDialog, and SpawnWaitDialog

The NewDialog control event is used to close one modal dialog box and open another. When a control that publishes this event is triggered, the Installer closes the current dialog box and puts up a new one in its place. The name of the new dialog box is stored in the Argument column of the ControlEvent table.

If you're designing a wizard-style interface for your Installer, the Back and Next buttons will usually publish NewDialog events to enable navigation between the various panels of the wizard.

The SpawnDialog event also opens a new modal dialog box. The difference between the NewDialog and SpawnDialog events is that the latter does not destroy the current dialog box.

The SpawnWaitDialog event also opens a new modal dialog box without closing the current dialog box. For the SpawnWaitDialog event you must include an expression in the Condition column of the ControlEvent table. The specified dialog box is shown as long as the condition evaluates to True and is destroyed as soon as it evaluates to False. For example, you might use this control event to display a "Please Wait" dialog box while the Installer computes component costs before displaying a dialog box with a SelectionTree control.

Reinstall and ReinstallMode

In most simple user interfaces, these two events will be published by the same control. The ReinstallMode event sets the flags that the Installer uses to control reinstallation actions. The Reinstall event specifies a feature to be reinstalled by supplying the name of that feature as the value of the Argument column. You can also use "ALL" as the Argument for the Reinstall event to reinstall all features in the product.

The argument to the ReinstallMode event consists of one or more of the options in Table 5.6. If you omit the argument, it defaults to "osum."

TABLE 5.6: Arguments to the ReinstallMode Event

Option	Meaning
a	Reinstall all files, regardless of checksum or version.
c	Reinstall if a file is missing or corrupt. This switch only operates on files with a checksum stored in the installation database's File table.
d	Reinstall if a file is missing, or a different version is installed.
e	Reinstall if a file is missing, or an earlier or equal version is installed.

TABLE 5.6: Arguments to the ReinstallMode Event *(continued)*

Option	Meaning
m	Recreate all Registry keys that are stored in the HKEY_LOCAL_MACHINE or HKEY_CLASSES_ROOT Registry hives. Also, rewrite all information from the Class, Verb, PublishComponent, ProgID, MIME, Icon, Extension, and AppID tables. Reinstall all qualified components.
o	Reinstall if a file is missing, or an earlier version is installed.
p	Reinstall if a file is missing.
s	Reinstall all shortcuts and icons, replacing any that are present or cached.
u	Recreate all Registry keys that are stored in the HKEY_CURRENT_USER or HKEY_USERS Registry hives.
v	Forces use of the package on the source media rather than any locally cached copy.

Remove

The Remove control event is similar to the AddLocal and AddSource control events. The Remove event sets a feature to be removed from the user's computer. The Argument column in the ControlEvent table must contain either the name of a feature from the Feature table or the string "ALL" to remove all features.

Reset

When a control publishes a Reset control event, all changes are rolled back on the current dialog box since it was displayed. You can think of this as a sort of dialog-level undo facility. One obvious place to use the Reset event is from the Cancel button on a Browse dialog box. By publishing a Reset event from the button, you can ensure that all of the installation directory properties are reset to their original values before the dialog box is closed.

ScriptInProgress

The Installer publishes a ScriptInProgress event when the user has finished choosing options and it is compiling the execution script to carry out the insallation. If a control subscribes to this event, it will display the value of the ScriptInProgress entry in the UIText table while this compilation proceeds.

SelectionAction, SelectionBrowse, SelectionDescription, SelectionIcon, SelectionNoItems, SelectionPath, SelectionPathOn, and SelectionSize

The SelectionTree control publishes all of these events as the user interacts with the control. Other controls on the same dialog box will typically subscribe to one of these events in order to supply updated help text.

SelectionAction control event   Published when the user chooses a new item in the tree. It publishes a string describing the action the highlighted item will take.

SelectionBrowse control event   Used to spawn a browse dialog box if the currently highlighted item allows selecting an installation location.

SelectionDescription control event   Published when the user chooses a new item in the tree. It publishes a string describing the item.

SelectionIcon control event   Published when the user chooses a new item in the tree. It publishes the icon handle of the icon for this item.

SelectionNoItems control event   Published whenever the highlighted item in the tree has no children.

SelectionPath control event   Published when the user chooses a new item in the tree. It publishes the path of the selected item.

SelectionPathOn control event   Published when the user chooses a new item in the tree. It publishes a boolean value indicating whether a path is associated with the selected feature.

SelectionSize control event   Published when the user chooses a new item in the tree. It publishes the size of the item.

SetInstallLevel

The SetInstallLevel sets the installation level for the current installation. The Installer determines which features to install by comparing the level of each feature to the level of the installation itself. A feature is only installed if the feature's level is less than or equal to the install level of the installation itself.

SetProgress

As the Installer proceeds with modifying the user's computer, it periodically reports its progress using the SetProgress event. If your user interface includes a ProgressBar control to display to the user the proportion of the installation that's completed, then you should use the EventMapping table to subscribe that ProgressBar control to this event.

SetProperty

The SetProperty event allows you to set the value of a property as the result of the user clicking a PushButton. Its syntax differs from that of the other control events. The Event column of the ControlEvent table contains the name of the property to be set. The property name must be enclosed in square brackets. The Argument contains the new value for the property. If this is a literal value, it is copied into the property specified in the Event column. If the Argument contains the name of another property instead (in square brackets), the value of the second property is copied to the value of the first property.

SetTargetPath

The SetTargetPath control event sets the target path for the installation. Usually you'll publish this event from the OK or Next button of a browse dialog to set the target path to that chosen by the user. If the user interface doesn't allow browsing for an installation location, you won't need this control event.

TimeRemaining

As the Installer is carrying out the installation, it publishes periodic TimeRemaining events with the number of seconds left in the installation. A control can subscribe to this event in the EventMapping table to display this information to the user. You might choose to ignore this event if you have a long and complex installation since the estimated time has a tendency to be inaccurate in such cases.

ValidateProductID

The ValidateProductID event checks the current value of the ProductID property to see whether it's accepted by the PIDKEY property. If there is a problem validating the ID, then the Installer displays an error message. Usually you'll want to call this event when the user is about to leave a dialog box that required entering a product ID in the first place.

Installer Actions

Now that you've seen the Installer database and the Installer user interface, you should have a good understanding of the static portion of the Installer. The third main piece of the puzzle explains the dynamic nature of the Installer. Sequence tables, which contain actions, define the activities that the Installer will perform and the order in which these actions will occur. In this chapter, I'll dig into sequence tables, show you what actions should be used in what order in an average installation, and introduce you to custom actions, which you can use to extend the Installer's built-in functionality.

Understanding Sequence Tables

You met the sequence tables in Chapter 4, "A Guide to the Installer Database." To recap, the six tables that control the order that the Installer uses to collect data, build, and execute installation scripts are in bold in the following list. They have been categorized by the installation for which they are used.

The InstallUISequence and InstallExecuteSequence tables Used to perform a normal install.

The AdvtUISequence and AdvtExecuteSequence tables Used to perform an advertised install.

The AdminUISequence and AdminExecuteSequence tables Used for an administrative install.

All six of these tables have the same three columns:

The Action column Contains the name of the action to execute. It can be either a built-in action or a custom action.

The Condition column Contains a conditional expression to evaluate. If present, this condition is evaluated before the action is executed. If it evaluates to False, the action is skipped. If the Condition column is blank, the action is always executed.

The Sequence column Used to order the actions in the table. Generally, the actions are run in increasing sequence order, but here are exceptions to this rule. Table 6.1 lists the special numbers you can use in this column.

T A B L E   6 . 1 :   Values for the Sequence Column of Sequence Tables

Value	Meaning
Positive number	Run the action in this sequence.
Zero	Don't run this action.
Null	Don't run this action.
-1	Run this action when an installation is successfully completed.
-2	Run this action when the user cancels during an installation.
-3	Run this action in case of a fatal error.

TABLE 6.1:   Values for the Sequence Column of Sequence Tables *(continued)*

Value	Meaning
-4	Run this action when the installation is suspended.
Other negative numbers	Don't run this action.

Sequence tables can contain both standard actions that are built into the Windows Installer and custom actions that are added on by other developers. In addition, they can contain dialog boxes that should be displayed during the installation. Some standard actions have dependencies on other standard actions. For example, the InstallFiles action must come after the InstallValidate action. I'll cover these dependencies later in the chapter as I discuss the individual standard actions.

Figure 6.1 shows a portion of one of the sequence tables from the Installer database for Microsoft Office 2000 Professional. Note that most of the sequence numbers have gaps between them. Sequence numbers need not be contiguous; the only restriction is that no two actions in the same table may have the same sequence number. By leaving gaps in the sequence numbers as you develop your sequence tables, you make it easier to insert new actions later if there's a need.

FIGURE 6.1

An example of a sequence table

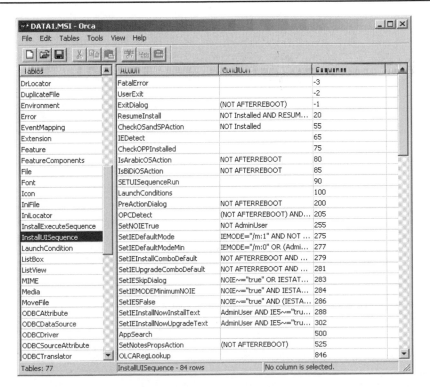

File Costing

In the context of the Windows Installer, *file costing* or *costing* refers to the process of determining how much disk space the software will take up and whether there's actually enough room on the user's hard drive for the selected features. The Installer uses quite sophisticated formulas to make file costing as accurate as possible. The following factors are considered:

- The raw size of the files to be installed
- The space that Registry entries and shortcuts will occupy
- The cluster size of the target hard drive(s)
- The extra room needed to support rollback
- The space saved by replacing old files instead of keeping them
- The space saved by deleting unneeded files and Registry entries

The goal is never to start an installation unless there's actually enough room for the selected features; the Installer does a good job of determining this.

Costing is done by a series of actions.

1. First, the CostInitialize action initializes the costing engine within the Installer.

2. Then, the FileCost action checks the files to be installed, compares their versions with those on the hard drive already, and collects other information.

3. Then, the CostFinalize action combines the collected information with the list of components to be installed in order to determine the actual costs of the installation.

4. Any time after the CostFinalize action is completed, you can display a dialog box containing a SelectionTree control and be assured that the control will be properly initialized. This gives your users a chance to change the selected components. If they make any changes, the SelectionTree will handle updating the Installer engine so that it can keep the cost calculations up-to-date.

5. Finally, when the user has made their final component selections (or you've done it for them, if you're not displaying a SelectionTree control), you should call the InstallValidate action, which compares the file cost information with the actual free space on the target drive(s) and also determines whether the installation should move forward.

Standard Actions

Most of what you'll ever need the Installer to do can be handled with standard actions. Indeed, if you think you need a custom action to perform a particular task, you should stop for a moment and review the list of standard actions. It's entirely possible that you've overlooked an easy way to take care of your installation needs.

In this section, I'll describe all of the standard actions. Later in the chapter, you'll see how these actions fit into a typical sequence table, but for now, I'll organize them by function. Standard actions can be classified into these major groups:

- Top-level actions
- File actions
- Registry actions
- ODBC actions
- Environment actions
- .ini File actions
- Service actions
- Publishing actions
- Upgrade Actions
- Miscellaneous actions

NOTE   As you read through the list of standard actions, you'll note that there is a close relationship between the Installer database tables you saw in Chapter 4 and the standard actions. Many actions exist only to process a single table from the Installer database. If a table (say, the Fonts table) has no entries in your particular Installer database, then there's no need for you to call the associated action (in this case, the RegisterFonts action).

ADMIN, ADVERTISE, and INSTALL

The three top-level actions are not actually called from within a sequence tables. Rather, they're the actions that the Installer executes in order to decide which sequence tables to use:

The ADMIN action   When the ADMIN action is executed, the Installer proceeds to work with the AdminUISequence and AdminExecuteSequence tables to do an administrative installation.

The ADVERTISE action   When the ADVERTISE action is executed, the Installer proceeds to work with the AdvtUISequence and AdvtExecuteSequence tables to do an advertised installation.

The INSTALL action   Whe the INSTALL action is executed, the Installer proceeds to work with the InstallUISequence and InstallExecuteSequence tables to perform a normal installation.

You can trigger one of these actions by launching the Installer with an appropriate command-line switch (as you learned in Chapter 2, "Running the Installer"). As you'll see in Chapter 8, "Using the Installer API," you can also use the Installer API MsiDoAction to launch a particular top-level action. Finally, you'll learn to use the DoAction method of the Session object to do the same in Chapter 9, "Using the Installer Automation Model."

File Actions

Many of the Installer actions deal with files in one way or another. These include the following:

AppSearch, CCPSearch, and RMCCPSearch   Check for existing files.

ResolveSource, CostInitialize, FileCost, CostFinalize, and InstallValidate   Manage the file costing process.

InstallFiles, IsolatedComponent, RemoveFiles, and RemoveDuplicateFiles Install or remove files.

BindImage, DuplicateFiles, MoveFiles, and PatchFiles   Manipulate files.

CreateFolders and RemoveFolders   Create or remove folders.

CreateShortcuts and RemoveShortcuts   Create or remove shortcuts.

I'll discuss each of these actions briefly in the following pages.

AppSearch

The AppSearch action processes the information in the AppSearch, CompLocator, IniLocator, DrLocator, and RegLocator tables to find existing files on the user's hard drive. It processes these tables in this order:

1. CompLocator
2. RegLocator
3. IniLocator
4. DrLocator

As it moves through the AppSearch table, it sets the properties specified in that table to the actual file names. These can be used later by other actions. Although the AppSearch action has no particular sequence dependencies of its own, it must be called before any action that depends on the information it writes to properties begins.

BindImage

The BindImage action uses the BindImage table to optimize some of the files that have been installed to the user's hard drive. This action calls the BindImageEx Windows API, which optimizes the addressing information for DLL functions contained within executable files.

The BindImage action can only be called after the InstallFiles action has been completed.

CCPSearch

The CCPSearch action is similar to the AppSearch action in that it searches the user's hard drive for existing files. It uses the CCPSearch table for this purpose. However, the CCPSearch action is intended for one specific use: *compliance checking*. This is the process of making sure that a previous version of a product, or of a competing product, is installed before an upgrade is allowed to be installed.

The CCPSearch action does not necessarily process all of the entries in the CCPSearch table. Rather, it processes rows from that table until it finds a matching file, at which point the Installer sets the CCP_Success property to 1 and terminates the action.

The CCPSearch action must come before the RMCCPSearch action.

CostFinalize

The CostFinalize action ends the internal file costing process. It must be executed after the CostInitialize and FileCost actions.

You must execute the CostFinalize action before showing any user interface that allows the user to modify the features to be installed. In particular, CostFinalize must be executed before any dialog box with a SelectionTree control is displayed.

In addition to computing file costs, the CostFinalize action makes sure that all target directories are writeable.

CostInitialize

The CostInitialize action tells the Installer to begin the file costing process. It must be called immediately before the FileCost action, and somewhere before the CostFinalize action.

During the execution of the CostInitialize action, the Installer loads both the Feature table and the Component table into memory. If you're somehow modifying those tables on the original source media, you must do it before this action is executed.

CreateFolders

The CreateFolders action uses the information in the CreateFolder table and the Component table to create any new folders needed by the installation. As you might guess, this action must appear in the sequence tables before the InstallFiles action, if any files are installed to new folders.

To have the Installer automatically remove folders during an uninstall, you need to include the RemoveFolders action in the sequence tables.

CreateShortcuts

The CreateShortcuts action uses the information in the Shortcut table to create shortcuts on the user's computer. Only shortcuts for components that are being installed or advertised are actually created. This action must come after both the InstallFiles action and the RemoveShortcuts action.

DuplicateFiles

The DuplicateFiles action uses the information in the DuplicateFiles table to make duplicate copies of files that were installed locally during this installation. Obviously, this action can only be executed after the InstallFiles action.

FileCost

The FileCost action tells the Installer to gather the information it needs to do the file costing for this installation. This action must come after the CostInitialize action and before the CostFinalize action.

InstallFiles

The InstallFiles action is at the heart of most installations. It's the action that actually copies files to the user's hard drive. It checks the Component table and installs all files for components that are marked to be installed locally at the time that the action is called.

The InstallFiles action also implements the version checking rules, copying files only if they're newer than versions already on the target computer. For each file, the action checks the source media to be sure that the correct disk is in the drive. If it's not, the prompt from the DiskPrompt column of the media table is displayed to the user.

The InstallFiles action deletes old files before copying new ones. If a problem occurs when copying a replacement file and the user chooses Ignore, then it's possible for a file to be deleted without being replaced.

The InstallFiles action must come after the InstallValidate action in the sequence tables.

InstallValidate

When the Installer executes the InstallValidate action, it makes a final check to be sure that there is enough free space on all of the target drives for the installation to proceed. If this check fails, the installation is terminated. This is because you might be running the installation in silent mode. If you're showing a user interface, you should perform your own check for free space before the user is allowed to proceed to the InstallValidate action.

InstallValidate also checks to see whether any file needing to be replaced is currently loaded. If there are any such files, it builds a list and calls the FilesInUse dialog box. The user can then take the appropriate action. If they leave the file loaded, the InstallValidate action makes an entry in the installation script that says that a reboot will be required after copying files.

The CostFinalize action, and any actions that allow the user to modify the list of components to be installed, must be called before the InstallValidate action.

IsolatedComponent

The IsolatedComponent action installs the files that are listed in the IsolatedComponent table. This table is used to install private copies of files that would otherwise be shared so that there's no risk of version conflicts with other applications. For example, if your application depends on a particular obsolete version of the Windows Common Control DLL, you could install that file as an isolated component rather than using the shared copy on the user's system.

The IsolatedComponent action can only be used in the InstallUISequence and InstallExecuteSequence tables. It must be placed after the CostInitialize action and before the CostFinalize action.

MoveFiles

The MoveFiles action processes the entries in the MoveFiles table. These entries are used to move or copy files that are already on the user's computer (not files that are being installed as part of the current product).

The MoveFiles action must come after the InstallValidate action but before the Install-Files action.

PatchFiles

The PatchFiles action processes the PatchFiles table, applying binary patches to files on the user's computer. These may be files that were installed by this product, or other files that were previously present. If any of the files being patched are installed as part of this installation, the PatchFiles action must occur after the InstallFiles action.

RemoveDuplicateFiles

The RemoveDuplicateFiles action is used to remove files that were created by the DuplicateFiles action. Typically, this action will have a conditional flag so that it's only called on uninstallation. The RemoveDuplicateFiles action must occur after the Install-Validate action and before the InstallFiles action.

RemoveFiles

The RemoveFiles action uses the information in the RemoveFiles table to remove files or empty directories from the user's computer. This action must be called after the InstallValidate action but before the InstallFiles action.

RemoveFolders

The RemoveFolders action removes folders that were created by the CreateFolders action. Like RemoveFiles, it is intended for use in uninstallation scenarios. If the RemoveFolders action isn't included in the sequence tables, then folders created by CreateFolders won't be deleted. This action must come after the RemoveFiles action, because it may depend on files being removed to leave folders empty.

RemoveShortcuts

The RemoveShortcuts action removes shortcuts for files that are being removed. It must be called after the InstallFiles action and before the CreateShortcuts action.

ResolveSource

The ResolveSource action tells the Installer to figure out where the source media for this installation is located. This is the action that sets the value of the SourceDir property for the current installation. The ResolveSource action must come after the CostInitialize action, but before any expression that depends on the value of the SourceDir property is evaluated.

RMCCPSearch

Like the CCPSearch action, the RMCCPSearch action is used to check for qualifying products for an upgrade installation. It uses the information in the CCPSearch table to identify qualifying products, but only searches for them on a removable drive. You must set the value of the CCP_DRIVE property to the root path of the drive to be searched before calling this action.

As soon as any qualifying product is found, this action stops searching and is terminated.

Registry Actions

Another large group of Installer actions manipulates the Windows Registry. The reason there are so many of these actions is that the Installer contains multiple tables to handle COM registration information. In this section, I'll briefly detail these actions.

AllocateRegistrySpace

The AllocateRegistrySpace action checks to make sure that there is enough room to add the number of bytes specified by the AVAILABLEFREEREG property to the Windows Registry. On Windows NT and Windows 2000, it actually allocates this number of bytes for the Registry. Typically, you'd use this action in conjunction with the AVAILABLE-FREEREG property to ensure there is enough space for any Registry modifications that are made by custom actions; otherwise the modifications won't be taken into account by the Installer when it's calculating available disk space. This action must be called after the InstallInitialize action.

RegisterClassInfo

The RegisterClassInfo action registers information on COM classes (that is, the information contained in the Class table) in the Windows Registry. If the system supports advertising OLE servers, then class information for every feature in the installation is registered. Otherwise, only class information for features being installed is registered.

The RegisterClassInfo action is one of a group of actions that must come after the InstallFiles action. The ordering within this group is fixed, although not every action in the group must be in the sequence tables. However, any of these actions that are in the sequence tables must be in this order:

1. UnregisterClassInfo
2. UnregisterExtensionInfo
3. UnregisterProgIdInfo
4. UnregisterMIMEInfo

5. RegisterClassInfo
6. RegisterExtensionInfo
7. RegisterProgIdInfo
8. RegisterMIMEInfo

You can determine whether a particular system supports advertising OLE servers by checking the OLEAdvtSupport property.

RegisterComPlus

The RegisterComPlus action registers the COM+ applications listed in the ComPlus table. This action must follow the InstallFiles action and the UnregisterComPlus action.

RegisterExtensionInfo

The RegisterExtensionInfo action registers information on extension servers (that is, the information contained in the Extension table) in the Windows Registry. If the system supports advertising extension servers, then extension information for every feature in the installation is registered. If this is not the case, only extension information for features being installed is registered.

You can determine whether a particular system supports advertising extension servers by checking the ShellAdvtSupport property.

See the earlier section on RegisterClassInfo for information on sequencing this action.

RegisterFonts

The RegisterFonts action registers installed fonts with the user's system. This action can only be called after the InstallFiles action has been completed. Only fonts belonging to a component that is installed locally are registered.

RegisterMIMEInfo

The RegisterMIMEInfo action uses the information in the MIME table to register MIME servers with the user's system. Only MIME servers for installed features are registered; MIME servers are never advertised.

See the list in the section on RegisterClassInfo for information on sequencing this action.

RegisterProgIdInfo

The RegisterProgIdInfo action registers information on COM ProgIDs (that is, the information contained in the ProgId table) in the Windows Registry. If the system supports advertising OLE servers, then ProgID information for every feature in the installation is registered. If the system doesn't support this, only ProgID information for features being installed is registered.

See the previous section on RegisterClassInfo for information on sequencing this action.

RegisterTypeLibraries

The RegisterTypeLibraries action puts information associated with type libraries into the Windows Registry. This information is taken from the TypeLib table. Only information for type libraries being installed as part of the current product is registered.

This action must come after the InstallFiles action.

RemoveRegistryValues

The RemoveRegistryValues action removes two types of values from the Registry:

- The associated entries from the Registry table are removed if a previously installed component is being uninstalled.
- The associated entries from the RemoveRegistry table are removed if a previously not installed component is being installed.

This action must come after the InstallValidate action and before any WriteRegistryValues, UnregisterMIMEInfo, or UnregisterProgIdInfo actions.

SelfRegModules

The SelfRegModules action uses the information in the SelfReg table to register self-registering files. It does this by calling the DllRegisterServer entry point of each file listed in the table.

This action can only be called after both the InstallValidate and InstallFiles actions have been completed.

Unlike most of the other standard actions, the SelfRegModules action is always performed with the default user's privileges instead of the elevated privileges of the Installer process.

SelfUnregModules

The SelfUnregModules action uses the information in the SelfReg table to unregister self-registering files. It does this by calling the DllUnegisterServer entry point of each file listed in the table.

The InstallValidate action must appear in the sequence tables before the SelfUnreg-Modules action. This action must appear before either the SelfRegModules action or the RemoveFiles action.

Unlike most of the other standard actions, the SelfUnregModules action is always per-formed with the default user's privileges instead of the elevated privileges of the Installer process.

UnregisterClassInfo

The UnregisterClassInfo action removes COM class information that was registered with the RegisterClassInfo action from the Registry.

See the section on RegisterClassInfo for information on sequencing this action.

UnregisterComPlus

The UnregisterComPlus action removed COM+ information that was registered with the RegisterComPlus action from the Registry. This action must be placed after the InstallFiles action but before the RegisterComPlus action.

UnregisterExtensionInfo

The UnregisterExtensionInfo action removes extension server information that was reg-istered with the RegisterExtensionInfo action from the Registry.

See the section on RegisterClassInfo for information on sequencing this action.

UnregisterFonts

The UnregisterFonts action removes font information that was registered with the RegisterFonts action from the Registry.

UnregisterMIMEInfo

The UnregisterMIMEInfo action removes MIME information that was registered with the RegisterMIMEInfo action from the Registry.

See the section on RegisterClassInfo for information on sequencing this action.

UnregisterProgIdInfo

The UnregisterProgIdInfo action removes COM ProgID information that was registered with the RegisterProgIdInfo action from the Registry.

See the section on RegisterClassInfo for information on sequencing this action.

UnregisterTypeLibraries

The UnregisterTypeLibraries action removes type library information that was registered with the RegisterTypeLibraries action from the Registry.

WriteRegistryValues

The WriteRegistryValues action writes miscellaneous information from the Registry table to the Windows Registry. The values from the table are written to the Registry if the corresponding component is set either to install locally or to run from source.

Both the InstallValidate action and the RemoveRegistryValues action must come before the WriteRegistryValues action.

ODBC Actions

Three Installer actions deal with ODBC:

- InstallODBC
- RemoveODBC
- SetODBCFolders

Oddly enough, there aren't any Installer actions to deal with OLE DB in the current release. If you have OLE DB drivers to install, you'll need to copy the files and make the proper Registry entries by hand.

NOTE ODBC, Open Database Connectivity, was the first Microsoft standard for database access. OLE DB is the newer COM-based standard that replaces ODBC.

InstallODBC

The InstallODBC action handles all the details of installing ODBC drivers, translators, and data sources. It uses information from the ODBCDriver, ODBCTranslator, ODBC-Attribute, and ODBCDataSource tables.

If your installation includes any ODBC pieces, you must also include a component named ODBCDriverManager, which contains the latest version of the ODBC Driver Manager, because you can't assume that this file is already present on the user's computer.

This action must be called after all actions that either install or remove files.

RemoveODBC

The RemoveODBC action is meant to be used during uninstallation. It uses the information in the ODBCDriver, ODBCTranslator, ODBCAttribute, and ODBCDataSource tables to undo the changes made by the InstallODBC action. Actual driver files are removed by this action only if their reference count drops to zero.

SetODBCFolders

The SetODBCFolders action makes sure that new copies of ODBC drivers being installed are placed in the same directories as existing copies of the same drivers. This action must come after the CostFinalize action but before the InstallValidate action.

Environment Actions

Two Installer actions manipulate the user's environment strings: WriteEnvironment-Strings and RemoveEnvironmentStrings.

WriteEnvironmentStrings

The WriteEnvironmentStrings action uses the information in the Environment table to create environment variables, either in the `autoexec.bat` file (for Windows 9x) or the Registry (for Windows NT and Windows 2000). The Installer only runs this action when a component is being installed. Because the inverse RemoveEnvironmentStrings action is only run when a component is being uninstalled, it doesn't matter which of these two actions comes first in a sequence table.

The InstallValidate action must be executed before the WriteEnvironmentStrings action.

RemoveEnvironmentStrings

The RemoveEnvironmentStrings action uses the information in the Environment table to remove environment variables, either from the `autoexec.bat` file (for Windows 9x) or the Registry (for Windows NT and Windows 2000). The Installer only runs this action when a component is being uninstalled.

The InstallValidate action must be executed before the RemoveEnvironmentStrings action.

.ini File Actions

The Installer implements two actions to manipulate .ini files: WriteIniValues and RemoveIniValues.

WriteIniValues

The WriteIniValues action uses the information in the IniFiles table to modify .ini files on the user's computer. The Installer only makes these modifications if the associated component is being installed; there's no advertising interaction with .ini files.

Both the InstallValidate action and the RemoveIniValues action must come before this action in the sequence tables.

RemoveIniValues

The RemoveIniValues action performs two tasks on the user's computer. First, if a component is being uninstalled, it removes any .ini file modifications that were made by WriteIniValues when the component was being installed. Second, it uses the information in the RemoveIniFile table to remove values when a component is being installed.

This action must come after the InstallValidate action but before the WriteIniValues action.

Service Actions

The Installer includes actions to install, delete, start, and stop services. None of these actions does anything useful in Windows 95 or Windows 98 because those operating systems don't have the concept of a system service.

InstallServices

The InstallServices action uses the information in the ServiceInstall table to install new system services. This action, along with the other service-related action, is part of a fixed sequence of actions:

1. StopServices.
2. DeleteServices.
3. File-related actions (InstallFiles, RemoveFiles, DuplicateFiles, MoveFiles, PatchFiles, RemoveDuplicateFiles) These actions are discussed in the File Actions section earlier in the chapter.
4. InstallServices.
5. StartServices.

DeleteServices

The DeleteServices action stops an existing service and removes its registration from the user's system. It uses information in the ServiceControl table to determine which services to stop.

See the list presented in the section on InstallServices for information on sequencing this action.

StartServices

The StartServices action uses the information in the ServiceControl table to start new system services on the user's computer. You could use this action to start an existing service, but you need to be absolutely sure that service will be present on the user's machine. In practice this is difficult to achieve.

See the previous section on InstallServices for information on sequencing this action.

StopServices

The StopServices action stops system services on the user's machine; it does this based on information it receives from the ServiceControl table. It does not remove the services.

See the section on InstallServices for information on sequencing this action.

Publishing Actions

The Publishing actions handle the advertisement activities of the Installer. Of course there are Unpublish actions as well as Publish actions. You can publish features, components, and products; and you can unpublish features and components. Note that you can't unpublish a product; once the Installer knows that a product exists, it always remembers.

PublishFeatures

The PublishFeatures action uses the information in the FeatureComponents, Components, and Features table to determine the state of each feature in the Installer package (installed, advertised, or absent). It then writes this state into the system Registry, along with a mapping indicating which features were installed by which components. This information is used if the Installer is reinvoked on the same product in the future—for example, to install an advertised feature locally, or to repair an installation.

The PublishFeatures action must come after the PublishProduct action.

PublishComponents

The PublishComponents action uses the information in the PublishComponents table (not in the main Components table) to make Registry entries for components that are actually being installed or advertised.

There are no sequence restrictions on PublishComponents, but to keep things organized, it makes sense to put it with PublishFeatures and PublishProduct in the sequence tables.

PublishProduct

The PublishProduct action handles the overall registration of a particular product as advertised. This action must come before the PublishFeatures action.

UnpublishComponents

When a feature is selected to be uninstalled, the UnpublishComponents action uses the information in the PublishComponents table to decide whether any components must be unadvertised as a result. If there are any such components, this action removes their information from the Registry, preventing other applications from using the Installer to automatically install those components. This action can appear anywhere in the sequence tables.

UnpublishFeatures

The UnpublishFeatures action removes all feature information from the Registry when an entire product is uninstalled. It can appear anywhere in the sequence tables.

Upgrade Actions

The Installer can execute four actions that are specific to upgrading an existing application. These actions can decide whether to upgrade an application or prevent an upgrade, set the state for features in the new version, and remove existing versions of products from the user's computer.

FindRelatedProducts

The FindRelatedProducts action is used to find products already installed on the user's system that can be upgraded by the current installation. It does this by using the list of products in the Upgrade table. For each of these products that is already installed on the system, the Installer appends the product's product code to the property specified in the ActionProperty column of the Upgrade table.

This action should be included in both the InstallUISequence and InstallExecute-Sequence tables, though the Installer will only run it once per installation (therefore, it runs from the InstallUISequence table if the user interface is displayed, and from the InstallExecuteSequence table if no user interface is displayed). It must come before the MigrateFeatureStates and RemoveExistingProducts actions.

PreventInstall

The PreventInstall action prevents the installation of an upgrade if a previous version of the product cannot be removed. This action can be overridden by setting the msiUpgradeAttributesIgnoreRemoveFailure bit in the Attributes column of the Upgrade table. It must come after FindRelatedProducts action.

MigrateFeatureStates

The MigrateFeatureStates action is useful when a new version has a feature tree that is identical (or nearly identical) with that of a previous version. When it encounters this action, the Installer queries the existing features for their state (installed locally, installed to run from source, or not installed) and applies the current state as the default state for the new features of the same name. This action should come immediately after the Cost-Finalize action in both the InstallUISequence and InstallExecuteSequence tables.

RemoveExistingProducts

The RemoveExistingProducts action removes old versions of products that are being upgraded. This action can be placed in several locations, but for the most efficient processing, it should occur directly after the InstallFinalize action. That way, the Installer will not waste time removing old files that have already been replaced with new versions. If anything goes wrong with the removal, both the old and new versions will be left on the computer.

Miscellaneous Actions

Finally, there are a number of actions that don't fit into any general categories. Many of these are actions that relate to the control of the Installer itself. In this section, I'll discuss these remaining standard actions:

- DisableRollback
- ExecuteAction
- ForceReboot
- InstallAdminPackage
- InstallExecute
- InstallFinalize

- InstallInitialize
- LaunchConditions
- ProcessComponents
- RegisterProduct
- RegisterUser
- ScheduleReboot
- SEQUENCE
- ValidateProductID

DisableRollback

The DisableRollback action can be used to disable all rollback processing for the remainder of the installation. If this action comes before the InstallInitialize action, it disables all rollback tracking.

You might conceivably want to use this action if you expect the end user to be low on disk space. You might also want to use this action if the results of an action can't be rolled back properly for some reason. Remember, though, that if you disable rollback and anything goes wrong with the installation, the user is stuck with whatever got installed.

There is no EnableRollback action. You can use the EnableRollback control event to turn rollback on if you're showing a user interface during installation.

ExecuteAction

The ExecuteAction action is used to transfer control from the UI sequence table to the matching Execute sequence table. For example, in a normal installation, the Install-UISequence table will contain all of the costing actions, followed by actions that occur while the user is interacting with the user interface. The last action in the Install-UISequence table is the ExecuteAction action, which tells the Installer to start running the actions listed in the InstallExecuteSequence table. These are the actions that do not require further interaction from the user.

NOTE   You'll recall from Chapter 4 that if the Installer is running with no user interface, the actions in the InstallUISequence table do not get executed. Because of this, you should include the costing actions in the InstallExecuteSequence table as well.

ForceReboot

The ForceReboot action can be inserted at any point in the sequence tables to tell the user that a reboot is required. The Installer tracks whether any files being installed are in use, and if any file in use needs to be replaced, it will prompt for a reboot automatically at the end of the installation. So, you only need to use the ForceReboot action if some custom action or other quirk of your installation requires a reboot that the Installer won't call for on its own.

When it encounters a ForceReboot action, the Installer puts up a dialog box telling the user that a reboot is necessary to continue, similar to the one shown in Figure 6.2.

FIGURE 6.2
A Reboot dialog box

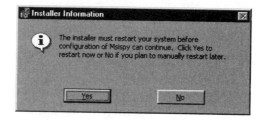

If the user clicks Yes, then their computer is rebooted immediately. If the user clicks No, then there is no reboot. In either case, further processing of the installation script is suspended until after the reboot. The Installer writes a command line to the RunOnce Registry key to automatically restart the installation after the next reboot.

You should always include a condition on the ForceReboot action so that it's not executed unnecessarily.

The ForceReboot action should come after any actions that require the source media to be present. This will keep the Installer from requesting the source media again after the reboot, which might be quite some time after the prompt if the user chose No. In particular, ForceReboot should be scheduled after these actions:

- RegisterProduct
- RegisterUser
- PublishProduct
- PublishFeatures
- CreateShortcuts
- RegisterMIMEInfo
- RegisterExtensionInfo
- RegisterClassInfo
- RegisterProgIdInfo

If the installation is being run without a user interface, then the computer is rebooted without asking the user for confirmation when a ForceReboot action is executed.

WARNING   It is vital to include a condition on any ForceReboot action in your action tables. At the minimum, this condition must include the NOT AFTERREBOOT clause. Otherwise, the Installer would reboot when it reached the same point in the script after the reboot, and in fact, it would never finish the installation.

InstallAdminPackage

During an administrative installation, the InstallAdminPackage action does the actual work of copying the product database to the administrative installation point (defined by the TARGETDIR property).

Typically, this action is only executed as part of the AdminExecuteSequence table, between the InstallInitialize and InstallFiles actions.

InstallInitialize

The InstallInitialize action must come before any actions that actually change the state of the user's system, such as InstallFiles or WriteRegistryValues. This action marks the start of the sequence of actions that make changes. It must come before any InstallExecute action and before the InstallFinalize action.

InstallExecute

The InstallExecute action causes the Installer to go ahead and actually run a script containing all of the pending operations to be performed on the user's system. In an installation package for a large product, you might use this action to commit some of the changes for an installation while other changes are still being calculated. This action is never required because the InstallFinalize action will always commit everything that's pending. If there is an InstallExecute action, it must be sequenced somewhere between the InstallIntialize and InstallFinalize actions.

InstallFinalize

The InstallFinalize action ends the transaction that started with the InstallInitialize action. It runs a script containing all remaining operations that need to be performed on the user's system. The script will contain all actions since the most recent InstallExecute action or since the InstallInitialize action, if there are no InstallExecute actions in the action table.

LaunchConditions

The LaunchConditions action should be the first action in a sequence table. This action evaluates the conditions in each row of the LaunchCondition table. If any of those conditions evaluate to false, the Installer aborts the installation immediately and displays the warning message from the Description column of the LaunchCondition table.

ProcessComponents

The ProcessComponents action determines the key path of each row in the Component table and stores that information for future use. It registers components that are being installed and unregisters components that are being uninstalled. The registered component information is then available to the MsiGetComponentPath API call.

RegisterProduct

The RegisterProduct records information about the product being installed on the local computer. It also caches a copy of the Installer database locally for future use.

The RegisterProduct action also handles the ARPNOMODIFY and ARPNOREMOVE properties. If ARPNOMODIFY is set, then the Modify button from the Control Panel Add/Remove Programs applet is suppressed for this product. If ARPNOREMOVE is set, then the Remove button from the Control Panel Add/Remove Programs applet is suppressed for this product.

RegisterUser

The RegisterUser action stores information about the registered user of a product for future use by the Installer. This action should be called after the ValidateProductID action.

ScheduleReboot

The ScheduleReboot action is very similar to the ForceReboot action. When the ScheduleReboot action is executed, the Installer notes that it should ask at the end of the installation whether the user would like to reboot. The only difference between ForceReboot and ScheduleReboot is that ScheduleReboot is deferred until the end of the installation, while ForceReboot is immediate. For other reboot issues, refer to the section on ForceReboot earlier in the chapter.

SEQUENCE

The SEQUENCE action can be used to run actions in a non-standard sequence table. You can add an additional table to an Installer database with the same schema as the existing action tables. If you store the name of this table in the SEQUENCE property, then the actions in it will be executed when the SEQUENCE action is encountered in another action table.

Unless your development circumstances are unusual, you're unlikely to need this action.

ValidateProductID

The ValidateProductID action confirms that a valid product ID exists. It does this by comparing the PIDKEY property (which can be passed on the command line or entered via the user interface) to the PIDTemplate property. If the PIDKEY property is valid, this action sets the ProductID property to the full product ID.

ActionData Messages

Some of the standard actions send ActionData messages as they're proceeding. You can use rows in the ActionText table to format these messages for display on the user interface. For example, the DeleteServices action sends an ActionData message with two fields. Field [1] contains the display name of the service, and field [2] contains the internal name of the service. You could create a format for this message by adding a row to the ActionText table with these columns:

- Action: DeleteServices
- Description: Deleting Service
- Template: Service [1] ([2])

At runtime, the Installer will build a message by matching the action name to the Action column of the ActionText table, and then concatenating the matching Description and Template columns. Placeholders in the Template column will be replaced with the actual fields from the message.

Table 6.2 lists all of the ActionData messages that the Installer sends during standard action execution.

TABLE 6.2:   ActionData Messages from Standard Actions

Action	Field	Data
AllocateRegistrySpace	[1]	Registry space allocated (in KB)
AppSearch	[1]	Property holding file location
AppSearch	[2]	File Signature
BindImage	[1]	File being optimized
CreateFolder	[1]	Folder name being created

TABLE 6.2: ActionData Messages from Standard Actions *(continued)*

Action	Field	Data
CreateShortcuts	[1]	File Name of the shortcut being created
DeleteServices	[1]	Service display name
DeleteServices	[2]	Service name
DuplicateFiles	[1]	Identifier of the duplicated file
DuplicateFiles	[6]	Size of the duplicated file (in bytes)
DuplicateFiles	[9]	Target directory for the duplicated file
InstallAdminPackage	[1]	Name of the database being installed
InstallAdminPackage	[6]	Size of database being installed (in bytes)
InstallAdminPackage	[9]	Target directory for administrative installation
InstallFiles	[1]	Name of the installed file
InstallFiles	[6]	Size of the installed file (in bytes)
InstallFiles	[9]	Target directory for the installed file
InstallODBC	[1]	Name of driver, translator or data source
InstallODBC	[2]	ComponentID
InstallODBC	[3]	Installation folder
InstallODBC	[4]	Data from the ODBCAttributes table
MoveFiles	[1]	Name of the moved file
MoveFiles	[6]	Size of the moved file (in bytes)
MoveFiles	[9]	Target directory for the moved file
PatchFiles	[1]	Name of the patched file
PatchFiles	[2]	Directory holding the patched file
PatchFiles	[3]	Size of the patched file (in bytes)
ProcessComponents	[1]	Product ID being registered or unregistered
ProcessComponents	[2]	Component ID being registered or unregistered
ProcessComponents	[3]	Key path (for registration only) being registered
PublishComponents	[1]	GUID from an advertised feature
PublishComponents	[2]	Qualifier of the published component
PublishFeatures	[1]	Name of feature being published
PublishProduct	[1]	Name of the product being published
RegisterClassInfo	[1]	GUID being registered
RegisterComPlus	[1]	Application ID of the COM+ application being registered

T A B L E 6 . 2 :   ActionData Messages from Standard Actions *(continued)*

Action	Field	Data
RegisterExtensionInfo	[1]	Extension being registered
RegisterFonts	[1]	Name of font being registered
RegisterMIMEInfo	[1]	MIME content identifier
RegisterMIMEInfo	[2]	Associated file extension
RegisterProduct	[1]	Information about product being registered
RegisterProgId	[1]	ProgID being registered
RegisterTypeLibraries	[1]	GUID of type library being registered
RemoveExistingProducts	[1]	Name of the product being removed
RemoveFiles	[1]	Name of the removed file
RemoveFiles	[9]	Directory holding the removed file
RemoveDuplicateFiles	[1]	Name of the removed file
RemoveDuplicateFiles	[9]	Directory holding the removed file
RemoveEnvironmentStrings	[1]	Name of the environment variable
RemoveEnvironmentStrings	[2]	Value of the environment variable
RemoveEnvironmentStrings	[3]	Flag indicating the action taken
RemoveFolders	[1]	Name of the folder being removed
RemoveIniValues	[1]	.ini file name
RemoveIniValues	[2]	Section name
RemoveIniValues	[3]	Item name
RemoveIniValues	[4]	Item value
RemoveODBC	[1]	Driver being removed
RemoveODBC	[2]	ComponentID being removed
RemoveODBC	[3]	SQL_REMOVE_DSN or SQL_REMOVE_SYS_DSN (only for data sources removed)
RemoveRegistryValues	[1]	Key containing the removed value
RemoveRegistryValues	[2]	Name of the value being removed
RemoveShortcuts	[1]	Name of the shortcut being removed
SelfRegModules	[1]	Name of the program being registered
SelfRegModules	[2]	Folder holding the program being registered
SelfUnregModules	[1]	Name of the program being unregistered
SelfUnregModules	[2]	Folder holding the program being unregistered

TABLE 6.2: ActionData Messages from Standard Actions *(continued)*

Action	Field	Data
SetODBCFolders	[1]	Driver description
SetODBCFolders	[2]	Original folder location
SetODBCFolders	[3]	Final folder location
StartServices	[1]	Service display name
StartServices	[2]	Service name
StopServices	[1]	Service display name
StopServices	[2]	Service name
UnpublishComponents	[1]	GUID of an advertised feature
UnpublishComponents	[2]	Component qualifier
UnpublishFeatures	[1]	Identifier of feature being unadvertised
UnregisterClassInfo	[1]	GUID of class being unregistered
UnregisterComPlus	[1]	Application ID of the COM+ application being unregistered
UnregisterExtensionInfo	[1]	Extension being unregistered
UnregisterFonts	[1]	Font being unregistered
UnregisterMIMEInfo	[1]	MIME identifier being unregistered
UnregisterMIMEInfo	[2]	MIME extension being unregisted
UnregisterProgIdInfo	[1]	ProgID being unregistered
UnregisterTypeLibraries	[1]	GUID of type library being unregistered
WriteEnvironmentStrings	[1]	Name of the environment variable
WriteEnvironmentStrings	[2]	Value of the environment variable
WriteEnvironmentStrings	[3]	Flag indicating the action taken
WriteIniValues	[1]	`.ini` file name
WriteIniValues	[2]	Section name
WriteIniValues	[3]	Item name
WriteIniValues	[4]	Item value
WriteRegistryValues	[1]	Registry key being written
WriteRegistryValues	[2]	Name of the Registry value being written
WriteRegistryValues	[3]	Data of the Registry value being written

Custom Actions

For most installations, you can do everything that needs to be done with the standard actions you've already seen in this chapter. But sometimes you have to stretch beyond what the Installer designers built in. In such cases, you will need to consider writing a custom action.

As you'll see in this section, custom actions can do just about anything you can think of. There are some pitfalls to beware of, the chief one being that custom actions are not automatically undone during a rollback (but see the section "Rollback and Commit Custom Actions" for information on rollback custom actions). Still, sometimes using custom actions is the only way to accomplish something. For example, you might have to install something such as the Microsoft Data Access Components (MDAC) that only comes as a self-extracting executable. You can't do this with the standard actions, but it's easy enough with a custom action.

Custom Action Summary

Custom actions are organized by types. Each custom action is listed in the Custom-Action table, which has four columns. The Action column gives the name of the custom action, an arbitrary identifier that you can create. This is also the name used to invoke the custom action from a sequence table. The Type column is one of the choices from Table 6.3. This table also shows how you should interpret the Source and Target columns for each type of custom action.

T A B L E 6 . 3 :   Custom Action Types

Type	Description	Source	Target
1	.dll stored in a binary stream	Key to a row in the Binary table	Name of the .dll entry point
2	.exe stored in a binary stream	Key to a row in the Binary table	Command-line string used to launch the .exe
5	JScript in a binary stream	Key to a row in the Binary table	Name of the JScript function to call
6	VBScript in a binary stream	Key to a row in the Binary table	Name of the VBScript function to call
7	Installation of a package nested inside of the first package	Name of the sub-storage containing database of nested application	Properties settings string

TABLE 6.3: Custom Action Types *(continued)*

Type	Description	Source	Target
17	.d11 installed as part of a product	Key to a row in the File table	Name of the .d11 entry point
18	.exe installed as part of a product	Key to a row in the File table	Command-line string used to launch the .exe
19	Displays a specified error message and returns failure, terminating the installation	Blank	Formatted text string; The literal message or an index into the Error table
21	JScript file installed as part of a product	Key to a row in the File table	Name of the JScript function to call
22	VBScript file installed as part of a product	Key to a row in the File table	Name of the VBScript function to call
23	Installation of a package that resides in the first application's source tree	Path of nested package specified relative to the root of the source location	Properties settings string
34	.exe in a known directory	Key to a row in the Directory table	Name of the executable file and any options. Use quotes to surround long file names
35	Directory set via formatted text	Key to the Directory table	Formatted text string that will be set as the directory path when this action is executed
37	JScript text	Null	A string of JScript code to execute
38	VBScript text	Null	A string of VBScript code to execute
39	Installation of an application that is advertised or already installed	Product Code for the application to install	Properties settings string
50	.exe named by a property	Property name or key to a row in the Property table	Command-line string used to launch the .exe
51	Property set via formatted text	Property name or key to the Property table	Formatted text string that will be stored in the property when this action is executed
53	JScript text stored in a property	Property name or key to a row in the Property table	Name of the JScript function to call
54	VBScript text stored in a property	Property name or key to a row in the Property table	Name of the VBScript function to call

If you look at the CustomAction table in existing Installer databases, you may see other values in the Type column than those listed above. That's because there are a series of flags that you can add to the type to modify the way the Installer treats the custom actions. These flags are listed in Table 6.4.

TABLE 6.4:   Custom Action Type Flags

Value added to Type	Effect
0	Synchronous execution. Fails if exit code is not zero. Must return one of the exit codes listed in Table 6.5. Always executed. Immediate execution.
+64	Synchronous execution. Exit code is ignored.
+128	Asynchronous execution. Fails if exit code is not zero. Must return one of the exit codes listed in Table 6.5.
+192	Asynchronous execution. Exit code is ignored
+256	Execute once. If the action is in both the UI and Execute sequence tables, it is executed only in the UI sequence table if the user interface is used, and it is executed only in the Execute sequence table if the user interface is not used.
+512	Execute once per process. If the action is in both the UI and Execute sequence tables, and both tables are read by the same process, it is executed only in the UI sequence table if the user interface is used, and only in the Execute sequence table if the user interface is not used.
+768	Execute only on client after UI sequence. This custom action is in the Execute sequence table, but it should not be run if the user interface is suppressed.
+1024	Deferred execution custom action (discussed later in this chapter).
+1280	Rollback custom action (discussed later in this chapter).
+1536	Commit custom action (discussed later in this chapter).
+3072	Deferred custom action run in the system process.

For example, in the Installer database for Microsoft Office 2000 Premium, there's a custom action named CAConfigureFPPWS with a type of 1089. This translates to 1024 + 64 + 1, so this is a custom action in a DLL stored in a binary stream in the Installer package, executed synchronously with no exit code, and set as a deferred execution custom action.

All custom actions run as a separate thread of execution from the main installation. If a custom action runs synchronously (the default), the Installer pauses the main thread until the custom action is completed. If the custom action runs asynchronously, then the Installer continues the main thread processing simultaneously with the custom action.

Custom actions can return one of a predefined set of constants to indicate their completion status to the Installer. These constants are listed in Table 6.5.

TABLE 6.5:   Custom Action Return Codes

Constant	Description
ERROR_FUNCTION_NOT_CALLED	Action not executed.
ERROR_SUCCESS	Completed successfully.
ERROR_INSTALL_USEREXIT	User terminated the action.
ERROR_INSTALL_FAILURE	An unrecoverable error occurred.
ERROR_INSTALL_SUSPEND	The sequence is suspended.
ERROR_NO_MORE_ITEMS	Skip remaining actions.

Rollback and Commit Custom Actions

As I've mentioned before, the Installer creates a rollback script as it carries out your installation. This script includes actions to undo every action that it performs. The Installer also saves copies of each file it deletes, just in case it needs to put them back. The rollback script and these duplicate files are deleted at the end of the installation if all goes well.

If there's a problem, though, the rollback script cannot automatically rollback changes made by custom actions. From the point of view of the Installer, your custom actions are black boxes. It didn't execute the code inside them, so it has no idea how to undo them.

The solution to this problem is the *rollback custom action*. When the Installer encounters a rollback custom action in a sequence table (that is, one which has had 1280 added to the Type column), it does not execute that action. Instead, it stores it in the rollback script. Only if a problem is encountered and the installation needs to be rolled back does this action get executed.

If your custom action makes some change to the system that is easily reversed (for example, installing a new printer), you should provide a corresponding rollback custom action to undo the change. This is just part of being a good developer citizen in the Installer universe.

A *commit custom action* (one with 1536 added to the Type column) is somewhat the reverse of a rollback custom action. Commit custom actions are only executed if an installation is successful. Specifically, when the Installer encounters a commit custom action, it sets it aside for later execution. If the InstallFinalize standard action is completed successfully, the Installer then runs all outstanding commit custom actions.

Deferred Execution Custom Actions

Normally the Installer executes custom actions when it comes to them in the sequence tables. For many actions, particularly those that modify the Installer database itself, this is a reasonable default. However, some custom actions should only be executed during the actual processing of an installation script, when the Installer is making other changes to the user's system. These are the *deferred execution custom actions*.

To create a deferred execution custom action, add 1024 to the Type of the custom action. You must also be sure that these actions are in the Execute sequence table and that they are somewhere between the InstallInitialize and InstallFinalize actions.

Sequencing Custom Actions

The Installer follows a simple algorithm to determine what the rows in a sequence table represent:

1. If the Action column contains the name of a standard action, run the standard action.

2. If the name is not that of a standard action, check to see whether it is a custom action. If the Action column contains the name of a custom action, run the custom action.

3. If the column contains neither a standard action nor a custom action, it must contain the name of a dialog box, so open the dialog box.

With the exception of deferred execution custom actions, custom actions can be inserted anywhere in the sequence tables. Deferred execution custom actions can only be inserted between the InstallInitialize and InstallFinalize standard actions.

Custom Actions and the Progress Bar

It is possible to integrate your custom actions with the Installer's progress bar. To do so, you'll need to use the MsiProcessMessage and MsiRecordSetInteger API calls that you'll learn about in Chapter 8.

The Installer measures time in arbitrary units called *ticks*. One tick is the time it takes to write one byte of data when copying a file. To add your custom action to the progress bar, follow these steps:

1. Decide how many total ticks your custom action is equivalent to. I'll call this amount TotalTicks.

2. Decide how many ticks you want to wait between updates to the progress bar. I'll call this amount IncrementTicks.

3. Send the Installer a message with the INSTALLMESSAGE_PROGRESS constant specifying the TotalTicks.

4. Send the Installer a message with the INSTALLMESSAGE_ACTIONSTART constant specifying the ActionText to be used for this action.

5. Send the Installer two messages each time the IncrementTicks amount of work passes. The first will have the INSTALLMESSAGE_ACTIONDATA constant and the ActionText record. The second will have the INSTALLMESSAGE_PROGRESS constant and the IncrementTicks value.

NOTE   Unless you have a very long-running custom action, it's probably not worth the effort to set up the API calls to hook up the progress bar.

Writing a Custom Action in VBScript

As an example of a custom action, I'll walk you through the process of adding a custom action to an existing Installer package. In particular, I'll use the Installer package for MsiSpy, the tool included in the Installer SDK for determining what the Windows Installer has published to your computer. You can download this utility, as well as the Orca editor that I'll use to modify it, from the Windows Installer SDK Web site msdn.microsoft.com/downloads/sdks/platform/wininst.asp.

To create the sample custom action, follow these steps:

1. Launch the Orca editor and load MsiSpy.msi. One of the interesting things about the Installer technology is that there are no secrets; you can use the editing tools to see what other developers are doing. This can save you a lot of development time.

2. The MsiSpy database doesn't contain a CustomAction table. This table isn't required and the database doesn't use any custom actions. To create one, choose Tables ➤ Add Table, check the CustomAction table in the Add Tables dialog, and click OK.

3. Now you need to add the custom action. To do so, click the CustomAction table in the left pane of Orca, then right-click in the right pane and choose Add Row. Figure 6.3 shows the Add Row dialog box filled out for this custom action. The value 1574 that you enter in theType textbox is composed of 38 (the type for a VBScript action contained directly in the CustomAction table) plus 1546 (the type modifier for a commit custom action). Click OK to add the new row to the table.

FIGURE 6.3
Adding a row to the
CustomAction table

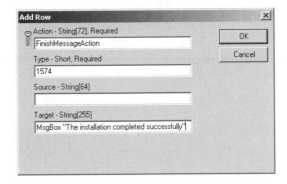

4. Click the InstallExecuteSequence table in the left pane of Orca. Click the Sequence column to sort this table in the order that actions will be executed. Because the custom action you're creating is a Commit custom action, it's deferred and must be inserted between the InstallInitialize and InstallFinalize actions. You can do this by adding a record with the Action column set to FinishMessageAction (the name of the action that you just inserted) and the Sequence column set to 6501.

5. Save the MsiSpy.msi file and close Orca. Now double-click the .msi file to install MsiSpy. When the installation completes successfully, you'll see the dialog box shown in Figure 6.4, which was produced by the FinishMessageAction custom action.

FIGURE 6.4
The FinishMessageAction
dialog box

WARNING   Because the Target column of the CustomAction table is limited to 256 characters, you can only run small custom actions by this method. For longer VBScript custom actions, you can use a type 6 or type 54 action.

A Typical Set of Sequence Tables

With all of the rules for sequencing actions that you've seen in this chapter it would be understandable if you were a bit confused. Fortunately, the Installer team has provided a set of recommended sequence tables as a starting point. In this section, I'll give you their recommendations in sequence number, together with some comments.

The InstallUISequence table should start with the actions shown in Table 6.6.

TABLE 6.6: Recommended InstallUISequence Table

Action	Condition	Sequence
ExitDialog		-1
UserExitDialog		-2
FatalErrorDialog		-3
LaunchConditions		100
PreActionDialog		140
AppSearch	APPS_TEST	400
CCPDialog	Not Installed AND CCP_TEST	500
RMCCPSearch	NOT Installed AND CCP_TEST	600
ValidateProductID		700
CostInitialize		800
FileCost		900
CostFinalize		1000
FirstRunDialog	NOT Installed	1230
FastMaintenanceDialog	Installed AND (RESUME OR Preselected)	1240
FirstMaintenanceDialog	Installed AND NOT Resume AND NOT Preselected	1250
ActionDialog		1280
ExecuteAction		1300

Here are some points to notice about the InstallUISequence table:

- The first three entries are for the default error and exit dialogs that must be present.
- Except for the special entries, all of the standard actions have sequence numbers divisible by 10. If you adhere to this standard, it's easy to tell standard actions from custom actions in the sequence tables.
- The sequence starts with the LaunchConditions action, to make sure that the installation should proceed. As soon as it's clear that the product can be installed, a PreActionDialog is displayed. This would typically be a simple text control reading "Please wait while the Installer is initialized."

- The compliance checking and product ID validation actions come next.
- The file costing actions come next.
- Then, depending on a series of conditions depending on properties that you'll learn about in Chapter 7, "Putting the Pieces Together," the Installer shows a dialog letting the user decide what to do.
- The table ends with an ExecuteAction action that transfers control to the InstallExecuteSequence table.

Table 6.7 gives the recommended sequence for the InstallExecuteSequence table.

T A B L E 6 . 7 : Recommended InstallExecuteSequence Table

Action	Condition	Sequence
LaunchConditions		100
AppSearch	APPS_TEST	400
CCPSearch	NOT Installed AND CCP_TEST	500
RMCCPSearch	NOT Installed AND CCP_TEST	600
ValidateProductID		700
CostInitialize		800
FileCost		900
CostFinalize		1000
SetODBCFolders		1100
InstallValidate		1400
InstallInitialize		1500
AllocateRegistrySpace	NOT Installed	1550
ProcessComponents		1600
UnpublishComponents		1700
UnpublishFeatures		1800
StopServices	VersionNT	1900
DeleteServices	VersionNT	2000
UnregisterComPlus		2100
SelfUnregModules		2200
UnregisterTypeLibraries		2300
RemoveODBC		2400
UnregisterFonts		2500
RemoveRegistryValues		2600

TABLE 6.7: Recommended InstallExecuteSequence Table *(continued)*

Action	Condition	Sequence
UnregisterClassInfo		2700
UnregisterExtensionInfo		2800
UnregisterProgIdInfo		2900
UnregisterMIMEInfo		3000
RemoveIniValues		3100
RemoveShortcuts		3200
RemoveEnvironmentStrings		3300
RemoveDuplicateFiles		3400
RemoveFiles		3500
RemoveFolders		3600
CreateFolders		3700
MoveFiles		3800
InstallFiles		4000
DuplicateFiles		4100
PatchFiles		4200
BindImage		4300
RegisterComPlus		4400
CreateShortcuts		4500
RegisterClassInfo		4600
RegisterExtensionInfo		4700
RegisterProgIdInfo		4800
RegisterMIMEInfo		4900
WriteRegistryValues		5000
WriteIniValues		5100
WriteEnvironmentStrings		5200
RegisterFonts		5300
InstallODBC		5400
RegisterTypeLibraries		5500
SelfRegModules		5600
InstallServices	VersionNT	5800
StartServices	VersionNT	5900

TABLE 6.7: Recommended InstallExecuteSequence Table *(continued)*

Action	Condition	Sequence
RegisterUser		6000
RegisterProduct		6100
PublishComponents		6200
PublishFeatures		6300
PublishProduct		6400
InstallFinalize		6600

Here are some things you should notice about the InstallExecuteSequence table:

- Most of the standard actions from the InstallUISequence table are repeated. That's because this table will contain the only actions that are executed if the installation is started with no user interface.
- Service-related actions are flagged only to occur on Windows NT or Windows 2000.
- Validation and costing is done early in the installation.
- There are no dialog boxes shown in the Execute table.
- Similar actions are grouped together.
- Actions that deal with removing components are completed before actions that deal with installing components are started.
- Product registration actions are at the very end of the installation.

The sequence tables for an administrative installation can be much simpler than those for a regular installation. That's because the administrative installation doesn't actually install the product; it merely prepares a network share point to hold a copy of the product that can be installed on other computers. Table 6.8 gives a recommended AdminUISequence table and Table 6.9 gives a recommended AdminExecuteSequence table.

TABLE 6.8: Recommended AdminUISequence Table

Action	Condition	Sequence
ExitDialog		-1
UserExitDialog		-2
FatalError		-3
PreActionDialog		140
CostInitialize		800
FileCost		900

TABLE 6.8: Recommended AdminUISequence Table *(continued)*

Action	Condition	Sequence
CostFinalize		1000
AdminWelcomeDlg		1230
ActionDialog		1280
ExecuteAction		1300

TABLE 6.9: Recommended AdminExecuteSequence Table

Action	Condition	Sequence
CostInitialize		800
FileCost		900
CostFinalize		1000
InstallValidate		1400
InstallInitialize		1500
InstallAdminPackage		3900
InstallFiles		4000
InstallFinalize		6600

Note that actions in the Admin tables have the same number as the same actions in the Install tables. The Installer doesn't require this (there's no reason, for example, that the InstallFiles action should always be sequenced as number 4000), but by adhering to this convention, you can make it easier for experienced developers to spot departures from the standards.

There is no suggested table for AdvtUISequence. In fact, the Installer team recommends that there should be no entries in this table, and that the Installer should be invoked with a command line that loads up the appropriate package with no user interface. This makes sense if you think about it. The main purpose of advertising is to make an application available without installing it, typically by pushing it out to clients on a network. In most such cases you don't want end users to have to make any decisions. They should just be presented with a product that "magically" works.

Table 6.10 shows the recommended actions for the AdvtExecuteSequence table.

Note that on the whole the AdvtExecuteSequence table just tells the Installer to perform those actions that are necessary to advertise a product (creating shortcuts, making Registry entries, and publishing features and components).

TABLE 6.10:   Recommended AdvtExecuteSequence Table

Action	Condition	Sequence
CostInitialize		800
CostFinalize		1000
InstallValidate		1400
InstallInitialize		1500
CreateShortcuts		4500
RegisterClassInfo		4600
RegisterExtensionInfo		4700
RegisterProgIdInfo		4800
RegisterMIMEInfo		4900
PublishComponents		6200
PublishFeatures		6300
PublishProduct		6400
InstallFinalize		6600

NOTE   In all cases you should use these recommended tables as a starting point. Remember, the Installer was designed to be data-driven so it would be flexible. If you have a good reason for reordering the actions in a table, and you're not breaking the Installer rules for sequencing, there's no harm in rearranging or augmenting the recommended sequences

chapter 7

Putting the Pieces Together

- Installer Properties

- Creating a New Installer Package

- Adding a File

- Adding a Shortcut

- Adding a Registry Key

- Adding a COM Server

- Searching for a Directory

- Installing MDAC

Now that you've seen all the major parts of the Installer Service, it's time to look at a few examples of how to put them together. In this chapter, I'll first review the available Installer properties, which come in handy when it's time to construct conditional expressions. Then I'll show you some examples of using the Installer tools you've seen in previous chapters to perform actual installation tasks.

Installer Properties

The Installer maintains a number of properties all by itself. These properties track the phase of the installation, the location of the user's Windows directory, and similar information. In addition, Installer package authors can add their own properties to the Installer database. In this section, I'll review the available properties and then show you some common expressions that make use of these properties.

Types of Properties

The Installer keeps track of two types of properties:

- Public properties can be changed by the user interface by applying a transform to the Installer database or by supplying their value on the command line used to launch the Installer. Public properties' names consist entirely of uppercase letters.
- Private properties can be changed only by the Installer itself or by the package author (by including their value in the Property table). Private properties' names contain at least one lowercase letter.

In addition, some public properties are *restricted*. These are public properties whose values can be changed by a system administrator. Restricted public properties are used to maintain a secure environment when the Installer is running with elevated privileges (for example, when installing an advertised product on a user workstation). The Installer maintains a default list of restricted public properties. You can add additional public properties to this list by supplying their names as the value of the SecureCustom-Properties property. Or, if you'd like to turn off the restrictions entirely, you can set the EnableUserControl property to True.

The Installer evaluates property settings in this order:

1. Values in the Property table
2. Values set by a transform
3. Properties set by the AdminProperties property
4. Properties set on the command line
5. Properties set by the operating environment

Thus, for example, if you have a public property named MYPROPERTY that is set in the Property table, set to a different value by a transform, and set to a third value by the command line, the actual value is the one set by the command line.

Public Properties

Most of the *public properties* have to do with the operation of the Installer itself. These include the following:

- Properties related to the operations the Installer is currently performing
- Properties used by the Add/Remove Software Control Panel applet
- Patching properties

Table 7.1 lists the public properties that the Installer uses. Of course, you can create your own properties by entering them into the Property table.

TABLE 7.1: Public Properties

Property	Description
ADVERTISE	A comma-delimited list of features to be advertised, or the value "All."
ADDDEFAULT	A comma-delimited list of features to be installed in their default state.
ADDLOCAL	A comma-delimited list of features to be installed locally.
ADDSOURCE	A comma-delimited list of features to be installed to run from source.
ARPAUTHORIZEDCDFPREFIX	URL of the update channel for the application.
ARPCOMMENTS	Add/Remove Control Panel comments.
ARPCONTACT	Add/Remove Control Panel contact name.
ARPHELPLINK	URL for technical support.
ARPHELPTELEPHONE	Phone number for technical support.
ARPINSTALLLOCATION	Full path to the application's primary folder, displayed by the Add/Remove Control Panel applet.
ARPNOREPAIR	If set to 1, disables the repair button in Add/Remove Control Panel.
ARPPRODUCTICON	Foreign key to the Icon table specifying the icon to display in Add/Remove Control Panel.
ARPREADME	Add/Remove Control Panel readme information.
ARPSIZE	Add/Remove Control Panel size of application in kilobytes.
ARPSYSTEMCOMPONENT	If set to 1, the application will not be displayed by the Add/Remove Control Panel applet.
ARPURLINFOABOUT	URL for information on the product.

TABLE 7.1: Public Properties *(continued)*

Property	Description
ARPURLUPDATEINFO	URL for information about product updates.
ARPNOMODIFY	If set to 1, disables Add/Remove Control Panel repair functionality.
ARPNOREMOVE	If set to 1, disables Add/Remove Control Panel remove functionality.
AVAILABLEFREEREG	Desired bytes free in the Registry after calling the AllocateRegistrySpace action.
CCP_DRIVE	Root path of the volume to be searched by the RMCPPSearch action.
COMPADDLOCAL	Comma-delimited list of Component IDs for components to be installed locally.
COMPADDSOURCE	Comma-delimited list of Component IDs for components to be installed to run from the source media.
COMPANYNAME	Name of the company of the user performing the installation. If this isn't set by another method, the Installer will read the value from the Registry.
DISABLEADVTSHORTCUTS	If set to 1, the Installer will generate regular shortcuts instead of advertised shortcuts.
DISABLEMEDIA	If set to 1, prevents the user from registering a different copy of the installation source. Useful if you are setting up an administrative source and want to ensure that all installs are from this source.
DISABLEROLLBACK	Set to 1 to disable all rollback processing, including the generation of the rollback script.
PATCHNEWPACKAGECODE	New Package code to set for a product after a patch is installed.
PATCHNEWSUMMARYCOMMENTS	New comments property for a product after a patch is installed.
PATCHNEWSUMMARYSUBJECT	New subject property for a product after a patch is installed.
PIDKEY	The part of the product ID entered by the user.
REBOOTPROMPT	If set to S or Suppress, the Installer automatically reboots at each reboot prompt, without actually prompting the user.
REMOVE	Comma-delimited list of features to be removed.
ROOTDRIVE	Default drive for the installation.
SOURCELIST	Semicolon-delimited list of available source paths for the installation.
TARGETDIR	Root location where the Installer package will be copied by an administrative installation.
USERNAME	Name of the user performing the installation. If this isn't set by another method, the Installer will read the value from the Registry.

Restricted Public Properties

Restricted public properties also have to do with the operation of the Installer. These properties are restricted because changing them could drastically change the software that's being installed. For example, you wouldn't want a user to be able to override the PRIMARYFOLDER property if you've set up an administrative installation that places the software in a standard location to make your corporate helpdesk's job easier. Table 7.2 lists the restricted public properties.

NOTE   You can extend the list of restricted public properties by using the SecureCustomProperties property, discussed in the next section.

TABLE 7.2:   Restricted Public Properties

Property	Description
ACTION	Reflects the top-level action being performed. Will be either INSTALL, ADVERTISE, or ADMIN.
AFTERREBOOT	Set to 1 after a reboot initiated by the ForceReboot action.
ALLUSERS	The ALLUSERS property determines whether a per-machine or per-user installation is done on Windows NT or Windows 2000 (it has no effect on Windows 9x). By default, all installations are per-user. If ALLUSERS is set to 1 and the user has administrative privileges, a per-machine installation is performed; if the user does not have administrative privileges, an error is returned. If ALLUSERS is set to 2 and the user has administrative privileges, a per-machine installation is performed; if the user does not have administrative privileges, a per-user installation is performed.
EXECUTEACTION	Set to the name of the top-level action being executed, for example INSTALL or ADMIN.
EXECUTEMODE	Set to None for a dry run that does not actually make any changes to the user's system. Set to Script to run the installation script. Any other value defaults to the Script setting.
FILEADDDEFAULT	Comma-delimited list of files to be installed in their default state.
FILEADDLOCAL	Comma-delimited list of files to be installed locally.
FILEADDSOURCE	Comma-delimited list of files to be installed to run from source.
INSTALLLEVEL	The level for which features are selected to install by default. Defaults to 1 if not set.
LIMITUI	Set to 1 to limit the user interface to the Basic level.
LOGACTION	Semicolon-separated list of actions for which action data messages will be logged.

TABLE 7.2: Restricted Public Properties *(continued)*

Property	Description
NOCOMPANYNAME	Set this to 1 to suppress the Installer's automatic filling in of the COMPANYNAME property. Useful if your application needs to be sure that it collects the current company name itself.
NOUSERNAME	Set this to 1 to suppress the Installer's automatic filling in of the USERNAME property. Useful if your application needs to be sure that it collects the current username itself.
PATCH	Full path of the current patch package (if any).
PRIMARYFOLDER	The main directory for the installation.
PROMPTROLLBACKCOST	Specifies how the installer should handle low-disk conditions if running with no UI or the basic UI. Set to P to prompt the user to disable rollback, D to disable rollback without prompting, or F to fail with a warning that there is not enough disk space.
REBOOT	Allows you to control some of the reboot-prompting behavior. If set to "Force," the Installer automatically prompts for a reboot after install. If set to "Suppress," the Installer doesn't prompt for a reboot unless it executes a ForceReboot action. If set to "ReallySuppress," the Installer doesn't prompt for a reboot even for a ForceReboot action.
REINSTALL	Comma-delimited list of features to be reinstalled.
REINSTALLMODE	A string of letters showing the actions to be performed by a reinstall. The choices are shown in Table 7.3. The default is "omus."
RESUME	Set to 1 when the current installation is a resumption of a previously suspended installation.
SEQUENCE	Specifies the name of a table to be used by the SEQUENCE action.
SHORTFILENAMES	Set this property to 1 to force the Installer to use short names for files and directories.
TRANSFORMS	List of transforms to be applied during the installation. See Chapter 11, "Merges and Transforms."
TRANSFORMSATSOURCE	Set this property to 1 to indicate that transforms are stored at the root directory of the installation.
TRANSFORMSSECURE	Set to 1 to cache transforms in a location where the user does not have write access.

TABLE 7.3: Valid Values for REINSTALLMODE

Value	Meaning-
p	Reinstall only if a file is missing.
o	Reinstall if a file is missing or older.
e	Reinstall if missing, older, or equal version.
d	Reinstall if missing or a different version is present.
c	Reinstall if missing or corrupt.
a	Reinstall all files regardless of checksum or version.
u	Rewrite all user-based Registry keys.
m	Rewrite all machine-based Registry keys and reinstall all qualified components.
s	Reinstall all shortcuts and icons.
v	Reinstall from the original source, ignoring the locally cached package.

Private Properties

Private properties cover several broad areas:

- Folder locations
- Machine information filled in by the Installer
- Required properties (such as ProductCode) that you must supply a value for in the Property table

Table 7.4 lists the default private properties.

TABLE 7.4: Private Properties

Property	Meaning
AdminProperties	A semicolon-delimited list of properties that should be "filled in" when an administrative install is performed. When the user later installs from the share point, this list is used instead of the values originally in the Installer database.
AdminToolsFolder	Full path to the directory that stores a user's administrative tools (for example, Microsoft Management Console files).
AdminUser	Set to True if the user has administrative privileges. Always set to True if running on Windows 9x.
Alpha	Set to the processor level if the Installer is running on an Alpha computer.
AppDataFolder	Full path to the directory that stores the user's application data.
BorderSide	Width of Windows dialog box borders in pixels.
BorderTop	Height of Windows dialog box borders in pixels.

TABLE 7.4: Private Properties *(continued)*

Property	Meaning
CaptionHeight	Height of a Windows caption in pixels.
ColorBits	Color depth for the current video settings.
CommonFilesFolder	Full path to the directory that stores the user's common files.
CommonAppDataFolder	Full path to the directory that stores the user's application data.
ComputerName	Name of the computer on which the installation is running. Set by the Installer by calling the GetComputerName API.
CostingComplete	This property is set to zero by the CostFinalize action. The Installer sets it to 1 when costing is completed.
Date	Current date as a text string.
DefaultUIFont	The name of the TextStyle to use by default on controls. You should set this in the Property table.
DesktopFolder	Full path to the current user's desktop.
DiskPrompt	String that the Installer uses to prompt for a new source disk.
EnableUserControl	Setting this to 1 has the effect of making all public properties unrestricted.
FavoritesFolder	Full path to the Favorites folder of the current user.
FontsFolder	Full path to the System Fonts folder.
Installed	Set to 1 if the product has already been installed for the current user, or on a per-machine basis. Useful to detect when you're in maintenance mode instead of installing for the first time.
Intel	Set to the processor level (4 for 486, 5 for Pentium, etc.) if the installation is running on an Intel-based computer.
IsAdminPackage	Set to 1 if the current installation is being run from a package created by an administrative installation.
LeftUnit	Set to 1 to display units to the left of numbers in such things as free space displays.
LocalAppDataFolder	Full path to the application data folder for non-roaming applications.
LogonUser	Name of the current user, set by a call to the GetUserName API.
NetHoodFolder	Full path to the Network Neighborhood folder. Although this property has been dropped from the most recent SDK documentation, it still works.
Manufacturer	Manufacturer of the product. You must set this property's value in the Property table.
MyPicturesFolder	Full path to the user's My Pictures folder.
OLEAdvtSupport	Set to True if the current system supports install-on-demand and advertisement.
OutOfDiskSpace	Set to True if any disk in the system doesn't have enough free disk space for the installation to be completed.

TABLE 7.4: Private Properties *(continued)*

Property	Meaning
OutOfNoRbDiskSpace	Set to True if any disk in the system doesn't have enough free disk space for the installation to be completed even if rollback is disabled.
PersonalFolder	Full path to the current user's Personal folder.
PhysicalMemory	Megabytes of actual RAM installed in the current computer.
PIDTemplate	String used as a template for the PIDKEY property.
Preselected	Set to 1 when the selection dialog has already been processed.
PrintHoodFolder	Full path to the user's Printer Neighborhood folder. Although this property has been dropped from the most recent SDK documentation, it still works.
PrimaryVolumePath	Path portion of the PRIMARYFOLDER property.
PrimaryVolumeSpace-Available	Number of bytes available on the primary volume, in units of 512 bytes.
PrimaryVolumeSpace-Required	Number of bytes required by all selected features on the primary volume, in units of 512 bytes.
PrimaryVolumeSpace-Remaining	Number of bytes remaining after installation on the primary volume, in units of 512 bytes.
Privileged	Set to 1 when the installation is running with administrative privileges.
ProductCode	GUID that identifies this product. You must set a value for this property in the Property table.
ProductID	Set to the product ID by the ValidateProductID action.
ProductLanguage	Language ID to use for internal Installer strings displayed to the user.
ProductName	Name of the product being installed. You must set a value for this property in the Property table.
ProductState	Will return −1 if the product is neither advertised nor installed, 1 if the product is advertised but not installed, 2 if the product is installed but for a different user, or 5 if the product is already installed for the current user.
ProductVersion	Product version represented as a string in the format 00.00.0000. You must set a value for this property in the Property table.
ProgramFilesFolder	Full path to the user's Program Files folder.
ProgramMenuFolder	Full path to the user's Program folder in the Start menu.
RecentFolder	Full path to the current user's Recent folder. Although this property has been dropped from the most recent SDK documentation, it still works.
RemoteAdminTS	Set to 1 when the system is configured for remote administration via Windows Terminal Services.
ReplacedInUseFiles	Set to 1 if the Installer replaces a file that's in use (thus requiring a reboot to finish the installation).

TABLE 7.4: Private Properties *(continued)*

Property	Meaning
RestrictedUserControl	Set to 1 if the user can't change the value of restricted public properties.
RollbackDisabled	Set to 1 whenever rollback has been disabled by any means.
ScreenX	Width of the screen (in pixels).
ScreenY	Height of the screen (in pixels).
SecureCustomProperties	Semicolon-delimited list of public properties that should be treated as restricted public properties.
SendToFolder	Full path of the Send To folder for the current user.
ServicePackLevel	Major revision number of the most recent service pack applied to the operating system.
ServicePackLevelMinor	Minor revision number of the most recent service pack applied to the operating system.
SharedWindows	Set to 1 when the system is operating in shared Windows mode.
ShellAdvtSupport	Set to 1 if the operating system supports advertising.
SourceDir	The root directory of the current installation package.
StartMenuFolder	Full path to the current user's Start Menu folder.
StartupFolder	Full path to the current user's Startup folder.
System16Folder	Full path to the Windows System folder.
SystemFolder	Full path to the Windows System32 folder.
SystemLanguageID	Default language for the system. The Installer sets this by calling the GetSystemDefaultLangID API.
TempFolder	Full path to the user's Temp folder.
TemplateFolder	Full path to the user's Templates folder.
TerminalServer	Set to 1 when the Installer is running on Windows Terminal Server.
TextHeight	Height of characters in the default font in Installer units.
Time	Current time in the format HH:MM:SS.
TTCSupport	Set to 1 if the system supports `.ttc` (TrueType Font Collection) files.
UILevel	2 for none, 3 for basic, 4 for reduced, or 5 for the full user interface.
UpdateStarted	Set to 1 when changes have been made to the user's system.
UpgradeCode	A GUID representing allowable upgrades. See Chapter 10, "Creating and Using Patch Packages," for more information on patches and upgrades.
UserLanguageID	The default language ID for the current user. The Installer sets this by calling the GetUserDefaultLangID API.

T A B L E   7 . 4 :   Private Properties *(continued)*

Property	Meaning
Version9X	If running on Windows 9*x*, this is set to 100 times the major version of Windows plus the minor version of Windows.
VersionDatabase	Numeric version of the Installer database for the package being installed.
VersionNT	If running on Windows NT or Windows 2000, this is set to 100 times the major version of Windows plus the minor version of Windows.
VirtualMemory	Size of the current page file in megabytes.
WindowsBuild	Build number of the operating system.
WindowsFolder	Full path to the Windows folder.
WindowsVolume	Root of the drive containing the Windows folder.

Sample Expressions

The main point of properties in the Installer is to let you write expressions that control the course of the installation. You can use expressions in any table that has a Condition column. This includes the following:

Component   A component is installed only if any condition evaluates to True.

Condition   A feature is installed only if any condition in the Condition table that references that feature evaluates to True.

Sequence table   An action in a sequence table is executed only if any condition evaluates to True.

LaunchCondition   If a condition in the LaunchCondition table evaluates to False, the entire installation is aborted.

ControlCondition   The ControlCondition table lets you make conditional alterations to dialog boxes.

ControlEvent   A control event is fired only if any associated condition evaluates to True.

NOTE   For more details on these tables and on the syntax for conditions, see Chapter 4, "A Guide to the Installer Database."

Table 7.5 lists some sample conditions, just to get you started.

TABLE 7.5: Sample Conditions

Condition	Effect
Version9X>=400	Evaluates to True only on Windows 9x.
Version9X>=410	Evaluates to True only on Windows 98.
VersionNT>=400	Evaluates to True only on Windows NT and Windows 2000.
VersionNT>=500	Evaluates to True only on Windows 2000.
(VersionNT>=400 AND VersionNT<=499)	Evaluates to True on any build of Windows NT 4.0 but not on Windows 2000.
(AdminUser Or Privileged)	Evaluates to True if either the current user or the Installer itself currently has administrative privileges.
ADMIN	Evaluates to True only during an administrative setup.
(VersionNT AND Intel)	Evaluates to True on any Windows NT or Windows 2000 PC with an Intel microprocessor.
NOT (SystemLanguageID=1033)	Evaluates to True on any version of Windows other than U.S. English.
(NOT AFTERREBOOT)	Evaluates to True only during the first part of an installation, before the computer is rebooted.

Creating a New Installer Package

It's time to get some hands-on experience with the Windows Installer. In the remainder of this chapter, I'll show you how to modify an Installer package to perform some common tasks.

As you've seen in the previous chapters, there is a tremendous amount of complexity to the Windows Installer. In order to avoid some of this complexity for now, I'm going to start with an existing Installer package and modify it, rather than creating a completely new package. In the examples in the remainder of this chapter, I'll use the MsiSpy.msi Installer package as a starting point. This package is available as part of the Windows Installer SDK.

NOTE You'll learn how to create a package completely from scratch in Chapter 12, "Installer Editing Tools," which covers tools for working with Installer databases.

In order to concentrate on the structure of the Installer database rather than the tools used, in the remainder of the chapter, I'll work with the simple Orca editor that ships as part of the Installer SDK.

To make the test package,

1. Make a copy of the `MsiSpy.msi` file (you'll find this file in the SampProd folder in the Installer SDK). Call the new file `TestSpy.msi`. Because this package uses external files, it's simplest to leave `TestSpy.msi` in the same folder as `MsiSpy.msi`.

2. Start the Orca editor, choose File ➢ Open, and open the `TestSpy.msi` package that you just created. Alternatively, you can right-click the `TestSpy.msi` package in Windows Explorer and choose Edit with ORCA.

3. Because we're going to be making changes to the package, we must assign a new ProductID to the package. I used the GUID generation sample from Chapter 3, "Basic Installer Concepts," to generate the GUID {FDB3BA7A-5AD4-43A3-B34B-541EA130617A} for my copy. Choose View ➢ Summary Information within Orca to enter the new ProductID. While you're there, you can update the other summary information for your new package. Figure 7.1 shows the Edit Summary Information dialog box with new information entered.

FIGURE 7.1
Summary information for
modified package

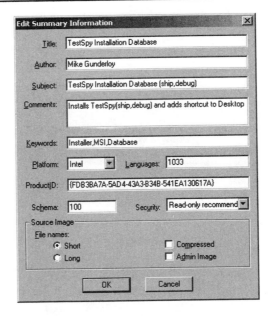

NOTE   The TestSpy package starts with the exact same components as the MsiSpy package. There's no need to change the ComponentIDs for these components because we're not making any changes to the components themselves. Shared components must use the same ComponentID across packages.

4. You must also change the ProductCode in the Property table. You can use the same GUID that you entered for the ProductID here.

5. You might also want to change some of the other properties in the Property table, such as the ProductName property and the Manufacturer Property, to further customize the test package. Of course, since you're not planning to distribute this package, you don't actually have to do this.

6. Use the Save button on the Orca toolbar to save your work.

Adding a File

I'll start the modifications by adding a new file to TestSpy.msi. To understand the mechanics of the process it doesn't really matter what file I add to the installation. I've added a file named Helpful.txt, which is a simple text file. It's stored in a folder named TestSpy under the root folder of the TestSpy installation, as shown in Figure 7.2.

> **NOTE** The readme.txt file in the sample project for this chapter explains how to set up the sample files on your hard drive to recreate this example.

FIGURE 7.2
A new file to be installed

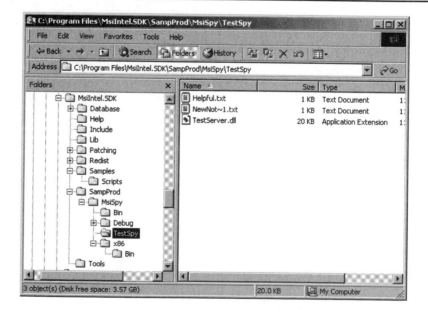

The files in the source tree for your installation must be laid out in the same relative positions that you want them installed on the user's hard drive.

Because this file is in a new folder, it requires a new entry in the Directory table. You can create this entry with Orca by following these steps:

1. Select Directory in the tables list on the left-hand side of Orca.
2. Right-click in the table and choose Add Row.
3. Fill in the values for the new row. The value for the Directory column is **TestSpy-Dir**, the value for the Directory_Parent column is **SPYEXEDIR**, and the value for the DefaultDir column is **TestSpy**. These define a directory with the name TestSpy, located directly under the root of the installation, and with the symbolic name of TestSpyDir.
4. Click OK to add the row to the table.

The new file doesn't really belong to any of the existing components, so it's also necessary to add a new row to the Component table. To do this, you'll need to generate another GUID to be the ComponentID. The new row should have these values:

- Component: **TestSpyFiles**
- ComponentID: **{F111E82A-B74D-4A68-AFCF-BC2095929863**
- Directory: **TestSpyDir**
- Attributes: **2**
- Condition: Null (that is, leave the property blank)
- KeyPath: **TestSpyMain**

Make sure that you leave Null columns blank! If you type in the word "Null," you're going to create hard-to-track-down errors. For example, a value of Null in the Condition column is completely different from an empty condition.

This creates a component that can be set to run either locally or from source, and that uses the file specified by TestSpyMain to determine whether it's already been installed. It's a good idea to create the entry in the file table while this information is still handy:

- File: **TestSpyMain**
- Component_: **TestSpyFiles**
- FileName: **Helpful.txt**

- FileSize: **41** (the actual size of the text file)
- Version: Null (this file has no version information)
- Language: **1033**
- Attributes: **0**
- Sequence: **13**

The Sequence number of 13 is one higher than the highest entry already in the table. This will force this file to be installed after all of the other files listed in the table.

Because you've increased the maximum sequence number in the file, you need to edit the Media table. The Media table tells the Installer which sequence numbers are found on which disk. In this case, all of the files are on a single disk. If you open the Media table in Orca, you'll find that it contains a single row with the LastSequenc column set to 12. Change this to 13 by clicking it and typing in the new value.

Having created entries in the Directory, Component, and File tables, you've defined the component; that is, the view of this file from the eyes of the developer. However, you still have to define it for the user. To do this, you need to add a row to the Feature table:

- Feature: **TestSpyMain**
- Feature_Parent: Null (this is a top-level feature)
- Title: **Files for TestSpy**
- Description: **Files required for the proper operation of TestSpy**
- Display: **14**
- Level: **1**
- Directory: Null
- Attributes: **0**

Finally, you need to associate the feature with the component by making an entry in the FeatureComponents table:

- Feature_: **TestSpyMain**
- Component_: **TestSpyFiles**

Once you've made these entries, the file is ready to test. Save your work, close Orca, and double-click the TestSpy.msi file. If you proceed through a custom installation, you can verify that your new feature shows in the feature tree, as seen in Figure 7.3. After the installation completes, you should be able to browse to the directory where you installed TestSpy and find a TestSpy folder containing a copy of Helpful.txt.

FIGURE 7.3
The modified feature tree

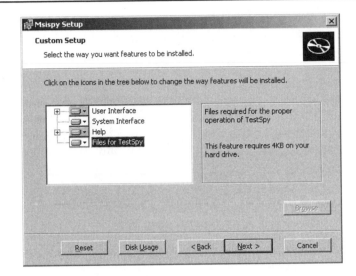

You might think that's a lot of work to add a single file to an installation, and you'd be right. In Chapter 12, you'll see how you can use some of the more sophisticated tools on the market to make the job easier.

Adding a Shortcut

Suppose you want to add a shortcut to a file. In this particular case, I'll add a desktop shortcut to open the Helpful.txt file that I added to the installation in the previous section.

Not surprisingly, you need to add a row to the Shortcut table to add a shortcut. Here are the details:

- Shortcut: **HelpfulShortcut**
- Directory: **DesktopFolder**
- Name: **Helpful**
- Component_: **TestSpyFiles**
- Target: **TestSpyMain**
- Arguments: Null
- Description: **This shortcut opens the Helpful text file**
- Hotkey: Null
- Icon: Null
- IconIndex: Null

- ShowCmd: Null
- WkDir: Null

This set of column values will create a shortcut to the key path file of the TestSpyMain feature—that is, to the `Helpful.txt` file. After you've made this entry, you can save and close the Installer package and run it. You'll find that you have created a new shortcut on the Windows desktop.

If you've previously installed TestSpy, you should uninstall it before you try reinstalling it. You can either do this from the Add/Remove Programs Control Panel applet, or by just running `TestSpy.msi` and choosing Remove from the maintenance menu.

WARNING   If you follow these directions, you'll find that the shortcut does not have the proper text file icon. To get the proper icon, you'd have to include it in a file in the Icon table.

Adding a Registry Key

Suppose that you want to create a couple of Registry keys when TestSpy is installed. I'll show you how to create two keys in this section:

- HKEY_LOCAL_MACHINE\Software\TestSpy\TestKey
- HKEY_CURRENT_USER\Software\TestSpy\TestKey

The HKLM key is simple. You can just add an entry to the Registry table and tie it back to the existing component that you created to install the TestSpy file.

WARNING   The TestSpy Installer database doesn't contain a Registry table by default. You can add one by choosing Tables ➤ Add Table from the Orca menus.

The first entry in the Registry table looks like this:

- Registry: **TestSpyHKLMkey**
- Root: **2**
- Key: **Software\TestSpy\TestKey**
- Name: **KeyName**
- Value: **#1**
- Component_: **TestSpyFiles**

The value of 2 for the root specifies that this key will be written to the HKLM Registry hive.

Adding the second key is a bit trickier. If there's a possibility that your software will be installed by two different users on the same computer, then correctly managing Registry entries to the HKCU hive requires that the Registry entry be the key path of a component. In this case, that means first adding another record to the Component table:

- Component: **TestSpyRegistry**
- ComponentID: **{735A3253-B221-4EEF-AA65-004F4595BF0E}**
- Directory_: **TestSpyDir**
- Attributes: **4**
- Condition: Null
- KeyPath: **TestSpyHKCUkey**

Now, you can add the corresponding row to the Registry table:

- Registry: **TestSpyHKCUkey**
- Root: **1**
- Key: **Software\TestSpy\TestKey**
- Name: **KeyName**
- Value: **#1**
- Component_: **TestSpyRegistry**

It's also useful to define a new feature to install this component:

- Feature: **TestSpyReg**
- Feature_Parent: **TestSpyMain**
- Title: **Registry keys for TestSpy**
- Description: **Registry keys for TestSpy**
- Display: **0**
- Level: **1**
- Directory: Null
- Attributes: **0**

Setting the display to zero and the level to 1 makes sure that this feature gets chosen whenever its parent feature is chosen. The user never gets to see a node for this feature in the SelectionTree control.

And of course, to make sure this component actually gets installed, you need to associate it with an appropriate feature by making an entry in the FeatureComponents table:

- Feature_: **TestSpyReg**
- Component_: **TestSpyRegistry**

Once you've made these entries, you should save and close the file and remove any previous installation of TestSpy. At this point, installing TestSpy should create the two Registry keys, as you can verify by examining the Registry with a tool such as regedit.

Adding a COM Server

If your installation includes any COM servers, you'll want to make sure that they're properly registered on the end user's computer. There are two ways to do this: the easy way and the right way. For illustration, I've prepared a simple COM server (a Visual Basic ActiveX DLL named TestServer that exposes a single class named TestObject).

The easy way to register a COM server is to add the file to your project and to the Self-Reg table. First, you need to make a copy of the `TestServer.dll` file to the TestSpy folder and add an entry to the Component table (remember, since this is a COM server, it must be the key path file for a component):

- Component: **TestServerFiles**
- ComponentID: **{8ADCBC87-AF9D-4880-976B-836CEA8141E0}**
- Directory: **TestSpyDir**
- Attributes: **2**
- Condition: Null (that is, leave the property blank)
- KeyPath: **TestServerMain**

Next you can create the entry in the File table:

- File: **TestServerMain**
- Component_: **TestServerFiles**
- FileName: **TestSe~1.dll | TestServer.dll**
- FileSize: **20480**
- Version: **1.0.0.0**
- Language: **1033**
- Attributes: **0**
- Sequence: **14**

Edit the Media table again, and change the LastSequence column of the single row in the table to the new value of 14 to include this new file.

NOTE   Note the use of the short filename/long filename pair in the FileName property. This is necessary because the name of the file does not conform to short filename rules.

This component can be associated with the same feature as the TestSpyFiles component. Remember, you don't need an individual feature for every component. You can just make an entry in the FeatureComponents table to associate this component with an existing feature:

- Feature_: **TestSpyMain**
- Component_: **TestServerFiles**

Now, to make this a self-registering component, enter the information in the SelfReg table (you'll have to use the Orca menus to create this table, if you're following along):

- File_: **TestServerMain**
- Cost: **20000**

Save your work, close Orca, and run the installation. You can check to make sure the COM server registration worked by opening a new Visual Basic project, choosing Project ➤ References, and verifying that the Test Server shows up in the list of available references, as shown in Figure 7.4.

FIGURE 7.4
Verifying the installation of a COM server

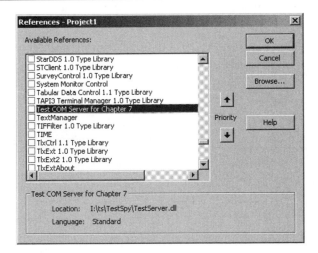

Although this method works, it's not ideal. As I mentioned in Chapter 4, there are a number of drawbacks to self-registration in the Windows Installer world:

- DllRegisterServer can't be safely rolled back if an installation fails, because there's no way to tell whether Registry keys are shared by other applications.
- The information that the Installer needs to advertise components isn't exposed.
- DllRegisterServer doesn't support the notion of per-user information in the HKCR Registry hive.
- Self-registering DLLs may fail in a "run from source" network installation.

To use the Registry tables instead of self-registration, you'll need to know what Registry entries the COM server requires to run. One way to do this is to use regedit to export the portion of the Registry that holds class information, and see what changes. To do this, follow these steps:

1. Open a command prompt and navigate to the folder in which you installed `Test-Server.dll`. Run the command **regsvr32 /u TestServer.dll** to unregister the server.

2. Start regedit.

3. Export the HKEY_CLASSES_ROOT hive.

4. In the command prompt, run **regsvr32 TestServer.dll** to reregister the server.

5. Export the HKEY_CLASSES_ROOT hive again. Use a different name for this second file.

Once you've got the "before" and "after" versions of the Registry, you'll need to find the differences. If your Registry is small, you can use the WinDiff tool that's installed with Visual Studio for that purpose. If it's large, you may have to use a professional text editor such as CodeWright or Visual SlickEdit.

Alternatively, you can just poke around in the Registry by searching for "TestServer" and "TestObject" to see what turns up.

In any case, you'll find that you have to make three table entries to handle the COM registration information for this simple server. If you'd like to actually add these entries to your Installer database, you should remove the call to selfregister the DLL so that it doesn't get registered twice. That wouldn't hurt anything, but it would waste time.

In the ProgId table,

- ProgId: **TestServer.TestObject**
- ProgId_Parent: Null
- Class: **{4623CB5A-3694-4BD4-A0E1-112F288EDC1C}**
- Description: **TestServer.TestObject**
- Icon_: Null
- IconIndex: Null

In the Class table,

- CLSID: **{4623CB5A-3694-4BD4-A0E1-112F288EDC1C}**
- Context: **InProcServer32**
- Component_: **TestServerFiles**

- ProgId_Default: **TestServer.TestObject**
- Description: **TestServer.TestObject**
- AppId_: Null
- FileTypeMask: Null
- Icon_: Null
- IconIndex: Null
- DefInProcHandler: Null
- Argument: Null
- Feature_: **TestSpyMain**

In the TypeLib table,

- LibId: **{DFF775CC-E403-4F75-85DE-77A721563272}**
- Language: **0**
- Component_: **TestServerFiles**
- Version: **256**
- Description: **Test COM Server for Chapter 7**
- Directory_: Null
- Feature_: **TestSpyMain**
- Cost: **20000**

From this simple example, you can see that adding a more complex COM server would be a difficult and error-prone task. As you'll see in Chapter 12, there are automated solutions available to make the proper entries in the COM-related Registry tables. If you can't use one of those solutions, I recommend that you stick to self-registration for your COM servers, despite the drawbacks to using self-registration.

Searching for a Directory

Suppose that your Installer package is putting an updated version of your product on the user's hard drive. In that case, you'd probably rather search for the previous version and use that folder as the location for the new version. You can make use of the Installer's search capabilities to do this.

To make this concrete, here's how you can add a file named NewNotes.txt to the Installer database for TestSpy and install it in the same folder where OldNotes.txt already exists. First, you need to define a file signature that will specify the existing file. You do this by adding a row to the Signature table:

- Signature: **OldNotesSignature**
- FileName: **OldNotes.txt**

- MinVersion: Null
- MaxVersion: Null
- MinSize: Null
- MaxSize: Null
- MinDate: Null
- MaxDate: Null
- Languages: Null

By leaving all the identifying information empty (except for the filename), you specify that you'll accept any file with that name as the one you're looking for.

Next, you need to add an entry to the AppSearch table:

- Property: **NOTESPATH**
- Signature_: **OldNotesSignatureDirectory**

You need to tell the Installer what to search for. It can search for directories and files, Registry keys, or .ini file keys. In this case, you need to make two entries to the Dr-Locator table. The first is for the actual file:

- Signature: **OldNotesSignature**
- Parent: Null
- Path: Null
- Depth: **2**

The second entry in the DrLocator table is for the directory:

- Signature: **OldNotesSignatureDirectory**
- Parent: **OldNotesSignature**
- Path: Null
- Depth: Null

When the Installer executes the AppSearch action, it looks at the various possible linked tables to determine what OldNotesSignatureDirectory should point to. Since this key is only in the DrLocator table, and not in the Signature table as well, it refers to a directory. The parent-child relationship with the OldNotesSignature row tells the Installer which file identifies the directory you want, and the row in the Signature table for OldNotesSignature specifies the file. With a search depth of 2 specified for the file, the Installer will check all fixed drives down to two levels below the root for the file. Once it's found, it will set the value of the NOTEPATH property to the location where the OldNotes file is found. You can use this property in a row in the Directory table:

- Directory: **NewNotesDir**
- Directory_Parent: **NOTESPATH**
- DefaultDir: **.:TestSpy**

The entry for DefaultDir indicates that the target directory is the one pointed to by NOTESPATH, but the source directory is the TestSpy directory on the source media. If you don't use this target:source notation, there's no way to handle a variable installation location.

Even though this directory will get set at runtime, you still need to include a default location in the directory tree. You can do this by adding one more record to the Directory table:

- Directory: **NOTESPATH**
- Directory_Parent: **SPYEXEDIR**
- DefaultDir: **.**

Now, create the entries for the NewNotes file, starting with the Component table:

- Component: **NewNotesFiles**
- ComponentID: **{C71F041C-0F6F-48E1-9524-C2331E12F2F4}**
- Directory: **NewNotesDir**
- Attributes: **2**
- Condition: Null (that is, leave the property blank)
- KeyPath: **NewNotesMain**

Now, create the corresponding entry in the File table:

- File: **NewNotesMain**
- Component_: **NewNotesFiles**
- FileName: **NewNot~1.txt | NewNotes.txt**
- FileSize: **41** (the actual size of the text file)
- Version: Null
- Language: **1033**
- Attributes: **0**
- Sequence: **15**

Update the LastSequence column in the Media table to 15 to include this new file. And of course, you need to create a feature to hold this file. You can't use an existing feature because none of the existing features are installed to this directory. So add an entry to the Feature table:

- Feature: **TestSpyNotes**
- Feature_Parent: **TestSpyMain**
- Title: **New Notes file**
- Description: **New Notes file**
- Display: **0**

- Level: **1**
- Directory: Null
- Attributes: **0**

Finally, associate the component with the feature by making an entry in the Feature-Components table:

- Feature_: **TestSpyNotes**
- Component_: **NewNotesFiles**

To test these changes, place a file named OldNotes.txt on the target drive for the installation and run the Installer package. When the dust clears, you should find a copy of NewNotes.txt in the same directory.

This example should give you some sense of the complexity that may be necessary to author even seemingly simple actions into an Installer package. You'll find that the tables are powerful enough to do almost anything you'd like and that custom actions are very seldom necessary. But it may take a bit of ingenuity to get the tables to do what you want.

Installing MDAC

I'll close this chapter with a brief discussion of some of the problems involved in installing the *Microsoft Data Access Components (MDAC)*. Many, many applications require this set of components to be installed in order to run properly. Microsoft distributes MDAC in the form of a self-extracting executable program named mdac_typ.exe.

In a perfect Installer world, Microsoft would also make available a Windows Installer merge module for MDAC. You could then just include this merge module in your Installer database, and all would be well. Unfortunately, there is no merge module for MDAC 2.1, the current version as I write this, and Microsoft has announced no plans to create one for MDAC 2.5, either.

Some developers are trying to work around this problem by including the files and Registry keys from the MDAC setup in their Installer database directly. Unfortunately, there are several problems with this approach. First, it's probably a license violation to redistribute the MDAC components in any fashion other than how Microsoft packaged them. Second, by rolling your own MDAC setup this way, you'd inevitably have to create your own ComponentId values for the files included. This would lead to multiple copies of the MDAC files being installed with different ComponentIds, and a good deal of chaos.

So, for the moment, the best bet is to simply include the entire `mdac_typ.exe` file in your Installer package and use a Type 18 custom action to execute the installation after the file has been copied to the user's hard drive. To get best results, you should use this command line:

```
mdac_typ.exe /q /C:"setup /QNT"
```

This command line will suppress the installation user interface, both when unpacking and when installing the data access components. The computer will need to be rebooted afterward, so you should be sure to author a ForceReboot action into your installation's sequence tables.

NOTE   Installing MDAC is a problem only on Windows 9x and Windows NT 4.0. Starting with Windows 2000, the data access components are included with the operating system. Thus, if you do install MDAC with a custom action, you should use a condition to prevent launching the setup on Windows 2000.

Using the Installer API

The Windows Installer provides a complete application programming interface (API) that can be used by other applications to access the Installer functions. Actually, the Installer provides two APIs. One set of functions lets external programs manipulate the Installer itself, while another set of functions lets external programs manipulate Installer databases. You may need to use both sets of functions in a single application, but it's convenient to think of them separately to get a sense of how the Installer API is organized.

In this chapter, I'll show you the broad outlines of the Installer API and then give some examples of its use from Visual Basic. This chapter is not a substitute for the help files in the Installer SDK. It would take many pages to list all the parameters of every API call thatthe Installer provides. Rather, I'll concentrate on some common tasks to give you a sense of what you can do with this API.

Before tackling the Installer API, you should also check the Installer automation model (covered in Chapter 9, "Using the Installer Automation Model") to see whether the functionality you need is available there. If it is, the automation model is often easier to use from Visual Basic than the Installer API.

Overview of the Installer API

The Installer API consists of 106 functions, counting both the core Installer API and the Installer database API. These functions can be broken down into 17 fundamental groups. For the core Installer API, there are eight groups:

- System status functions
- Product query functions
- Installation and configuration functions
- Application-only functions
- Component-specific functions
- User interface and logging functions
- Handle management functions
- Patching functions

For the Installer database API, there are nine groups:

- General database access functions
- Summary information property functions
- Installer location functions
- Installer selection functions
- User interface functions

- Database management functions
- Record processing functions
- Installer action functions
- Installer state access functions

I'll discuss each of these groups of functions in turn in the following pages. As you can see, the division between the core and database APIs is somewhat arbitrary. You can use some of the core APIs to retrieve information from the database, and some of the database APIs to cause the Installer to perform useful work.

Installer Functions

The core Installer API functions let you perform actions such as these:

- Locate products and components registered on the computer.
- Request features.
- Install entire applications.
- Reinstall an application or a component.
- Remove an advertised application.

In general, to work with already-installed applications, you'll want to consider the functions in the core API.

System Status Functions

The 12 *system status functions* allow you to retrieve information about products, features, and components that are known to the Installer Service on this particular computer.

The MsiEnumProducts API returns the GUIDs of all products that have either been installed or advertised. It returns the product codes of these products, one on each call to the API, until it returns the constant ERROR_NO_MORE_ITEMS. In fact, there are a whole group of functions that work this way:

MsiEnumProducts   Enumerates products.

MsiEnumRelatedProducts   Enumerates products with a specific upgrade code.

MsiEnumFeatures   Enumerates published features.

MsiEnumComponents   Enumerates the components of *all* installed products.

MsiEnumClients   Enumerates the products that use a particular component.

MsiEnumComponentQualifiers   Enumerates the advertised qualifiers for a particular component.

Given a product code, the MsiQueryProductState API will tell you whether that product is installed for the current user, installed for another user, advertised, or not on the computer at all. Similarly, MsiQueryFeatureState takes a product code and feature ID and tells you whether the feature is installed locally, installed to run from source, advertised, or not installed at all.

MsiGetFileVersion looks at any file on your hard drive and tells you the version string and language string for that file in the format that the Installer uses.

The MsiGetFeatureUsage API returns information on the number of times that an installed feature has been used.

The MsiGetUserInfo API gets the user and company information that was registered for a particular product.

The MsiGetProductInfo API allows you to retrieve properties for products that have been installed or advertised. For example, you can use this API to retrieve the installation date, product language, or product name of a particular product. You'll see an example of this API in use later in this chapter.

Product Query Functions

The five *product query functions* are used to retrieve product information or to prepare a product for other API calls.

MsiOpenProduct opens a product for other core API functions that need access to the details of the Installer database. It returns an Installer handle, which is a long integer uniquely identifying the open product. Any time you want to use an API that requires a product handle, you'll need to call MsiOpenProduct first. The similar MsiOpenPackage API opens a disk file containing an Installer package, and is primarily intended for validation of the package.

The MsiGetProductProperty API returns the value of a property for an installed product.

MsiGetFeatureInfo returns information describing an installed feature: the name, localized name, attributes, and description of the feature.

MsiVerifyPackage checks an arbitrary disk file and tells you whether it is an installation package.

Installation and Configuration Functions

The 11 *installation and configuration functions* are at the heart of the core API. These are the functions that let you change what's installed as part of a given product.

The MsiInstallProduct API takes the path to a package and installs or uninstalls an entire product. The MsiConfigureProduct API does the same thing based on a product code. The MsiConfigureProductEx API performs the same operation as MsiConfigure-Product, and also allows you to pass command-line arguments to the Installer to customize the installation.

MsiInstallMissingComponent installs a single component. It does this by installing the feature using the component that takes the least amount of disk space. MsiInstall-MissingFile functions similarly except that it starts with the name of a file rather than with a component ID.

MsiReinstallProduct is used to repair or reinstall products. It takes a parameter that indicates which repair activities should be performed, similar to the command-line switches for repair. MsiReinstallFeature performs the same function but on a specified feature rather than an entire product.

MsiConfigureFeature allows you to change the installed state of a particular feature. You can use this to install a feature locally, install it to run from the source, advertise it, remove it, or install it according to the default in the Installer database.

The MsiSourceListAddSource can be used to modify the list of network locations that can supply files for an advertised product. MsiSourceListClearAll removes all sources from this list of locations. The MsiSourceListForceResolution API tests the list of sources until it finds one that actually holds a valid copy of the product.

Application-Only Functions

The four *application-only functions* are utility functions designed to be called from within a running program that was installed by the Installer Service.

MsiCollectUserInfo is used by applications that require a user to register on first use. It runs the FirstRun dialog from within the Installer package to collect the information.

MsiUseFeature increments the usage count for a feature. MsiUseFeatureEx does the same but also returns the installation status of the feature.

MsiGetProductCode returns the product code of the application, given the component code of the application's main executable file.

Component-Specific Functions

The five *component-specific functions* are used to install and locate components.

MsiProvideComponent can be used to arrange "just-in-time" installation from within your application code. It returns the path to a component, but if necessary, it will install that component first. MsiProvideQualifiedComponent does the same for a qualified component. MsiProvideQualifiedComponentEx will do the same, prompt for the source if necessary, and increment the usage count of any features involved.

MsiGetComponentPath will, given a component ID, return the disk or registry path to that component. This API requires the product code for the product that contains the component. Given only the component ID, the very similar MsiLocateComponent call will return the full path to a component.

WARNING   MsiLocateComponent is not guaranteed to return the path to the component actually installed by the current application. For example, if two products install different qualified versions of the same component, MsiLocateComponent might return the path to either one.

User Interface and Logging Functions

The three *user-interface and logging functions* work in conjunction with the other core APIs (notably, the installation and configuration functions) to control the user experience while the API is in action.

MsiSetInternalUI allows you to choose which level of user interface (none, reduced, basic, full, default) should be used for subsequent API calls.

MsiSetExternalUI allows another program to install itself as the default user interface. Of course, it must properly handle the messages from the Installer engine.

MsiEnableLog sets the level of logging to be used for subsequent API calls. Its parameters allow you to specify the same logging levels that you can specify from the command line.

Handle Management Functions

The two *handle management functions* are used to cleanly shut down an Installer session triggered via the API.

The MsiCloseHandle API closes an Installer handle (for example, one supplied by MsiOpenPackage).

The MsiCloseAllHandles API closes all handles that were opened by the current thread of execution.

WARNING   The Installer SDK recommends that you only call MsiCloseAllHandles for "diagnostic" purposes. Under normal circumstances, you should close each open handle with a separate call to MsiCloseHandle.

Patching Functions

Finally, the three *patching functions* allow you to automate the upgrade of Installer-enabled products.

MsiApplyPatch applies a patch to an existing installation.

MsiEnumPatches lets you list all the patches that have been applied to a particular product.

Given a patch code, the MsiGetPatchInfo API will tell you where the patch package has been cached on the local hard drive.

Installer Database Functions

The *Installer database API functions* are designed to let you view and manipulate information stored in an Installer database. These functions are the means by which the various editing tools interact with Installer databases (see Chapter 12, "Installer Editing Tools"). They can also be useful if you need to perform other database functions from your own code:

- View or change the contents of any of the Installer database tables.
- Set the source or target folder for an installation.
- Add records to the database tables during an installation.

The Installer database functions are useful when you're working on a tool to help build such databases or when you need to interact with the database during an installation.

General Database Access Functions

The 12 *general database access functions* include some functions that allow you to open views and fetch records from an Installer database, as well as some metadata functions. With most of the database functions, you'll need to obtain a database handle before proceeding.

MsiGetActiveDatabase returns a database handle, given an Installer handle. If you're not running an installation, use the MsiOpenDatabase API call instead to return a database handle, given the filename of the Installer package.

MsiDatabaseOpenView takes a SQL query string and a database handle and opens the corresponding view. MsiViewExecute can be used to execute a parameterized query with specific parameter values. Once a view is open, you use the MsiViewFetch API to fetch records one by one. MsiViewClose releases the result set from a view once you're done with it.

You can modify a record in a view with MsiViewModify. If there's any problem modifying a record, the MsiViewGetError API will return the most recent error.

The MsiDatabaseCommit API commits all pending changes to the on-disk version of the database. You should always call this function when you're done making changes to the database.

The Windows Installer provides these three metadata functions for inquiring about the structure of the database:

MsiDatabaseGetPrimaryKeys   Returns the names of the primary key columns for a specified table.

MsiDatabaseIsTablePersistent   Tells you whether a particular table is temporary or permanent.

MsiViewGetColumnInfo   Returns column names or definitions.

NOTE   Several of these functions require you to write SQL statements. I'll discuss the SQL syntax for the Installer after reviewing the rest of the Installer database API calls.

Summary Information Property Functions

The five *summary information property functions* allow you to read and write the summary information stream within an Installer package.

MsiGetSummaryInformation returns a handle to the summary information stream, given a database handle.

MsiSummaryInfoGetPropertyCount returns the number of properties in the summary information stream.

MsiSummaryInfoGetProperty retrieves a single property from the summary information stream. MsiSummaryInfoSetProperty allows you to set a new value for a property from the summary information stream. If you do make any changes, you need to call MsiSummaryInfoPersist to write them back out to the Installer database.

Installer Location Functions

The three *Installer location functions* allow you to work with the source and target paths for components in an installation.

MsiGetSourcePath returns the full source path for a folder in the Directory table. For a running installation, this will tell you, for example, whether you're installing from a local or a network drive.

MsiGetTargetPath returns the full target path for a folder in the Directory table.

The MsiSetTargetPath API will let you specify a different path for an entry in the Directory table. This can be used to change the install location "on the fly" from a custom action or from within an application.

Installer Selection Functions

The nine *Installer selection functions* are designed to work with the state of an installation and the features and components within the installation.

MsiGetComponentState supplies the current state of a component (installed, incomplete, missing, run from source, and so on). MsiGetFeatureState supplies the same information for a feature.

MsiSetComponentState lets you move a particular component to be installed locally or from source, or to be removed entirely. MsiSetFeatureState performs the same operation for a feature.

MsiGetFeatureValidStates indicates whether a particular feature can be installed locally, run from source, or advertised.

MsiGetFeatureCost returns the amount of space that a feature takes up, optionally including parent and child features.

MsiSetFeatureAttributes lets you modify the information that is stored in the Attributes column of the Feature table.

MsiSetInstallLevel controls which features will be installed during an installation.

MsiVerifyDiskSpace takes an Installer handle and checks to see whether there is enough free disk space to complete the current installation.

User Interface Functions

The three *user interface functions* help you inspect the user interface contained within an installation package.

MsiEnableUIPreview puts the Installer into a mode in which it can display dialog boxes outside the flow of execution of a sequence table. This API is primarily useful when you're writing an external tool to manipulate Installer dialog boxes. Once you've called MsiEnableUIPreview, you can use the MsiPreviewDialog API to display any dialog box from the Installer database as a modeless, inactive dialog box.

MsiPreviewBillboard lets you view billboards from an Installer database without actually running the installation. You must call MsiEnableUIPreview before calling MsiPreviewBillboard.

Database Management Functions

The seven *database management functions* handle operations that affect an Installer database as a whole.

MsiDatabaseExport exports a table from an Installer database to a text file. Conversely, MsiDatabaseImport imports a table from a text file to an Installer database. These two functions allow you to easily link external table-generation tools to a database.

The MsiGetDatabaseState API will check an open database to see whether it's read-only or read-write.

MsiDatabaseMerge merges two Installer databases together. You can call this API to add a merge module to an existing Installer database.

MsiDatabaseGenerateTransform looks at two Installer databases and generates a transform of the differences between them. MsiDatabaseApplyTransform applies a transform to an Installer database.

The MsiCreateTransformSummaryInfo creates a summary information stream within a transform. As a side effect, it also validates the transform and returns information on any errors it contains.

NOTE   You'll learn more about merges and transforms in Chapter 11, "Merges and Transforms."

Record Processing Functions

The 12 *record processing functions* work with records returned as part of views from an Installer database.

MsiRecordGetInteger returns an integer value from a field in a record. MsiRecordGetString returns a text value from a field in a record. MsiRecordReadStream will transfer the contents of a stream from a record to a buffer. There are also corresponding functions for writing integers, strings, and streams back to records. These are MsiRecordSetInteger, MsiRecordSetString, and MsiRecordSetStream.

MsiRecordGetFieldCount returns the number of fields in a given record. MsiRecord-DataSize returns the size of a particular field in a record. This is the size of the actual data stored in the field, not the maximum size of the data that the field can hold. Msi-RecordIsNull will tell you whether a particular field currently contains a Null value.

MsiRecordClearData sets all the fields in a record to Null.

The MsiCreateRecord API creates a new, blank record with a specified number of fields.

MsiFormatRecord is used to resolve symbols in a record according to the usual Installer rules. For example, a substring of the form [propertyname] is replaced with the current value of the property.

Installer Action Functions

The four *Installer action functions* let you interact with sequence tables and individual actions.

The MsiDoAction API call executes an action from within an Installer database. This call can also be used to display a live dialog box by supplying the dialog box name as the action name. MsiSequence executes all the actions in a sequence table according to their stored ordering and conditions.

MsiEvaluateCondition uses the Installer rules to evaluate a conditional expression, returning True, False, or "syntax error."

MsiProcessMessage sends an error message to the Installer to be logged.

Installer State Access Functions

The six *Installer state access functions* let you retrieve information about the internal state of the Installer engine.

MsiGetLanguage returns the LangID of the current installation.

MsiGetLastErrorRecord returns information on the most recent error (if any) from any of the other Installer APIs.

MsiGetMode lets you check some of the internal Installer flags. Table 8.1 lists the flags you can check with this API. MsiSetMode allows you to set only the flags that indicate a deferred or immediate reboot is necessary.

MsiGetProperty gets the current value of an Installer property. The corresponding MsiSetProperty API lets you set a new value for an Installer property.

TABLE 8.1: Constants for MsiGetMode

Constant	Returns True If
MSIRUNMODE_ADMIN	An administrative install is being performed.
MSIRUNMODE_ADVERTISE	Advertisements are being made or a product is being installed or updated.
MSIRUNMODE_CABINET	Files are being installed from cabinets.
MSIRUNMODE_COMMIT	A custom action is being called from a commit script.
MSIRUNMODE_LOGENABLED	Logging is being performed.
MSIRUNMODE_MAINTENANCE	An installation is being modified, or a new product is being installed.
MSIRUNMODE_OPERATIONS	Operations from the Execute table are being executed.
MSIRUNMODE_REBOOTATEND	A reboot is necessary at the end of the installation.
MSIRUNMODE_REBOOTNOW	An immediate reboot is necessary.
MSIRUNMODE_ROLLBACK	A custom action is being called from a rollback script.
MSIRUNMODE_ROLLBACKENABLED	Rollback is enabled.
MSIRUNMODE_SCHEDULED	A custom action is being called from the installation script.
MSIRUNMODE_SOURCESHORTNAMES	Short filenames are being used on the source.
MSIRUNMODE_TARGETSHORTNAMES	Short filenames are being used on the target.
MSIRUNMODE_WINDOWS9X	The operating system is Windows 95 or Windows 98.
MSIRUNMODE_ZAWENABLED	The operating system supports installation on demand.

Installer SQL

The MsiDatabaseOpenView, MsiViewExecute, and MsiViewModify APIs accept SQL strings to control their actions. *SQL (Structured Query Language)* is a catchall term for a standardized language for writing database queries. The Installer accepts an extremely limited form of the SQL syntax. This section details the SQL statements that the Installer understands.

To select a group of records, use a SELECT statement:

```
SELECT [DISTINCT] column_list
FROM table_list
[WHERE operation_list]
[ORDER BY column_list]
<column_list>::= * | [table_name].column_name [,…n]
```

```
<table_list>::= table_name [,...n]
<operation_list>::=
 column_name = column_name |
 column_name comparison constant |
 column_name comparison ? |
 column_name IS [NOT] NULL
 [AND | OR operation_list] [...n]
<comparison>::=
 = | <> | > | < | >= | <=
```

NOTE In these syntax diagrams, SQL keywords are capitalized. Italics indicate markers to be replaced. Some of these markers are expanded later in the syntax diagram; for example, the column_list marker can be replaced with an asterisk, a column name, a table name plus column name, or a combination of these things. The "...n" notation indicates that an element can be repeated. The vertical bar indicates a choice between alternatives. Square brackets enclose optional items.

In the SELECT statement (and elsewhere in Installer SQL), you can escape a column name or table name that conflicts with a keyword by enclosing it in backquotes. Escaping the name in this fashion tells the Installer to interpret it as a name rather than as a keyword. In fact, it's safe to always escape names. For example, you might refer to a particular column this way:

```
`Dialog`.`Width`
```

You can use the ? operator in a WHERE clause for a parameter that will be filled in at the time a query is evaluated. If you include the DISTINCT keyword, any duplicate rows will be eliminated from the resulting view.

You can delete records from a table with a DELETE statement:

```
DELETE FROM table_name
[WHERE operation_list]
```

You can modify existing records using an UPDATE statement:

```
UPDATE table_list
SET column = constant [,...n]
[WHERE operation_list]
```

To add records to a table, use an INSERT statement:

```
INSERT INTO table_name
(column_list)
VALUES (constant [,...n])
TEMPORARY
```

There must be as many constants in the VALUES clause as there are columns in the column list. If you specify the TEMPORARY keyword, this row is not saved to the permanent database on disk.

Installer SQL also supports three statements useful for manipulating the database schema:

CREATE TABLE   To add a new table to the database

DROP TABLE   To eliminate a table from the database

ALTER TABLE   To add or drop a column, or lock or free a temporary table

You're unlikely to need these statements for most common applications. If you need them, you can refer to the Installer SDK for their full syntax.

WARNING   Table names and column names in Installer SQL are always case-specific.

Using the Installer API

In the rest of this chapter, I'll show you some examples of using the Installer API. The sample code is all written in Visual Basic 6.0 with Service Pack 3, and it's all in the InstallerAPI sample project.

I'll cover these areas of the API:

- Enumerating products and user information
- Inspecting summary information properties
- Viewing records in a table
- Using MsiProvideQualifiedComponent to install a new component
- Setting the user interface level

To use the Installer API from Visual Basic, you need to have installed the msi.dll library. This library is available on any computer that has used the Windows Installer to install any product, and on any Windows 2000 computer. Normally, this library will be installed in the Windows System directory and will be available in Visual Basic by choosing Project ➤ References.

Enumerating Products and User Information

For the first example, I'll show you how to enumerate all the products that the Installer knows about on the current computer, together with their product names and user information. Figure 8.1 shows the frmEnumProducts form in the InstallerAPI sample project displaying this information. As you'll see, even this simple example demonstrates that the Installer API is rather hostile to Visual Basic users. Before deciding to use the API for anything, you should check the Installer automation model (see Chapter 9) and see whether an easier, COM-based alternative exists.

FIGURE 8.1

Retrieving product and user information

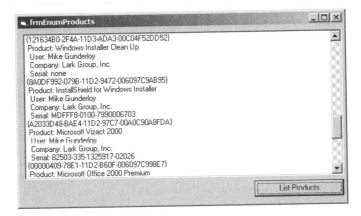

Listing 8.1 shows the source code for frmEnumProducts (without the variable declarations). Although it's fairly straightforward, I want to walk through this example to give you an idea of what you need to do to work with the Windows Installer via the API.

Listing 8.1: frmEnumProducts

```
' Loop through all products using MsiEnumProducts, which
    ' returns the product codes
    Do While MsiEnumProducts(lngIndex, strGUID) = ERROR_SUCCESS
        lboProducts.AddItem strGUID
        strProductName = Space(128)
        lngProductNameLen = 128
        ' Use MsiGetProductInfo to get the product name
        If MsiGetProductInfo(strGUID, _
         INSTALLPROPERTY_INSTALLEDPRODUCTNAME, _
         StrPtr(strProductName), lngProductNameLen) = _
         ERROR_SUCCESS Then
            strProductName = _
             Left(StrConv(strProductName, vbUnicode), _
             lngProductNameLen)
            lboProducts.AddItem " Product: " & strProductName
        End If
        strUserName = Space(128)
        strOrganization = Space(128)
        strSerial = Space(128)
        lngUserNameLen = 128
        lngOrganizationLen = 128
```

```
      lngSerialLen = 128
      ' And use MsiGetUserInfo to get some product details
      If MsiGetUserInfo(strGUID, _
       StrPtr(strUserName), lngUserNameLen, _
       StrPtr(strOrganization), lngOrganizationLen, _
       StrPtr(strSerial), lngSerialLen) = _
        USERINFOSTATE_PRESENT Then
          strUserName = Left(StrConv(strUserName, vbUnicode), _
           lngUserNameLen)
          strOrganization = _
           Left(StrConv(strOrganization, vbUnicode), _
           lngOrganizationLen)
          strSerial = Left(StrConv(strSerial, vbUnicode), _
           lngSerialLen)
          lboProducts.AddItem "  User: " & strUserName
          lboProducts.AddItem "  Company: " & strOrganization
          lboProducts.AddItem "  Serial: " & strSerial
      End If
      lngIndex = lngIndex + 1
  Loop
```

NOTE   I'm not showing the Visual Basic declarations for the Installer API calls. All of the calls I use in this chapter are contained in basAPI in the InstallerAPI sample project. Unfortunately, the Installer SDK does not provide the Visual Basic declarations for the API calls; you need to convert them yourself. You can use the supplied code in basAPI for guidance, or refer to a reference on using API calls, such as Ken Getz and Michael Gilbert's *VB Language Developer's Handbook* (Sybex Inc., 2000).

The loop here uses MsiEnumProducts to retrieve all the products known to the Installer on this computer. This includes both installed products and advertised products. MsiEnumProducts is a good example of an API that's a bit off the beaten path. In the Windows API in general, enumeration APIs tend to take the form of GetFirstXXX and GetNextXXX, where you call GetFirstXXX to get the first instance and then call GetNextXXX to get all the rest. MsiEnumProducts works as if there were a collection of products behind the scenes and lets you fetch from that collection by position. You start by fetching the zeroth item, then the first, and so on. When it runs out of products, the function returns a value other than ERROR_SUCCESS, and you know that the fetching process is done.

MsiEnumProducts uses a simple zero-terminated string to hold the product codes that it returns. The strings used by the other API calls in this function (MsiGetProductInfo and MsiGetUserInfo) are not as straightforward. Here's the declaration for MsiGet-ProductInfo:

```
Public Declare Function MsiGetProductInfo Lib "msi.dll" _
    Alias "MsiGetProductInfoA" _
    (ByVal szProduct As String, ByVal szAttribute As String, _
    ByVal lpValueBuf As Long, pcchValueBuf As Long) As Integer
```

You'll note that although the two values that are strictly inputs (the product code and the property to retrieve) are strings, the declaration of the buffer to hold the returned value consists of a pair of longs. The first is a pointer to a buffer to hold the information, and the second is a pointer to a variable that holds the length of the buffer (the total length going in, and the used length coming back). To call this API, you need to follow these steps (which you can find in the source code in Listing 8.1):

1. Declare a string variable to hold the information.

2. Initialize the string variable to a known length with the Space() function.

3. Initialize the length variable to the length of the string.

4. Pass the address of the string variable by using the StrPtr() function. This little-used function returns the address of a Visual Basic string.

5. Pass the address of the length variable by passing its name.

In another little bit of VBA-hostility, what comes back is a Unicode string and the number of characters that are valid in the string, even though the function was declared to use the ANSI version of the API call! You need to both convert the string to ANSI and truncate it at the correct length to make it usable in the Visual Basic interface:

```
strProductName = _
    Left(StrConv(strProductName, vbUnicode), _
    lngProductNameLen)
```

The strings returned by MsiGetUserInfo are treated the same way.

Overall, the design of the frmEnumProducts form is fairly straightforward: Fetch each product, fetch the product name and user information for each product, and add the information to the list box. It's just the details of the Installer API that blow this simple idea up to such a substantial lump of code.

Inspecting Summary Information Properties

The next code sample demonstrates how to retrieve the properties that the Installer stores in the summary information stream. These are the properties that are available to the Windows Explorer interface. Figure 8.2 shows the result of right-clicking an Installer database and choosing Properties in Windows Explorer using Windows 2000.

FIGURE 8.2

Viewing the Summary
Information Stream in
Explorer

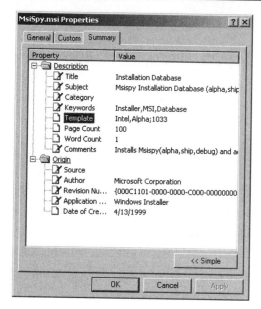

FIGURE 8.2

Viewing the Summary
Information Stream in
Explorer

You can retrieve this same information via the Installer API. The frmSummaryInfo
form in the InstallerAPI sample database demonstrates this technique. Figure 8.3 shows
this form viewing summary information for the MsiSpy Installer database that's
shipped with the Installer SDK.

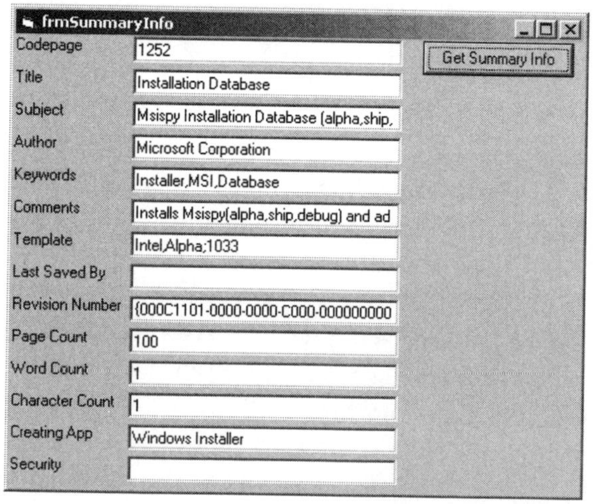

FIGURE 8.3

Viewing Summary Informa-
tion on frmSummaryInfo

The code starts by getting a handle to the summary information stream. A *handle* is an arbitrary number the Installer API uses to refer to the stream:

```
If MsiOpenDatabase(strDatabaseName, _
    MSIDBOPEN_READONLY, hDatabase) = ERROR_SUCCESS Then
      If MsiGetSummaryInformation(hDatabase, 0, 0, _
        hSummaryInfo) = ERROR_SUCCESS Then
```

In this case, the code first obtains a database handle and then uses that handle to get the summary information stream handle. The MsiGetSummaryInformation API can actually take either a filename or a database handle (but not both) to identify the database to work with. An alternative way to get the same summary information stream handle would be

```
If MsiGetSummaryInformation(0, strDatabaseName, 0, _
    hSummaryInfo) = ERROR_SUCCESS Then
```

Of course, if you're not using the database handle for any other reason, this second alternative is simpler.

Once you've got the summary information stream handle, you can use it to retrieve properties from the summary information stream. For example, this code retrieves the Title property:

```
strValueBuf = Space(32)
lngValueBufLen = 32
If MsiSummaryInfoGetProperty(hSummaryInfo, _
 PID_TITLE, VT_LPSTR, _
 intValue, ftvalue, strValueBuf, _
 lngValueBufLen) = ERROR_SUCCESS Then
     txtTitle = Left(strValueBuf, _
       lngValueBufLen)
End If
```

The MsiSummaryInfoGetProperty takes seven arguments:

- The handle to the summary information stream
- A constant indicating the property to retrieve (PID_TITLE, in this case)
- A constant indicating the data type of the property (VT_LPSTR, in this case)
- A variable that can hold an integer return value
- A variable that can hold a FILETIME return value
- A variable that can hold a string return value
- A variable indicating the length of the string return value

Although you need to supply all of these pieces of information when you call the MsiSummaryInfoGetProperty API, they're not all used. Only one of the return value variables will be filled in, depending on the data type of the property that you've retrieved. Of course, the constant indicating the data type must be the correct one for the property.

When the code is done retrieving properties, it closes the open handles, in the reverse order of their opening:

```
        End If
        intRet = MsiCloseHandle(hSummaryInfo)
    End If
    intRet = MsiCloseHandle(hDatabase)
End If
```

Viewing Records in a Table

You can use the Installer database API calls to perform just about any action you'd like with the data in an Installer database. I'll show you how to read records in this example, but the sequence of API calls is similar for deleting or changing records. You might use this technique, for example, to display a set of features from within your application. Users could choose a feature and have your code install it.

Figure 8.4 shows the frmReadTable sample form from the InstallerAPI sample project. In this case, it's displaying a list of component IDs and component names from the MsiSpy Installer database.

FIGURE 8.4

Retrieving information from the Installer database

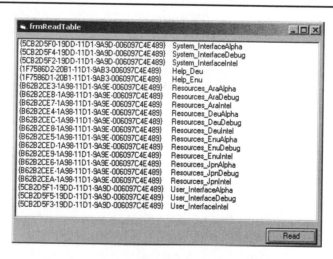

The code for this form starts out by opening a database handle and a view handle:

```
If MsiOpenDatabase(strDatabaseName, _
    MSIDBOPEN_READONLY, hDatabase) = ERROR_SUCCESS Then
        strQuery = "SELECT Component, ComponentId FROM Component"
```

```
If MsiDatabaseOpenView(hDatabase, strQuery, hView) = _
ERROR_SUCCESS Then
    If MsiViewExecute(hView, 0) = ERROR_SUCCESS Then
```

Note that calling MsiDatabaseOpenView does not, despite the name, retrieve any data into the view. Rather, this API call is the equivalent of preparing a stored procedure; it gets the query ready to execute but does not actually perform the query. The MsiView-Execute API is the one that actually loads data into the view.

Once you've called MsiViewExecute, you can call MsiViewFetch repeatedly to get the records from the view. Installer views are always forward-only. You can retrieve one record at a time until you get to the end; you can't go backward or fetch records at random. Each call to MsiViewFetch returns a record handle, and you must close this handle before another call to MsiViewFetch. The loop for fetching records looks like this:

```
Do While MsiViewFetch(hView, hRecord) = _
ERROR_SUCCESS

    ...
    intRet = MsiCloseHandle(hRecord)
Loop
```

Within the loop, you can call MsiRecordGetString (or MsiRecordGetInteger) to retrieve the information from the view. This API takes the record handle, the number of the field that you'd like to retrieve, a buffer to hold the data, and a variable that gets the length of valid data in the buffer. If you're unsure how much space you need, pass an empty string and check the value of the length variable; this will tell you how long the buffer needs to be to hold all the data, and you can then call the API again. The field numbering starts at 1 (actually, there is a zeroth field in Installer records, but it's used only for internal bookkeeping).

```
strValue = Space(40)
lngValueLen = 40
intRet = MsiRecordGetString( _
 hRecord, 2, strValue, lngValueLen)
strLine = Left(strValue, lngValueLen)
```

Once all of the records have been fetched (and in this case, printed out to the user interface), all that remains is to close the open handles:

```
    intRet = MsiCloseHandle(hView)
End If
intRet = MsiCloseHandle(hDatabase)
End If

Debug.Print MsiCloseAllHandles()
```

Note the final call to MsiCloseAllHandles. This is a useful technique to apply while you're developing Installer API code. If this prints zero, you've already cleaned up everything. If it prints any other number, then somewhere in your code you've orphaned a handle that you should have closed.

Working with Qualified Components

In Chapter 4, "A Guide to the Installer Database," you learned about qualified components: components that share a single Component ID but come in multiple versions distinguished by strings called *qualifiers*. Qualified components provide an easy way for your application to call the Windows Installer to add new components on the fly while the application is running.

For example, Microsoft Excel 2000 uses qualified components for the Excel add-ins. Figure 8.5 shows the frmQualifiedComponent form from the Installer API sample project listing these components. All of these add-ins have the same Component ID but can be installed individually.

FIGURE 8.5

Qualified components from Microsoft Excel 2000

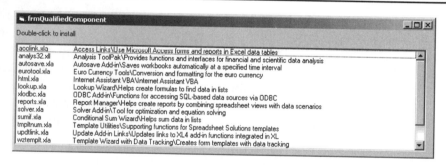

To list all of the qualified components belonging to a single ComponentID, you use the MsiEnumComponentQualifiers API. This API works similarly to MsiEnumProducts in that you enumerate the components by asking for successively higher indexes until the call no longer returns ERROR_SUCCESS:

```
'Component ID for Excel addins
strComponentID = _
 "{44DC336F-8798-11D1-A0C0-00A0C9054277}"

strQualifier = Space(128)
lngQualifierLen = 128
strApplicationData = Space(128)
lngApplicationDataLen = 128
```

```
Do While MsiEnumComponentQualifiers(strComponentID, _
  lngIndex, StrPtr(strQualifier), lngQualifierLen, _
  StrPtr(strApplicationData), lngApplicationDataLen) _
  = ERROR_SUCCESS
    lboComponents.AddItem _
    Left(StrConv(strQualifier, vbUnicode), _
    lngQualifierLen) & "        " & vbTab & _
    Left(StrConv(strApplicationData, vbUnicode), _
    lngApplicationDataLen)
    lngIndex = lngIndex + 1
    strQualifier = Space(128)
    lngQualifierLen = 128
    strApplicationData = Space(128)
    lngApplicationDataLen = 128
Loop
```

You'll see that this code has the Component ID hard-coded. That's safe, because Component IDs are stable. On any computer, with any future version of Excel, that component ID should still return Excel add-ins (of course, the code won't run on a computer that doesn't have Excel 2000, or some later version of Excel, available). Note also that you don't have to tell the Installer anything about what product is involved here; it figures that out based simply on the Component ID.

When you double-click an add-in, in this case, the code uses the MsiProvideQualified-Component API to actually install the component:

```
' Component ID for Excel addins
strComponentID = _
  "{44DC336F-8798-11D1-A0C0-00A0C9054277}"

' Install or repair as needed
lngMode = INSTALLMODE_DEFAULT

intSpace = InStr(1, lboComponents.Text, " ")
strQualifier = Left(lboComponents.Text, intSpace - 1)

intRet = MsiProvideQualifiedComponent(strComponentID, _
  strQualifier, lngMode, 0&, 0&)
```

As you can see, this code is extremely simple. In your own code, you'll probably know the component ID and the qualifier that you're interested in, and will only need a single line of code to invoke the Installer. If you actually run this code, you'll see the Installer's progress dialog come up on-screen as the add-in gets installed. The Installer may also ask for the original source CD that Office was installed from, if it's not currently available.

Installing Features

While installing components makes sense from the developer's point of view, you may wish to present users with a way to install features, instead. There are actually three separate tasks to consider here:

1. Enumerating the available features
2. Retrieving the state of any given feature
3. Installing a feature

The frmInstallFeature form in the InstallerAPI sample project demonstrates all three of these tasks. Figure 8.6 shows this form displaying all of the features from the MsiSpy project together with their current installation status.

FIGURE 8.6
Displaying feature
information

To enumerate the available features, you can use the MsiEnumFeatures API. This is similar to the other enumeration API calls that you've seen earlier in this chapter:

```
' Product ID for MsiSpy
mstrProductID = _
 "{8FC72000-88A0-4B41-82B8-8905D4AA904C}"

strFeature = Space(MAX_FEATURE_CHARS)
strParent = Space(MAX_FEATURE_CHARS)
```

```
Do While MsiEnumFeatures(mstrProductID, lngIndex, _
 strFeature, strParent) = _
ERROR_SUCCESS

    ...
    strFeature = Space(MAX_FEATURE_CHARS)
    strParent = Space(MAX_FEATURE_CHARS)
    lngIndex = lngIndex + 1
Loop
```

The Installer API defines a constant, MAX_FEATURE_CHARS, that is the maximum length of a feature name (it happens to be 38 characters, the same as the maximum length of a product code, but that's just a coincidence). The MsiEnumFeatures API takes a product code and an index and returns sequentially all of the features associated with that product.

Of course, if you're writing some general-purpose application and don't know the product code of interest in advance, you can use MsiEnumProducts to get a list of all the possible product codes, as you saw earlier in this chapter.

Each feature is returned along with the name of its parent feature (if any). Using this information, you can build a tree of the feature hierarchy if you wish. You'll see from Figure 8.6 that feature names tend to be a bit cryptic. If you want to do a bit of extra work, you can also retrieve the feature descriptions by running a query against the Installer database for the product:

```
SELECT Feature, Title, Description FROM Feature
```

Once you've got the feature name, you can use the MsiQueryFeatureState API to retrieve the current status of the feature. The frmInstallFeature code uses this API to create a string with the installation state based on the return value from this API:

```
Select Case _
 MsiQueryFeatureState(mstrProductID, strFeature)
   Case Is < 0
       strInstallState = "Error"
   Case INSTALLSTATE_ADVERTISED
       strInstallState = "Advertised"
   Case INSTALLSTATE_ABSENT
       strInstallState = "Not Installed"
   Case INSTALLSTATE_LOCAL
       strInstallState = "Installed"
   Case INSTALLSTATE_SOURCE
       strInstallState = "Run from Source"
End Select
```

Finally, installing a feature, once you know the product code and the feature name, is simply a matter of calling the MsiConfigureFeature API:

```
intRet = MsiConfigureFeature( _
  mstrProductID, _
  strFeature, _
  INSTALLSTATE_LOCAL)
```

Table 8.2 shows the possible return values from MsiQueryFeatureState. The non-error values in this table are also the values that you can use with MsiConfigureFeature to choose a new state for the feature.

TABLE 8.2: Feature Installation States

Constant	Meaning
INSTALLSTATE_NOTUSED	The component is disabled.
INSTALLSTATE_BADCONFIG	The Installer configuration data is corrupt.
INSTALLSTATE_INCOMPLETE	An installation is suspended or in progress.
INSTALLSTATE_SOURCEABSENT	Component is set to run from source, but the source is unavailable.
INSTALLSTATE_MOREDATA	Return buffer overflow.
INSTALLSTATE_INVALIDARG	Invalid function argument.
INSTALLSTATE_UNKNOWN	Unrecognized product or feature.
INSTALLSTATE_BROKEN	The feature is in need of repair.
INSTALLSTATE_ADVERTISED	Advertised feature.
INSTALLSTATE_REMOVED	Component being removed (action state, not settable).
INSTALLSTATE_ABSENT	The feature is not installed.
INSTALLSTATE_LOCAL	The feature is installed on local drive.
INSTALLSTATE_SOURCE	The feature is installed to run from source, CD or net.
INSTALLSTATE_DEFAULT	Install the feature to use the default, local or source.

Setting the User Interface Level

If you tested either the component installation or feature installation examples, you'll have noticed that the Installer displays a simplified user interface while the component or feature is being configured. By default, the Installer uses the basic user interface level (consisting of a progress meter but suppressing the wizard dialogs that might be in the Installer database) when it's called through the API.

Of course, this isn't always the appropriate user interface for your application. Sometimes you might want to display no user interface at all if the user doesn't even need to know that product configuration is going on behind the scenes. Other times you might want to display the entire Wizard interface together with a dialog when the process is finished.

Figure 8.7 shows the frmUILevel form from the InstallerAPI sample project. This form lets you experiment with the different available interface levels while installing features. (There's no need to install multiple features to test this form; installing the same feature multiple times works just as well).

FIGURE 8.7
The frmUILevel form

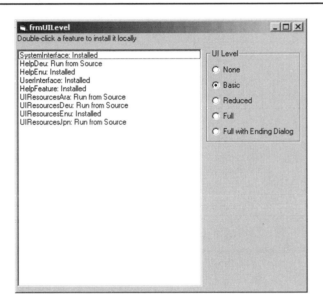

The work of changing the user interface level is done by the MsiSetInternalUI API. For example, when you choose the reduced user interface, this procedure is called:

```
Private Sub optReduced_Click()
    MsiSetInternalUI INSTALLUILEVEL_REDUCED, 0
End Sub
```

The first argument to MsiSetInternalUI is the user interface level to set. The second argument is the window handle of the window that should own the Installer dialogs. By default, this is the desktop window, which always has a window handle of zero. You can also pass a Null here to leave the owning window unchanged. Table 8.3 shows the user interface levels that you can choose with this function.

TABLE 8.3: User Interface Level Arguments for MsiSetInternalUI

Constant	Meaning
INSTALLUILEVEL_DEFAULT	Use the default level authored into the Installer database.
INSTALLUILEVEL_NONE	No user interface (silent install).
INSTALLUILEVEL_BASIC	Progress bar and error messages, if necessary.
INSTALLUILEVEL_REDUCED	Minimal user interface from the Dialog table.
INSTALLUILEVEL_FULL	Full user interface, including all wizard dialogs.
INSTALLUILEVEL_ENDDIALOG	Add to the other constants to display a confirmation dialog when the installation is finished.
INSTALLUILEVEL_PROGRESSONLY	Valid only when added to INSTALLUILEVEL_BASIC. Displays progress bar but no error messages.

Using the Installer Automation Model

In the last chapter, you saw how to control the Installer by use of its API functions. However, if you're writing programs in Visual Basic or VBA, the API function method is probably not the easiest way to make the Installer do what you want. The reason for this is because the Installer allows you to take advantage of Visual Basic's COM support by exposing an automation model in addition to the core and database APIs. While the automation model does not cover every single facet of the Installer that the APIs do, it exposes more than enough for most purposes. In this chapter, I'll introduce you to the Installer automation model and its component objects, and then I'll show you a few examples of how to use these objects.

The Installer Object Hierarchy

Figure 9.1 shows the objects that are exposed by the Windows Installer.

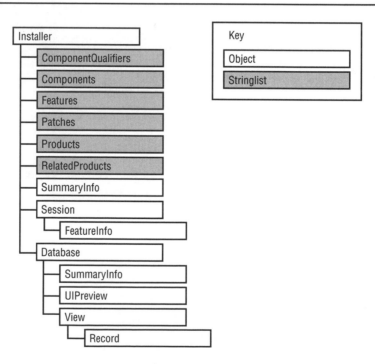

FIGURE 9.1
Windows Installer Objects

As you can see, the Installer object model is fairly simple, especially when compared with, say, the object models for Microsoft Office programs. There are only 13 objects to worry about, and some of them (such as the UIPreview object) are not very complex.

The Installer exposes six objects that you might think would be collections: Component-Qualifiers, Components, Features, Patches, Products, and RelatedProducts. Instead of being collections, these are actually instances of a special Installer object called the StringList. The StringList object is a collection of strings. It exposes Count and Item properties, as well as the _NewEnum method necessary to support enumerating the members with a For Each loop. However, you can't declare variables of any of the StringList types, nor can you add or delete members of these lists.

The Installer Object

Everything you do with the Windows Installer via automation starts with the Installer object. This is the top-level object in the Installer hierarchy from which all other objects are created. It represents the Installer Service itself, and has quite a number of properties and methods. I've summarized these properties and methods in Table 9.1.

NOTE The tables in this chapter are meant only to give you a quick reference to the Installer objects. In these tables, "M" indicates a method and "P" indicates a property. For full details, you'll want to refer to the Installer SDK.

TABLE 9.1: Properties and Methods for the Installer Object

Name	Type	Description
Components	P	Returns the Components StringList object, containing the components for all installed products
ComponentPath(Product, Component)	P	Full path to an installed component
ComponentQualifiers(Category)	P	Returns the ComponentQualifiers StringList object for a particular category of component
Environment(Variable)	P	Current value of an environment variable
Features(Product)	P	Returns the Features StringList object for a particular product
FeatureParent(Product, Feature)	P	Feature ID of the parent of the selected feature
FeatureState(Product, Feature)	P	State of the feature (absent, installed locally, and so on)
FeatureUsageDate(Product, Feature)	P	Date the feature was last used
FeatureUsageCount(Product, Feature)	P	Number of times the feature has been used
FileAttributes(filePath)	P	Attributes of the selected file

TABLE 9.1: Properties and Methods for the Installer Object *(continued)*

Name	Type	Description
Patches(Product)	P	Returns the Patches StringList object for a particular product
PatchInfo(Patch, Attribute)	P	Value of an attribute of a particular patch
PatchTransforms(Product, Patch)	P	Semicolon-delimited list of the transforms in a particular patch
Products	P	Returns the Products StringList object
ProductInfo(Product, Attribute)	P	Value of an attribute of a particular product
ProductState(Product)	P	State of the product (installed, advertised, and so on)
QualifierDescription(Category, Qualifier)	P	Localizable string describing a qualified component
RelatedProducts(UpgradeCode)	P	Returns the RelatedProducts StringList object
SummaryInformation(packagePath, maxProperties)	P	Returns the SummaryInfo object for a particular package
UILevel	P	User interface level for the current Installer session
Version	P	Version of the Windows Installer Service that's running
AddSource(Product, User, Source)	M	Adds a valid source for network installations
ApplyPatch(PatchPackage, InstallPackage, InstallType, CommandLine)	M	Applies a patch to a package
ClearSourceList(Product, User)	M	Clears the list of valid sources for network installations
CollectUserInfo(Product)	M	Invokes a dialog box to collect user and company information
ConfigureFeature(Product, Feature, InstallState)	M	Set the specified feature to the specified state
ConfigureProduct(Product, InstallLevel, InstallState)	M	Set the specified product to the specified state
CreateRecord(count)	M	Returns a new, blank Record object with the specified number of fields
EnableLog(logMode, logFile)	M	Sets the level of logging desired
FileSize(path)	M	Size of the specified file
FileVersion(Path, Language)	M	Version string from the specified file
ForceSourceListResolution(Product, User)	M	Forces the Installer to search for a valid source path rather than using any cached information

TABLE 9.1: Properties and Methods for the Installer Object *(continued)*

Name	Type	Description
GetShortcutTarget(Shortcut)	M	Examines a shortcut and returns the product, feature, and component that it refers to
InstallProduct(packagePath, propertyValues)	M	Opens a package and starts installing a product
LastErrorRecord	M	Returns a Record object with information on the most recent error (if any)
OpenDatabase(name, OpenMode)	M	Opens a database and returns the corresponding Database object
OpenPackage(packagePath)	M	Opens a package and returns the corresponding Session object
OpenProduct(productCode)	M	Opens a product and returns the corresponding Session object
ProvideComponent(Product, Feature, Component, InstallMode)	M	Does any installation necessary to make the selected component available and returns the path to the component
ProvideQualifiedComponent(Category, Qualifier, InstallMode)	M	Does any installation necessary to make the selected component available and returns the path to the component
RegistryValue(root, key, value)	M	Returns a value from the Registry
ReinstallFeature(Product, Feature, ReinstallMode)	M	Reinstalls or repairs the specified feature
ReinstallProduct(Product, ReinstallMode)	M	Reinstalls or repairs the specified product
UseFeature(Product, Feature, InstallMode)	M	Increments the usage count for a feature and returns the installation state for that feature

As you can see from the table, a number of the properties and methods of the Installer object have direct analogs in the Installer API. The ProvideQualifiedComponent method, for example, performs the same work and takes the same arguments as the MsiProvideQualifiedComponent API. Whether you choose the API or the object model to provide a qualified component is a decision that you can make based strictly on ease of development.

The Products StringList

The Products StringList is an Installer pseudo-collection that contains the product code for every product known to the Windows Installer on the current computer. This includes both products that are installed and those that have only been advertised to this computer. Here's a bit of code (from the frmStringList form in the Installer-Automation sample project) that shows you how you can work with this StringList:

```
Private Sub cmdProducts_Click()

    Dim objInstaller As WindowsInstaller.Installer
    Dim slProducts As WindowsInstaller.StringList
    Dim varProduct As Variant

    Set objInstaller = _
     CreateObject("WindowsInstaller.Installer")
    Set slProducts = objInstaller.Products

    lboDisplay.Clear

    For Each varProduct In slProducts
        lboDisplay.AddItem varProduct
    Next varProduct

End Sub
```

A few points to note here:

- You can't use the New syntax to create an Installer object. You need to use Create-Object for this purpose.
- The Installer automation library supplies a StringList data type, which you can use to hold any of the StringList objects.
- You can use a variant variable to loop through any StringList object.
- If you run this code, you'll find that it displays a list of the GUID product codes that are available on the computer. That's all of the information about products that is contained in this StringList. If you need further information (such as the name of the product or the current installation state), you can use other properties of the Installer object once you know the product code.

The Features StringList

The Features StringList object contains all of the feature names for a particular product. To retrieve this object, you must supply the product code for a particular product to the

Installer.Features property. Figure 9.2 shows the features for Office 2000 Premier being displayed on the frmStringList form in the InstallerAPI sample project.

FIGURE 9.2

Listing the features for a particular product

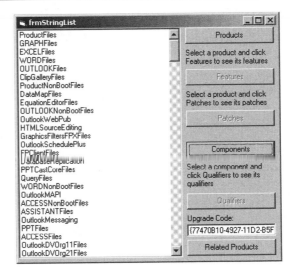

As you can see in the figure, the features are returned in no particular order. All that the Features StringList returns is the raw names of the features. In this case, the form uses this procedure to display those names:

```
Private Sub cmdFeatures_Click()

    Dim objInstaller As WindowsInstaller.Installer
    Dim slFeatures As WindowsInstaller.StringList
    Dim varFeature As Variant

    Set objInstaller = _
     CreateObject("WindowsInstaller.Installer")
    Set slFeatures = objInstaller.Features(lboDisplay.Text)

    lboDisplay.Clear

    For Each varFeature In slFeatures
        lboDisplay.AddItem varFeature
    Next varFeature

    cmdFeatures.Enabled = False
    cmdPatches.Enabled = False

End Sub
```

If you want more detail about a feature than just its name, you can use the Installer's FeatureParent or FeatureState properties, or you can use the Database object (discussed later in this chapter) to open a view on the Features table.

The Components StringList

Unlike features, components are not associated with any particular product. Thus, when you retrieve the Components StringList object from the Installer.Components property, you're retrieving a list of the component IDs (GUIDs) for every component that has been installed on or advertised to your computer. As with the other StringLists, these are returned in no particular order, and with no additional information beyond the component ID. To retrieve additional information about a component, you can use the Installer's ComponentPath property, or open a View on the Components table in the appropriate Installer package.

The ComponentQualifiers StringList

The ComponentQualifiers StringList object requires you to provide a category ID for the qualifiers that you're interested in. A category ID is any component ID for a component that actually has qualified versions (that is, one that's listed in the PublishComponent table). If you try to retrieve the ComponentQualifiers StringList for a component that's not a category, you'll get error −2147352560, "Invalid Callee." The code behind the frm-StringList form in the InstallerAutomation sample project works around this by simply ignoring the error and returning if the StringList object can't be retrieved:

```
Private Sub cmdQualifiers_Click()

    Dim objInstaller As WindowsInstaller.Installer
    Dim slComponentQualifiers As _
     WindowsInstaller.StringList
    Dim varQualifier As Variant

    Set objInstaller = _
     CreateObject("WindowsInstaller.Installer")
    On Error Resume Next
    Set slComponentQualifiers = _
     objInstaller.ComponentQualifiers(lboDisplay.Text)
    If slComponentQualifiers Is Nothing Then
        Exit Sub
    End If

    lboDisplay.Clear
```

```
For Each varQualifier In slComponentQualifiers
    lboDisplay.AddItem varQualifier
Next varQualifier

cmdQualifiers.Enabled = False

End Sub
```

Once you've obtained a component qualifier, you can get more information by opening a view on the PublishComponents table.

The Patches StringList

The Patches property of the Installer object returns the Patches StringList object for a particular product code. This list holds the package IDs of all of the patches that have actually been applied to the specified product. Until developers start shipping revised versions of their products in the form of patches, this object is going to remain of little use. If there are no patches for a particular product, it simply returns an empty StringList.

The RelatedProducts StringList

The Installer.RelatedProducts property requires a GUID that is the upgrade code of a particular product to return the RelatedProducts StringList object. On the frmStringList form in the InstallerAutomation sample project, I've supplied the upgrade code of the Microsoft Office 2000 Premier package. You can determine the upgrade code of any package by opening the Installer Database and inspecting the value of the UpgradeCode property in the Property table.

Related products are products that share the same upgrade code—that is, products that can all be upgraded by application of the same patches. You'll learn more about patches and upgrades in Chapter 10, "Creating and Using Patch Packages."

The SummaryInfo Object

To instantiate a SummaryInfo object, you call the Installer object's SummaryInformation property, supplying the full path to an Installer package and a number which represents the maximum number of properties that you're going to add or change while this object is open.

This is one of those rare cases in which the object and the property that refers to it do not have exactly the same name.

Figure 9.3 shows the frmSummaryInfo form in the InstallerAutomation sample project. This shows the variety of information that you can retrieve from the Summary-Info object.

FIGURE 9.3

Retrieving summary information

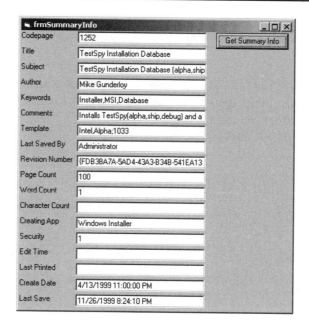

The code for populating this form is relatively simple:

```
Private Sub cmdGetSummaryInfo_Click()

    Dim strPackage As String
    Dim objInstaller As WindowsInstaller.Installer
    Dim objSummaryInfo As WindowsInstaller.SummaryInfo

    Set objInstaller = _
     CreateObject("WindowsInstaller.Installer")

    dlgOpen.ShowOpen
    strPackage = dlgOpen.FileName
```

```
Set objSummaryInfo = _
  objInstaller.SummaryInformation(strPackage, 0)

txtTitle = objSummaryInfo.Property(PID_TITLE)
txtSubject = objSummaryInfo.Property(PID_SUBJECT)
txtAuthor = objSummaryInfo.Property(PID_AUTHOR)
txtKeywords = objSummaryInfo.Property(PID_KEYWORDS)
txtComments = objSummaryInfo.Property(PID_COMMENTS)
txtTemplate = objSummaryInfo.Property(PID_TEMPLATE)
  ' Similar calls for other properties omitted here
End Sub
```

The SummaryInfo object supports two properties and a single method. The Property property, as shown in the code sample above, retrieves an individual property from the summary information stream of the selected package. Unfortunately, there is no way to iterate through all the properties as though they were a collection; you must retrieve individual properties as shown here. The PropertyCount property simply returns the number of properties in the stream. The Persist method writes any changed properties back to the summary information stream. Once you've called the Persist method, you must close and reopen the SummaryInfo object if you want to make any further changes.

WARNING   If you open the SummaryInfo object with a maxProperties value greater than zero and do not call the Persist method, all of the summary information will be deleted from the package.

The Session Object

The Session object represents a single active session of the Windows Installer: that is, it represents an installation actually in progress. This does not need to include going through all of the actions in the sequence tables. However, once the Session object is instantiated, you have the power to make changes to the way a product is installed.

You can instantiate a Session object in one of two ways:

- If you know the path to an Installer package, you can open a Session object by calling the Installer.OpenPackage property.
- If you know the product code of a product that's already installed or advertised on the computer, you can open a Session object by calling the Installer.OpenProduct property.

Either way, the Session object supports a wide variety of properties and methods. Table 9.2 summarizes the functionality of the Session object.

TABLE 9.2: Properties and Methods for the Session Object

Name	Type	Description
ComponentCurrentState(component)	P	Current installation state for the specified component.
ComponentRequestState(component)	P	Action currently being taken on this component.
Database	P	Returns a Database object for the current session.
FeatureCost(feature, costTree, state)	P	Returns the disk space required by the specified feature.
FeatureCurrentState(feature)	P	Current installation state for the specified feature.
FeatureRequestState(feature)	P	Action currently being taken on this feature.
FeatureValidStates(feature)	P	Bit field of valid states for the feature.
Installer	P	Returns the Installer object, which is the parent of this Session object.
Language	P	Language ID in use by the current session.
Mode(flag)	P	A general-purpose inquiry function. Depending on the flag value, the Mode property will tell you what type of install is being performed, whether rollback is enabled, whether logging is active, and more. See "Using the Session.Mode property," later in this chapter for more details.
ProductProperty(name)	P	Value of a property in the Property table.
Property(name)	P	Value of a property in memory.
SourcePath(folder)	P	Retrieves the full source path being used by an entry in the Directory table.
TargetPath(folder)	P	Retrieves the full target path being used by an entry in the Directory table.
VerifyDiskSpace	P	Boolean that tells you whether there's enough room available to proceed with the installation or not.
DoAction(action)	M	Performs one of the standard or custom Installer actions.
EvaluateCondition(condition)	M	Returns the result of a conditional expression.
FeatureInfo(Feature)	M	Returns a FeatureInfo object for the specified feature.
FormatRecord(record)	M	Returns a formatted record based on raw data and a template.
Message(kind, record)	M	Sends an Installer error or status message.
Sequence(table)	M	Executes the actions stored in a sequence table.
SetInstallLevel(InstallLevel)	M	Sets the default installation level for the current session.

The Session object is your key to performing any of the normal Installer actions through code. You won't typically make much use of this from an application. However, if you're writing a custom action in VBScript, you can connect back to the Session object to have that action integrate better with the rest of the setup.

The FeatureInfo Object

The FeatureInfo object allows you to retrieve some information about a particular feature inside of a product without having to directly create a database view. The Feature-Info object exposes three properties:

Title   Returns the title of the feature.

Description   Returns the description of the feature.

Attributes   Returns the attributes of the feature.

All three of these properties get their data directly from the Feature table in the Installer database.

Initially, the FeatureInfo object looks promising as a way to display some additional information on features from within your application. However, it proves to only be useful if you're running code during an actual installation (for example, as part of a custom action). That's because the FeatureInfo object is really just an object wrapper around the MsiGetFeatureInfo API call, and that API call will only succeed after the Cost-Initialize action has been performed.

The Database Object

The Database object provides you with COM access to the Installer database. You instantiate this object by calling the OpenDatabase method of the Installer object, specifying the full path and file name of the package containing the database you're interested in. Alternatively, you can retrieve the database for an active session by using the Database property of the Session object. Because you can open a Session object by knowing only the product code, the latter alternative is useful for cases in which you don't know the location of the package.

Table 9.3 lists the details of the Database object.

TABLE 9.3: Properties and Methods of the Database Object

Name	Type	Description
DatabaseState	P	Indicates whether changes can be made to the database
SummaryInformation(maxProperties)	P	Returns the SummaryInfo object corresponding to the summary information stream in this database
TablePersistent(table)	P	Distinguishes between temporary and permanent tables
ApplyTransform(storage, errorConditions)	M	Applies a transform to the database
Commit	M	Commits all changes to the database
CreateTransformSummaryMethod-(reference, storage, errorConditions, validation)	M	Creates a summary information stream for a transform
EnableUIPreview	M	Puts the user interface into preview mode and returns a UIPreview object
Export(table, path, file)	M	Exports a table to a text file
GenerateTransform(reference, storage)	M	Generates a transform that consists of the differences between the current database and the reference database
Import(path, file)	M	Imports a table from a text file
Merge(reference, errorTable)	M	Merges the reference database into the current database
OpenView(sql)	M	Opens a SQL statement and returns a View object
PrimaryKeys(table)	M	Returns a Record object containing the names of the primary key columns for the specified table

The Database object is particularly useful if you need to get some of the information out of an existing Installer database. For example, you might want to display a list of features along with their descriptions so that users can decide whether to install any of those features. One easy way to do this is to open the Database object and then use the OpenView method to query against the Feature table directly.

WARNING Note that if you allow a Database object to go out of scope without explicitly calling the Commit method, all changes are automatically rolled back.

The UIPreview Object

The UIPreview object exists mainly as an adjunct to package authoring. This object allows you to preview but not change any dialog or billboard in the Installer database.

The UIPreview object supports one property and two methods:

Property property   Retrieves the value of a property from the Property table in the Installer database.

ViewBillboard method   Previews a billboard.

ViewDialog method   Previews a dialog.

In the InstallerAutomation sample database, you can use the frmUIPreview form to experiment with the UIPreview object. The code that displays a dialog is simple:

```
Private Sub lboDialogs_Click()

    Dim objInstaller As WindowsInstaller.Installer
    Dim objDatabase As WindowsInstaller.Database
    Dim objUIPreview As WindowsInstaller.UIPreview

    Set objInstaller = CreateObject _
     ("WindowsInstaller.Installer")
    Set objDatabase = objInstaller.OpenDatabase( _
     mstrPackage, msiOpenDatabaseModeReadOnly)
    Set objUIPreview = objDatabase.EnableUIPreview

    objUIPreview.ViewDialog (lboDialogs.Text)

    frmDismiss.Show vbModal

End Sub
```

Note that this procedure displays a model form after showing the preview. That's because as soon as the UIPreview object goes out of scope the dialog it's previewing is removed from the screen.

WARNING   You can only retrieve a UIPreview object from a Database if the Database was opened using the Installer.OpenDatabase method. If you use the Session.Database property to open the Database object, attempting to retrieve the UIPreview object will result in an error. This makes sense since there's no use in previewing dialogs during an actual installation session, but it's not mentioned in the documentation.

The View Object

The View object represents a set of records retrieved from the Installer database by calling first the OpenView and then the Execute methods of the Database object. Views are defined by a SQL statement that conforms to the Installer SQL dialect. (You can review the syntax of Installer SQL in Chapter 8, "Using the Installer API.") A View object has one property and five methods:

ColumnInfo property Retrieves metadata about a specific column.

Close method Terminates the view.

Execute method Retrieves the records for the view.

Fetch method Retrieves the next record for the view.

GetError method Retrieves the most recent error that occurred.

Modify method Lets you save changes to the current record.

The Record Object

The Record object represents a single record retrieved from an Installer View. Table 9.4 shows the details of the Record object.

TABLE 9.4: Properties and Methods of the Record Object

Name	Type	Description
DataSize(field)	P	Size of the data in the specified field
FieldCount	P	Number of fields in the Record
IntegerData(field)	P	Numeric data from the specified field
IsNull(field)	P	Returns true if the specified field contains a null
StringData(field)	P	String data from the specified field
ClearData	M	Sets all fields in the current record to Null
FormatText	M	Formats text in a record according to a template in the zeroth field
ReadStream(field, length, format)	M	Reads bytes from a field holding stream data
SetStream(field, filePath)	M	Inserts a file into a field holding stream data

The data fields in a Record object are always referred to by number. The numbering is 1-based; the zero field is reserved for a formatting template for the FormatText method.

The frmUIPreview form in the InstallerAutomation sample project uses the View and Record objects together to retrieve a list of the dialogs in the selected database. First, the code opens the database in a specific package, selected by browsing on the user's hard drive:

```
dlgOpen.ShowOpen
mstrPackage = dlgOpen.FileName

lboDialogs.Clear

Set objInstaller = CreateObject _
 ("WindowsInstaller.Installer")
Set objDatabase = objInstaller.OpenDatabase( _
 mstrPackage, msiOpenDatabaseModeReadOnly)
```

Next, the View object is instantiated by calling the OpenView method, with a SQL statement specifying the records that the form needs to retrieve. The form then uses the Execute method to get data into the View, and the Fetch method to retrieve the first record into a Record object:

```
Set objView = objDatabase.OpenView( _
 "SELECT Dialog FROM Dialog")
objView.Execute
Set objRecord = objView.Fetch
```

From there, the code loops through all the records by repeatedly calling the Fetch method. Installer Views are always forward-only; you can fetch the next record, but you can never move backwards.

```
Do Until objRecord Is Nothing
    lboDialogs.AddItem _
     objRecord.StringData(1)
    Set objRecord = objView.Fetch
Loop
```

Finally, the procedure closes and cleans up the open objects:

```
objView.Close

Set objDatabase = Nothing
Set objInstaller = Nothing
```

Using the Automation Model

In the remainder of this chapter, I'll show you some of the operations you can perform with the Windows Installer via the automation model. Of course, these small examples just scratch the surface. If you'd like, you could write an entire front end to perform installations without invoking the user interface within the Installer package. But you're not likely to need that level of control.

I'll cover these techniques, which I hope you'll find useful in your own applications:

- Checking the Installer version
- Retrieving special folders
- Checking feature status
- Installing an advertised feature
- Using the Session.Mode property
- Modifying an Installer database

NOTE   To use any of the Installer automation objects in Visual Basic, you need to set a reference to the Microsoft Windows Installer Object Library. This library is in the `msi.dll` file that the Installer places on every system where it has ever been run. You may have to register this file before it can be used. To do so, open a command prompt, navigate to the System32 folder, and enter the command `regsvr32 msi.dll`.

Checking the Installer Version

Depending on the other actions you intend to perform, you may need to know the version of the Installer that's functioning on the computer where your application is running. Fortunately, this information is easy to retrieve. There's an example on the frmMenu form in the InstallerAutomation sample project:

```
Private Sub cmdVersion_Click()
    Dim objInstaller As WindowsInstaller.Installer
    Set objInstaller = CreateObject( _
     "WindowsInstaller.Installer")
    MsgBox "The Installer version on this computer is " & _
     objInstaller.Version
End Sub
```

Currently, you're likely to find version 1.0 on a computer that has had Office 2000 installed, or version 1.1 on a computer that has had Windows 2000 or a more recent application installed. The 1.1 upgrade includes these new features that you won't be able to use if the computer only has version 1.0 of the Installer:

- The MsiEnumRelatedProducts, MsiSetFeatureAttributes, MsiSourceListForce-Resolution, MsiSourceListAddSource, MsiGetShortcutTarget, and MsiSourceList-ClearAll API calls

- The Complus, Upgrade, and IsolatedComponent tables
- The Description column in the ServiceInstall table
- The Attributes column in the Class table
- The RegisterComPlus, UnregisterComPlus, FindRelatedProducts, PreventInstall, MigrateFeatureStates, RemoveExistingProducts, and IsolatedComponent actions
- Type 7, 23, and 39 custom actions
- The AdminToolsFolder, LocalAppDataFolder, CommonAppDataFolder, MyPictureFolder, ServicePackLevelMinor, TRANSFORMSSECURE, Remote-AdminTS, and REBOOTPROMPT properties
- The Password attribute for Edit controls
- The ERROR_SUCCESS_REBOOT_INITIATED, ERROR_SUCCESS_REBOOT_REQUIRED, ERROR_PATCH_TARGET_NOT_FOUND, and ERROR_INSTALL_REMOTE_DISALLOWED return codes
- MsiSetComponentState can return ERROR_INSTALL_USEREXIT

If you discover that the user's computer has the 1.0 Installer and you need the 1.1 version, you can put up a warning message instructing them to install the 1.1 version (from the redistributable file) and then exit.

Retrieving Special Folders

In the earliest releases of Windows, the only special folder was the one named "Windows," and you could count on this folder being at c:\Windows on more than 99 percent of all computers. These days, the situation is much more complicated. There are special folders for Windows, for system components, for user data, for application data, for pictures, and for administrative tools, to name just a few of the possibilities. Even worse, from the viewpoint of the applications developer, is that these folders can be located in many different places depending on user preferences, security requirements, and hardware setup.

In the past, some developers resorted to hard-coding paths such as "c:\My Documents," checking undocumented Registry keys that store these paths, or prompting the user. Fortunately, the Installer service provides a way to retrieve these paths much more easily and reliably. After all, the Installer itself needs this information to successfully install software. Because this information is exposed in the automation model it's available to any developer.

The key to finding special folders is to use the Property property of the Session object. All of the special folder information is available via default properties of the Installer, and the Property property can return the value of any property from this list. Because the Installer determines this information dynamically, you must initiate an Installer session before you can get these property values. However, as you'll see in the code below, you can do this without displaying the Installer user interface to your users.

Figure 9.4 shows the frmFolders form from the InstallerAutomation sample project. This form displays all of the special folders that the Installer is aware of. As you can see, there's quite a variety.

FIGURE 9.4

Retrieving special folders

Listing 9.1 shows the entire source code for this form. A few of points to note here:

- The code stocks an array with the property names of all of the special folder properties. This is necessary because the Session object doesn't expose a Properties collection; you must retrieve individual properties by name. Of course, you'll just want to use the properties that are important to your own application.
- By setting the UILevel property of the Installer object to msiUILevelNone before instantiating the Session object, the code keeps the Installer splash screen from displaying.
- The code uses the first product known to the Installer, whatever that product might be, to instantiate the Session object. Because the properties of interest are not specific to any particular product, it doesn't matter what product the code uses. In your own code, you might want to fill in the GUID for your own product.

Listing 9.1: frmFolders

```
Private Sub Form_Load()

    Dim objInstaller As WindowsInstaller.Installer
    Dim objSession As WindowsInstaller.Session
    Dim astrFolders(23) As String
    Dim intFolder As Integer
    Dim strGUID As String

    Screen.MousePointer = vbHourglass

    astrFolders(1) = "AdminToolsFolder"
    astrFolders(2) = "AppDataFolder"
    astrFolders(3) = "CommonAppDataFolder"
    astrFolders(4) = "CommonFilesFolder"
    astrFolders(5) = "DesktopFolder"
    astrFolders(6) = "FavoritesFolder"
    astrFolders(7) = "FontsFolder"
    astrFolders(8) = "LocalAppDataFolder"
    astrFolders(9) = "MyPicturesFolder"
    astrFolders(10) = "NetHoodFolder"
    astrFolders(11) = "PrintHoodFolder"
    astrFolders(12) = "ProgramFilesFolder"
    astrFolders(13) = "ProgramMenuFolder"
    astrFolders(14) = "RecentFolder"
    astrFolders(15) = "SendToFolder"
    astrFolders(16) = "StartMenuFolder"
    astrFolders(17) = "StartupFolder"
    astrFolders(18) = "System16Folder"
    astrFolders(19) = "SystemFolder"
    astrFolders(20) = "TempFolder"
    astrFolders(21) = "TemplateFolder"
    astrFolders(22) = "WindowsFolder"
    astrFolders(23) = "WindowsVolume"

    Set objInstaller = CreateObject("WindowsInstaller.Installer")
    objInstaller.UILevel = msiUILevelNone
    strGUID = objInstaller.Products(0)
    Set objSession = objInstaller.OpenProduct(strGUID)
    For intFolder = 1 To 23
        lboFolders.AddItem astrFolders(intFolder) & vbTab & _
            objSession.Property(astrFolders(intFolder))
    Next intFolder

    Screen.MousePointer = vbDefault

End Sub
```

Checking Feature Status

Just about any application these days can be broken up into multiple features. The Windows Installer makes it easy to install just a subset of features to the local hard drive, and update the installed features later. However, this flexibility comes at the cost of complexity. If users of your application try to use a particular feature, you may need to check and see whether that feature is in fact installed.

Figure 9.5 shows the frmFeatures form in the InstallerAutomation sample project. This form lets you select any product and then retrieves the feature state for every feature in that product. Of course, in your application, you'll know exactly which feature you need to check at any given time, but the code will be much the same.

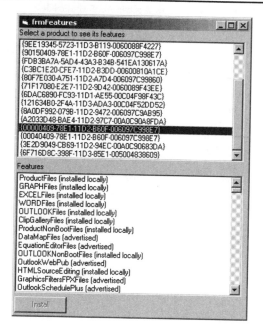

FIGURE 9.5

Retrieving feature states

To retrieve the state of a feature, you need to follow these steps:

1. Create and instantiate the Installer object.

2. Call the Installer.FeatureState property, supplying the product ID and the feature ID.

In the code behind the frmFeatures form, I've used a loop to retrieve the feature state for every feature in the particular product (determined by iterating through the Features

StringList object). Note that the Installer provides symbolic constants for each possible state, and that these constants are defined in the type library:

```
For Each varFeature In slFeatures
    Select Case objInstaller.FeatureState( _
        lboProducts.Text, varFeature)
        Case msiInstallStateAbsent
            lboFeatures.AddItem varFeature & _
            " (not installed)"
        Case msiInstallStateAdvertised
            lboFeatures.AddItem varFeature & _
            " (advertised)"
        Case msiInstallStateLocal
            lboFeatures.AddItem varFeature & _
            " (installed locally)"
        Case msiInstallStateSource
            lboFeatures.AddItem varFeature & _
            " (run from source)"
        Case msiInstallStateInvalidArg
            lboFeatures.AddItem varFeature & _
            " (invalid argument)"
        Case msiInstallStateUnknown
            lboFeatures.AddItem varFeature & _
            " (unknown)"
        Case msiInstallStateBadConfig
            lboFeatures.AddItem varFeature & _
            " (bad configuration data)"
        Case Else
            lboFeatures.AddItem varFeature & _
            " (unexpected state)"
    End Select
Next varFeature
```

Installing an Advertised Feature

Of course, knowing the state of a feature doesn't help all that much if you can't also change the state. Fortunately, the Installer automation model also makes it easier to change the state of a feature. The frmFeatures form in the InstallerAutomation sample project shows how you can install an advertised feature to the user's local hard drive.

Once again, the code is simple. All you need to do to install a figure locally is to call the Installer's ConfigureFeatureState method with the proper arguments: the product ID, the feature ID, and the state that you wish the feature to be in when the Installer is done.

In the frmFeatures form in the InstallerAutomation sample, the only complexity comes about in extracting the feature ID from the listbox:

```
Private Sub cmdInstall_Click()

    Dim objInstaller As WindowsInstaller.Installer
    Dim strFeature As String

    strFeature = Left(lboFeatures.Text, _
     InStr(1, lboFeatures.Text, "(") - 2)

    Set objInstaller = _
     CreateObject("WindowsInstaller.Installer")
    objInstaller.ConfigureFeature lboProducts.Text, _
     strFeature, msiInstallStateLocal

End Sub
```

You can use ConfigureFeature to place a feature in any available state. The possible values for the third argument are listed below:

msiInstallStateAdvertised To advertise the feature.

msiInstallStateLocal To install to the local hard drive.

msiInstallStateAbsent To uninstall the feature.

msiInstallStateSource To install the feature to run from source.

msiInstallStateDefault To install the feature to the default (local or source) specified in the Feature table in the Installer database.

Using the Session.Mode Property

The Mode property of the Session object is actually a sort of catch-all property. Really, there ought to be a Modes collection that you could iterate, but it appears that the Installer team lacked the development time to implement that idea. So instead, there's a single property that you use with a set of constants to retrieve information about the current session. Table 9.5 shows the available constants.

TABLE 9.5: Constants for the Session.Mode Property

Constant	Value	Returns True if
msiRunModeAdmin	0	An administrative install is being performed.
msiRunModeAdvertise	1	Products or features are being advertised.
msiRunModeMaintenance	2	The Installer is in maintenance mode.
msiRunModeRollbackEnabled	3	Rollback is enabled.
msiRunModeLogEnabled	4	Installer actions are being logged.

TABLE 9.5: Constants for the Session.Mode Property *(continued)*

Constant	Value	Returns True if
msiRunModeOperations	5	The Installer is executing or spooling actions.
msiRunModeRebootAtEnd	6	A reboot is required.
msiReunModeRebootNow	7	An immediate reboot is required.
msiRunModeCabinet	8	Files are being installed from cabinets and files.
msiRunModeSourceShortNames	9	Short file names are in use on the source.
msiRunModeTargetShortNames	10	Short file names are in use on the target.
msiRunModeWindows9x	12	The target computer is running Windows 95 or Windows 98.
msiRunModeZawEnabled	13	The operating system supports advertised products.
msiRunModeScheduled	16	A custom action is being executed from the installation script.
msiRunModeRollback	17	A custom action is being executed from a rollback script.
msiRunModeCommit	18	A custom action is being executed from a commit script.

The primary use for the Mode property of the Session object is to enable custom actions to make decisions based on the context in which they are called. For example, you might have a custom action that maintains a file of its operations only if rollback is enabled, or one which needs to perform different functions if the installation script is running on Windows 95 instead of Windows NT.

Modifying an Installer Database

Finally, I'll show you how to modify an Installer database directly. This technique is most useful if you're writing a tool that is used to create or update Installer databases. For instance, you might want to automatically update the version of a file that your database refers to when you rebuild the file.

To make a change to an Installer database, you can follow this general outline:

1. Use the OpenDatabase method of the Installer object to open the database that you want to work with.

2. Use the OpenView method of the Database object to define a view that includes the record that you want to change.

3. Use the Execute method of the View object to load the record of interest.

4. Call the Fetch method of the View object (repeatedly, if necessary) to get the actual record that you want to modify.

5. Make changes to the record.

6. Call the Modify method of the View object to save changes back to the database.

7. Call the Close method of the View object to release the records.

8. Call the Commit method of the Database object to save the changes.

The frmModify form in the InstallerAutomation sample project demonstrates this process, using a copy of the TestSpy.msi Installer database that I created for Chapter 7, "Putting the Pieces Together." When you're writing code to modify Installer databases, you should definitely experiment on copies and scratch databases before risking anything that you've invested serious work in.

The form starts its work by obtaining the proper Installer and Database objects:

```
Dim objInstaller As WindowsInstaller.Installer
Dim objDatabase As WindowsInstaller.Database
Dim objView As WindowsInstaller.View
Dim objRecord As WindowsInstaller.Record

Set objInstaller = CreateObject( _
  "WindowsInstaller.Installer")

Set objDatabase = objInstaller.OpenDatabase( _
  App.Path & "\TestSpy.msi", msiOpenDatabaseModeDirect)
```

Next, it opens a view on the entire File table. Since I know exactly what file I want to work with, I could use a WHERE clause to get just that record back, but it's easy to loop in application code as well:

```
Set objView = objDatabase.OpenView( _
  "SELECT File, Version FROM File")

objView.Execute
Set objRecord = objView.Fetch
```

The code loops through records until it finds one for a particular file listed in the table:

```
Do Until objRecord.StringData(1) = "TestServerMain"
    Set objRecord = objView.Fetch
Loop
```

The next step is to get the new data and insert it into the table. The StringData property of the Record object is read/write, so you can use it both to retrieve the existing data and to set the new data (for numeric data you can use the IntegerData property instead).

```
objRecord.StringData(2) = _
  InputBox("Enter new version:", _
  "frmModify", objRecord.StringData(2))
```

The final task is to save the changes to the View and to the Database, and then to clean up all the objects that the code opened:

```
objView.Modify msiViewModifyUpdate, objRecord

objView.Close
objDatabase.Commit

Set objRecord = Nothing
Set objView = Nothing
Set objDatabase = Nothing
Set objInstaller = Nothing
```

WARNING   One pitfall to watch out for if you've worked with other database object libraries such as ADO or DAO: the Fetch method returns an object, it doesn't just move the record pointer. If you should happen to call objView.Fetch *without* assigning the results to a Record object, your code will just mysteriously hang at that point, and you'll have to use Task Manager to kill the program to proceed.

Creating and Using Patch Packages

- What Is a Patch Package?

- Types of Updates

- Preparing for Future Upgrades

- Creating a Patch Package

- Applying Patches

Software applications are not static things. Unless all funding for a project ceases, it's typical for a new version to be being worked on even before the old version is distributed to your users. Because of this, it's necessary to come up with a strategy for updating applications that you've already delivered to users. The Windows Installer provides such a strategy in the form of patch packages. In this chapter, I'll show you what patch packages are and discuss how you can create them.

WARNING	While patch packages are theoretically supported by the 1.0 version of the Windows Installer, the support is almost completely nonexistent before version 1.1. The examples in this chapter were tested with the Windows Installer version 1.1, and I recommend you use this version (or a later one) when you're working with patch packages.

What Is a Patch Package?

A *patch package* is an alternative type of file (different than the normal installation package) that is understood by the Windows Installer Service. Unlike a regular installation package, though, a patch package does not contain an Installer database. Rather, a patch package consists of two parts:

- A database transform that can alter the contents of an existing Installer database
- A cabinet file stream that contains new files, revised files, and binary patches for existing files

When you use the Installer to apply a patch to an existing product (using the /p option on the msiexec command line), the Installer reads the information in the patch package and uses it to modify the existing Installer database. In effect, the existing Installer database becomes the Installer database for a new version of the product.

WARNING	If an application has been installed with elevated privileges (for example, if it contains items that require administrative rights to install on Windows NT), then it can only be patched by a user with administrative privileges.

By default, patch packages use the file extension .msp (as compared to the .msi extension used by a regular Installer package). Also, the summary properties for a patch package differ from those for an Installer database. Table 10.1 lists the summary properties for a patch package. Most of these are available by right-clicking the package in the Windows Explorer and choosing Properties.

TABLE 10.1:   Patch Package Properties

Property	Contains
Title	"Patch".
Subject	Short description of the patch.
Author	Manufacturer property from the Installer database.
Keywords	Source path for the patch.
Comments	Typically "This patch contains the logic and data necessary to modify <Product Name>".
Template	Semicolon-delimited list of product codes for products to which this patch can be applied.
Last Saved By	Semicolon-delimited list of transforms in the order that they should be applied.
Revision Number	Patch code (GUID) for this patch. Optionally this may be concatenated with the patch codes for patches that are superseded by this patch.
Create Time/Date	Time the patch was created.
Last Saved Time/Date	Time the patch was last modified.
Word Count	Must be set to 1 for Installer version 1.1. In the future, this will be used to indicate the engine that was used to create the patch.
Creating Applications	Software used to create the patch.
Security	4 (Enforced read-only).

Types of Updates

The Windows Installer Service distinguishes between three types of updates you can make to an existing product: small updates, minor upgrades, and major upgrades. The distinction depends on the size of the changes to be made to the existing installation, and it dictates how you should handle the mechanics of updating.

Small update   Designed to update only a few of the files in an existing installation. The ProductCode and ProductVersion properties of the package do not change for a small update. The Revision Number summary property must be changed.

Minor upgrade   Makes changes to multiple files in an existing installation, but it doesn't qualify as a new installation. The ProductCode property for the package remains constant, but the ProductVersion property should be changed for a minor upgrade. The Revision Number summary property must be changed.

Major upgrade   Represents an entirely new version of a product. For a major upgrade, the package should be assigned an entirely new ProductCode property (of course the ProductVersion property changes as well). The Revision Number summary property must be changed.

NOTE   Remember, the Revision Number summary property is used to store the unique Package Code, which is a GUID. You must change this to a different GUID if you make *any* change to a package, no matter how minor.

One easy way to distinguish between a small update and a minor upgrade is to consider the effect that the change has on future versions of the product. If future versions will need to be able to tell the difference between the current and the updated product, you should use a minor upgrade instead of a small update.

Any of these types of update may be shipped as a full installation package or as a patch package (or both). If you ship an update as a full installation package, it works like any other installation package. When you run the package, it goes through all the actions in the appropriate sequence tables, replaces files depending on their versions, and so on. The rest of this chapter will only consider the other alternative: shipping your application's update as a patch package.

Because they contain only the parts of the product that have changed, patch packages can be much smaller than full installation packages. This can be especially beneficial if you offer the update for download from the Internet; using a patch package will minimize download time.

When to Change the Product Code

How do you decide what type of update to create when you're ready to update your product? One thing to look at is whether you're required to assign a new product code to the new version. For a small update or a minor upgrade, you must keep the same product code. But the Windows Installer has rules for when you must change the product code. So, depending on the changes you make, you might be forced to call your update a major upgrade, no matter how small you think it is.

To keep the same product code, your changes must adhere to these guidelines:

- You can enlarge or reduce the feature tree (as described by the hierarchy relationships in the Feature table), but you can't reorganize the tree. That is, you can't change the value of the Feature_Parent column for an existing feature.

- You can add new features to the feature tree without changing the product code.
- You can remove a feature from the feature tree without changing the product code, but if you do, you must also remove all the child features in the tree beneath that feature.
- You can add a new component, but only if that component is associated with a new feature via the FeatureComponents table.
- You cannot change the component code of an existing component.
- You cannot change the name of an existing component's key path file because this in turn requires changing the component code of the component.
- You cannot change the name of the .msi file. You must, of course, change the package code of the Installer package if you make any changes.
- You can modify files, registry keys, and shortcuts of components that are only associated with a single feature.
- You can modify files, registry keys, and shortcuts of components that are associated with more than one feature, but you can do this only if the changed version is 100 percent backward-compatible with all features that use this component. Remember that a component can be shared across multiple applications, and you need to consider all applications that use this component when deciding whether changes are compatible.

If it's necessary to be able to install both the original version of the application and the changed version on the same computer, you must change the product code.

Preparing for Future Upgrades

Even if you don't intend to ever revise your product, it's still a good idea to prepare your original application for the upgrading process. That way, if you do make a mistake and need to issue a revised file, you're covered.

Fortunately, you don't have to do very much to make sure that an Installer package can be patched. To prepare for the possibility of patching the package in the future, follow these steps:

1. Assign a unique Product Code to the Installer package. This is a GUID that is stored as the ProductCode property in the Property table.
2. Assign a value to the ProductVersion property in the form AA.BB.CCCC. This property is also stored in the Property table.

3. Determine the language of the product and enter the language ID as the Product-Language property in the Property table.

4. Determine whether you need a new Upgrade Code, or if you can reuse an existing Upgrade Code (see below). Store the Upgrade Code in the UpgradeCode property in the Property table. To determine whether you need to create a new Upgrade Code, consider these points:

   - If this is the first version of your product, create a new Upgrade Code using GUIDGEN or another GUID generation tool.
   - If this is a version of an existing product in a new language, use the Upgrade Code from the existing product.
   - If this is a newer version of an existing product, use the Upgrade Code from the existing product.

That's it! Once you've equipped your Installer package with these four properties, the Installer will be able to apply future patches to the package. These properties are those which the Installer uses to recognize a particular package as the one to be patched.

Creating a Patch Package

To create a patch package, you use functions in a Microsoft-supplied library named Mspatchc.dll. This library looks at two versions of an installation and figures out how to build a patch that will change the first version into the second version. To demonstrate the process, I'll walk you through the steps of creating a patch package to upgrade a simple Installer package.

NOTE   You can use the same steps to create the patch package no matter which type of update you're preparing (small update, minor upgrade, or major upgrade).

Before and After Packages

I'll start with HelloWin.msi. This is an Installer package (created, in this particular case, with the Wise for Windows Installer software, which you'll learn more about in Chapter 12, "Installer Editing Tools") that installs a single executable file named HelloWin .exe. As you might guess, this is a "Hello Windows" program that displays a message box when it's run. Figure 10.1 shows HelloWin in action.

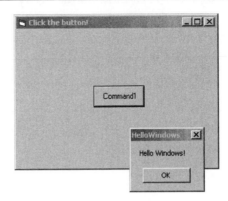

FIGURE 10.1
The Hello Windows
program

Now, suppose that after shipping version 1 of HelloWin, you discover a problem—namely, that the readme file was accidentally omitted from the Installer package. You'd like to ship version 1.0.0.1 that includes the readme file, and create a patch package to convert existing 1.0.0.0 installations to the new version.

The first step is to fix HelloWin.msi to include the new file. That requires following these steps:

1. Make a copy of HelloWin.msi in a new folder. It's important to work with a copy rather than modifying the original file, because you'll need both the old and the new versions to create the patch file.

2. Open the new copy in an Installer editor.

3. Add the new readme.txt file to the File table.

4. Change the version resource for the package to 1.0.0.1. This updates the Revision Number summary property. Because this is a small update, there's no need to generate a new product code.

After creating the before and after versions of your Installer package, the next step is to perform administrative installations of both packages (to separate folders). This is essential because the patch generation process requires all of the files in the package to be uncompressed. Suppose, for example, that the original packages are located at

```
c:\HelloWin\1000\HelloWin.msi
c:\HelloWin\1001\HelloWin.msi
```

In this case, you can perform the necessary administrative installations by executing these two command lines:

```
C:\>msiexec /a c:\HelloWin\1000\HelloWin.msi
    ↳/qn+ TARGETDIR="c:\HelloWinAdmin\1000"
C:\>msiexec /a c:\HelloWin\1000\HelloWin.msi
    ↳/qn+ TARGETDIR="c:\HelloWinAdmin\1000"
```

> **NOTE** Remember, the **/a** option specifies an administrative install, and the **/qn+** option tells the Installer to suppress the user interface except for the completion message. Setting the value of the TARGETDIR public variable tells the Installer where to put the expanded files.

Creating the PCP File

The next step in the process is to create a *.pcp file*. This is a file that tells the patching DLL what it is that you want to do when you're creating a patch. A `.pcp` file is a database with the same binary format as an Installer package (though containing different tables), so it can be edited with any tool that will edit an Installer package.

The Installer SDK contains two `.pcp` files:

Template.pcp   Is a blank `.pcp` file containing the necessary tables. You can use a copy of this file to start your own application's `.pcp` file.

Example.pcp   Is a `.pcp` file with some sample data filled in to make it easier for you to see the use of the various columns.

There are nine tables in a `.pcp` file (although some of them may be empty):

- Properties
- ImageFamilies
- UpgradedImages
- TargetImages
- UpgradedFiles_OptionalData
- FamilyFileRanges
- TargetFiles_OptionalData
- ExternalFiles
- UpgradedFilesToIgnore

The Properties Table

A good place to start is with the Properties table. This table has two columns:

Name (String, K)   The name of the property.

Value (String)   The default value of the property.

Table 10.2 shows the properties that you may want to set in a .pcp file, and Figure 10.2 shows the Properties table from the HelloWin.pcp sample file that I'm using to build a patch.

T A B L E   1 0 . 2 :   Properties in the .pcp File

Property	Description
AllowProductCodeMismatches	Set to 1 if the product code differs between the target and upgraded images.
AllowProductVersionMajorMismatches	Set to 1 if the major product version differs between the target and upgraded images.
ApiPatchingOptionFlags	A set of flags that can be used to control the internal operation of the patching DLL. For most purposes, you should use the default value of 0x00100000. You can find the list of flags in **patchapi.h**, which is part of the Installer SDK.
ApiPatchingSymbolFlags	A set of flags that can be used to control the symbol generation of the patching DLL. For most purposes, you should use the default value of 0x00000000. You can find the list of flags in **patchapi.h**, which is part of the Installer SDK.
DontRemoveTempFolderWhenFinished	Set to1 to save temporary files generated while building the patch package. You might want to set this for debugging if you're having a problem.
IncludeWholeFilesOnly	Set to 1 to include changed files instead of generating binary patches.
ListOfPatchGUIDsToReplace	List of GUIDs for patch packages that this patch package supersedes.
ListOfTargetProductCodes	A semicolon-delimited list of Product Codes for packages that can be patched by this patch. You can set this to "*" to automatically generate the list from the target installation.
MsiFileToUseToCreatePatchTables	Full path and filename of an Installer file that contains Patch and PatchPackage tables to use. This is optional and need only be supplied if you've customized those tables.
PatchGUID	Unique identifier for the patch package to be generated. This must be unique for every patch package.

TABLE 10.2: Properties in the `.pcp` File *(continued)*

Property	Description
PatchOutputPath	Full path and filename of the patch package to generate.
PatchSourceList	List of network sources that hold copies of the patch file. This probably is not useful unless you're generating patches on an intranet.

FIGURE 10.2
Sample Properties table
from `HelloWin.pcp`

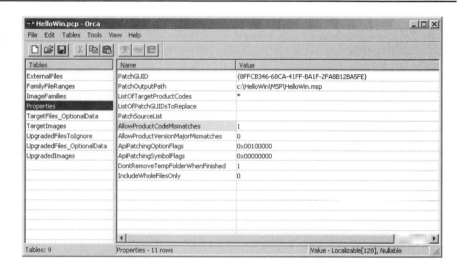

The ImageFamilies Table

The ImageFamilies table describes new entries to be made to the Media table during the patching process. It includes these fields:

Family (String, K)   This field is limited to eight alphanumeric or underscore characters and provides a way to group patches that all work on the same product.

MediaSrcPropName (String)   Use this value in the Source column of the new row added to the Media table.

MediaDiskID (Integer)   Use this value in the DiskId column of the new row added to the Media table.

FileSequenceStart (Integer)   Use this value in the LastSequence column of the new row added to the Media table.

DiskPrompt (String)   Use this value in the DiskPrompt column of the new row added to the Media table.

VolumeLable (String)   Use this value to use in the VolumeLabel column of the new row added to the Media table.

When a patch is applied, the information in the ImageFamilies table is used to create a new row in the Media table of the Installer package. This new row specifies where the patch files may be found. Figure 10.3 shows the ImageFamilies table in `HelloWin.pcp`.

FIGURE 10.3
Sample ImageFamilies table

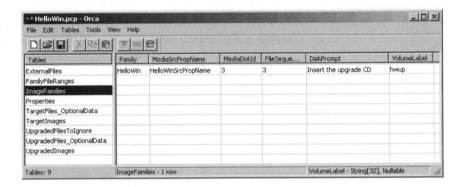

The UpgradedImages Table

The UpgradedImages table will generally have just one row, describing the administrative installation of the newer version of the product. This table has these columns:

Upgraded (String, K)   An arbitrary primary key, which is limited to 13 characters.

MsiPath (String)   Full path and filename of the `.msi` file for the upgraded version.

PatchMsiPath (String, N)   Full path and filename to another Installer package containing extra resources that need to be copied. Usually, you can leave this blank.

SymbolPaths (String, N)   Optional semicolon-delimited list of paths containing symbol files for the patched application.

Family (String)   Foreign key referring to the Family column in the ImageFamilies table.

Figure 10.4 shows the UpgradedImages table from `HelloWin.pcp`.

FIGURE 10.4
Sample UpgradedImages
table

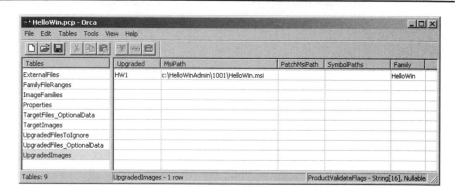

The TargetImages Table

The TargetImages table will generally have just one row, describing the administrative installation of the older version of the product (that is, the one that has already been distributed and that needs to be patched). This table has these columns:

Target (String, K) An arbitrary primary key, which is limited to 13 characters.

MsiPath (String) Full path and filename of the .msi file for the target version.

SymbolPaths (String, N) Optional semicolon-delimited list of paths containing symbol files for the patched application.

Upgraded (String) Foreign key that points to the Upgraded column in the UpgradedImages table.

Order (Integer) The order of previous versions, if there are multiple rows in this table.

ProductValidateFlags (String) A bitmap column that specifies what information the Installer should verify before applying a patch. Generally, you should leave this set to the default of 0x00000922, which checks version, product, and upgrade codes. Note that this field is stored as a string even though it appears to be a hexadecimal integer.

IgnoreMissingSrcFiles (Integer) If set to 1, files missing from the target installation are ignored (assuming that they haven't been changed).

Figure 10.5 shows the TargetImages table from HelloWin.pcp.

FIGURE 10.5

Sample TargetImages table

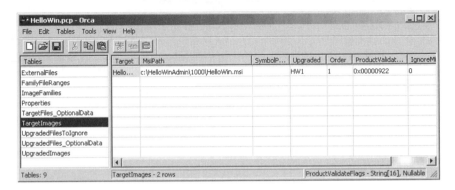

NOTE   If you want your patch to work on more than one version of your product, you'll have multiple rows in the TargetImages table. For example, a patch that could be used to update either version 1.0.0.0 or version 1.0.0.1 to version 1.0.0.2 would require two rows in the TargetImages table.

The UpgradedFiles_OptionalData Table

The UpgradedFiles_OptionalData table can be used to ensure special handling for particular files. It has these columns:

Upgraded (String, K)   Foreign key to the UpgradedImages table.

FTK (String, K)   Foreign key to the Files table of the Installer database for the upgraded installation.

SymbolPaths (String, N)   Additional paths to search for symbols for this particular file.

AllowIgnoreOnPatchError (Integer)   Setting this to 1 allows the Installer to continue patching if a particular file can't be patched. For example, you might want to set this for a readme or other non-critical file that the user can delete without affecting the operation of the product.

IncludeWholeFile (Integer)   Setting this to 1 forces the patch generation library to include the entire file from the upgraded image rather than generating a binary path. You'd want to set this if a particular file contains registration information or other data that can vary from machine to machine.

In the sample .pcp file, this table is empty.

The FamilyFileRanges Table

The FamilyFileRanges table lets you specify sections in an existing file that should not be overwritten when the file is patched. This could be useful for files that contain registration information that must be retained or user customizations. This table has these columns:

Family (String, K)   Foreign key to the ImageFamilies table.

FTK (String, K)   Foreign key to the Files table of the Installer database for the upgraded installation.

RetainOffsets (String)   Comma-delimited list of offsets (measured in bytes) to the start of ranges to retain unchanged.

RetainLengths (String)   Comma-delimited list of lengths (measured in bytes) of the ranges to be retained.

In the sample .pcp file, this table is empty.

The TargetFiles_OptionalData Table

The TargetFiles_OptionalData table has these columns:

Target (String, K)   Foreign key to the TargetImages table.

FTK (String, K)   Foreign key to the Files table of the Installer database for the target installation.

SymbolPaths (String, N)   Semicolon-delimited list of additional paths to search for symbol tables for this file.

IgnoreOffsets (String, N)   Comma-delimited list of offsets (measured in bytes) to the start of ranges that do not have to match the original target file.

IgnoreLengths (String, N)   Comma-delimited list of lengths (measured in bytes) of ranges that do not have to match the original target file.

RetainOffsets (String)   Comma-delimited list of offsets (measured in bytes) to the start of ranges to retain unchanged.

Ignored ranges are not considered when the Installer is determining whether a file should be patched, but they may still be overwritten with new data from the path. In the sample .pcp file, this table is empty.

The ExternalFiles Table

The ExternalFiles table allows the patch to alter files that aren't included in the target's File table. This table has these columns:

Family (String, K)   Foreign key to the ImageFamilies table.

FTK (String, K)   Foreign key to the Files table of the Installer database for the target installation.

FilePath (String, K)   Full path and filename of the file to patch.

SymbolPaths (String, N)   Additional paths to search for symbol tables for this file.

Order (Integer)   Relative order to patch this file.

IgnoreOffsets (String, N)   Comma-delimited list of offsets (measured in bytes) to the start of ranges that do not have to match the original target file.

IgnoreLengths (String, N)   Comma-delimited list of lengths (measured in bytes) of ranges that do not have to match the original target file.

RetainOffsets (String)   Comma-delimited list of offsets (measured in bytes) to the start of ranges to retain unchanged.

In the sample .pcp file, this table is empty.

The UpgradedFilesToIgnore Table

The UpgradedFilesToIgnore table allows you to include files in the patch that aren't installed on the target machine. For example, you might have a readme file that only needs to be seen by administrators. This table has these columns:

Upgraded (String, K)   Foreign key to the UpgradedImages table, or * to include all rows in that table.

FTK (String, K)   Foreign key to the File table of the upgraded image, indicating the file to not install.

In the sample .pcp file, this table is empty.

Generating the *.msp* File

Once you've got the target (before), upgraded (after) administrative installations, and finished the .pcp file, you're ready to create the actual patch file, which has the extension .msp by default. To do this, you need to call a variety of functions in the MsPatchC.dll file supplied by Microsoft. If you'd like all the details, you can find them in the SDK topic on "Creating a Patch Package."

I'm not going to go into the low-level details of creating the .msp file here because few if any developers will actually call MsPatchC.dll directly. Rather, you'll want to use a wrapper program of one sort or another that makes the correct calls in the correct sequence for you. For this chapter, I'm going to use a program named PatchWiz developed by Gaël Fraiteur. This program is a wrapper around code supplied by Microsoft that does the actual patch package creation. You can find PatchWiz on the Web site for this book in the file `patchwiz.zip`.

Figure 10.6 shows PatchWiz in action. You need to supply the location of the `.pcp` file and the location where you'd like to place the `.msp` file. In this case, I'm creating the `.msp` file in a folder named MSP. Then just press the Start button, and PatchWiz will handle the details of building your patch package. If there are any problems with the source files, you'll see an error message in the main PatchWiz box.

FIGURE 10.6
Generating a patch
package with PatchWiz

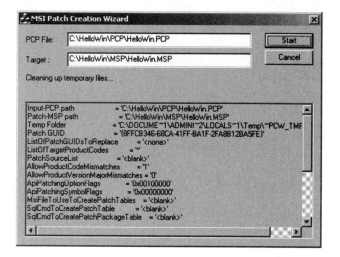

Applying Patches

Once you've created the patch file, you can distribute it to your users with a simple batch file to apply it. The batch file only needs to contain a single line to apply the patch, invoking msiexec with the /p option. For example, with the directories I've used in this chapter, you can apply the patch using

```
msiexec /p c:\HelloWin\MSP\HelloWin.msp
```

Once the user invokes this command (either from a batch file or directly at the command prompt), the Installer will open the original package in maintenance mode. Choosing to reinstall will automatically apply the patches from the patch package to the existing installation.

Merges and Transforms

- Understanding Merge Modules

- Understanding Transforms

- Localizing Packages

In the previous chapter, you saw how to use patch packages to modify a project after it has been installed. In this chapter, I'll explain two other ways to modify an Installer database, using merge modules (sometimes just called merges) and transforms. The changes from merges and transforms are applied to an Installer package before the product is installed, rather than after. A developer can use a merge module to add a piece of functionality (for example, the Microsoft Windows common controls) to a package under development. An administrator can use a transform to modify a package before it's installed (for example, to change the user interface of a product from English to French).

Understanding Merge Modules

Most developers understand the benefits of writing reusable code. That is, once you've written and debugged a piece of software, it makes sense to use that piece again when you need the same functionality. The more pre-tested software you can reuse, the fewer bugs you're likely to have in the final product.

One important facet of reusable code is the notion of shared components. All versions of Microsoft Windows make heavy use of shared components. For example, take a look at Windows Explorer. The toolbar at the top, the status bar at the bottom, the treeview to the left and the listview to the right are all shared components. Any application on the system that wants to use a treeview can actually use the exact same treeview component that was first developed for Windows Explorer. Shared components can be visual (such as the ones I've just mentioned) or invisible infrastructure (such as the Microsoft Data Access Components [MDAC], which handle OLE DB operations).

Merge modules extend the notion of reusable components to the software installation process. The basic notion is simple: once you've developed a way to install a reusable component, you can also reuse the installation process. Merge modules are a tool for the setup developer, not for the end user. Once you've merged the information from a merge module into a full Installer package, there's no need to have the merge module remain available to the end user.

There's another, perhaps less obvious, benefit to merge modules. Recall that the Windows Installer Service expects a particular version of a particular file to always belong to the same component. By allowing multiple developers to share a single component, merge modules lessen the chance of a file being accidentally included in more than one component. Strictly speaking, if someone else is responsible for creating a file that you use, you should ask that person to supply a merge module rather than including the file directly in your own Installer packages.

In this section, I'll discuss the contents of a merge module and show how to create them and how to merge them with a larger installation.

What's in a Merge Module

A merge module is very similar in structure to an Installer package. The major difference is that it doesn't contain everything a complete package holds so that the component can't be installed by the Installer just by using the merge module. Instead, the merge module contains the tables and binary information used by the component that, when added to a full package, make it possible for that package to install the component. Merge modules are delivered as files with the extension .msm, but the internal structure of these files is the same as for regular .msi Installer packages. That means that you can use the same tools for editing merge modules that you use for editing Installer packages.

There are three essential parts to a merge module:

- The summary information stream describing the merge module
- A set of database tables (some shared with regular package tables, some unique to merge modules)
- A cabinet file included as a stream named `MergeModule.CABinet`

WARNING   The files installed by a merge module must be contained in a cabinet file in an internal stream. They cannot be stored externally.

Merge Module Summary Information Stream

The summary information stream for a merge module is similar to that for a patch package or a regular package, but there are differences. Table 11.1 lists the properties stored in the summary information stream in a merge module.

TABLE 11.1: Merge Module Summary Properties

Property	Contains
Title	"merge module"
Subject	ProductName property from the Installer database
Author	Manufacturer property from the Installer database

TABLE 11.1: Merge Module Summary Properties *(continued)*

Property	Contains
Keywords	"Merge Module, MSI, database"
Comments	Description of the merge module and its contents
Template	Platforms and languages supported by this merge module
Last Saved By	Platform and languages of the database after the merge
Revision Number	GUID for this merge module
Create Time/Date	Time the merge module was created
Last Saved Time/Date	Time the merge module was last modified
Word Count	Must be set to 2 if the merge module uses long file names, or 3 if the merge module uses short file names
Creating Application	Software used to create the merge module
Security	2 (Read-only recommended)

Primary Keys in a Merge Module

The primary keys in all tables in a merge module must follow a particular naming convention, which uses the GUID assigned to the merge module as a part of the name. This prevents names in different merge modules from conflicting if they are merged into the same Installer database.

The GUID must be transformed before appending it to the key name. This transformation requires removing the curly braces, changing all of the dashes to underscores, and adding a period at the start of the GUID. Figure 11.1 shows a table from a merge module; it demonstrates the use of this particular merge module's GUID as a part of the primary key values.

Values that are not specific to the merge module need not be modified with the merge module GUID. In Figure 11.1, for example, the SystemFolder directory is intended to be the same as any SystemFolder directory that's already present in the target database.

FIGURE 11.1
Constructing key columns
in a merge module

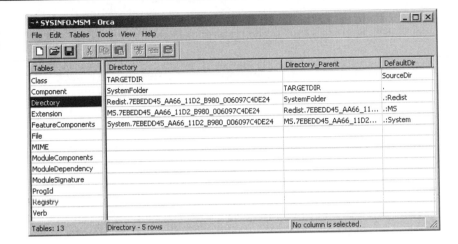

The Component Table

Every merge module must have a Component table. The Component table in a merge module has the same schema as the Component table in a regular Installer database. The Component table specifies the components that the merge module will add to the installation.

NOTE   For more information on the schema of the tables that are shared with regular Installer databases, see Chapter 4, "A Guide to the Installer Database."

The Directory Table

Every merge module must have a Directory table. The Directory table in a merge module has the same schema as the Directory table in a regular Installer database. The Directory table must form a tree structure, with a single directory named TARGETDIR as the root of the tree. When the developer merges the merge module with an Installer database they can choose where on the main tree to locate this directory root.

Components in a merge module should never be installed directly into TARGETDIR. Rather, they should be installed to directories beneath TARGETDIR in the Directory table.

The FeatureComponents Table

Every merge module must have a FeatureComponents table. The FeatureComponents table in a merge module has the same schema as the FeatureComponents table in a regular Installer database.

The FeatureComponents table in a merge module must be empty. Its sole purpose is to provide an empty table to be merged if the target database does not already have a FeatureComponents table of its own. Do not make any entries in this table. While regular databases contain both components and features, a merge module contains only components. It's up to the developer to assign these to features in their own Installer database after the merge has been completed.

The File Table

Every merge module must have a File table. The File table in a merge module has the same schema as the File table in a regular Installer database. All files contained in the File table must also be contained in the `MergeModule.CABinet` stream within the merge module. The file names and file sequence must be identical between the File table and the stream.

The ModuleSignature Table

The ModuleSignature table is a required table. In a merge module, the ModuleSignature table contains a single record that identifies the contents of the merge module. When the merge module is merged into a regular database, the ModuleSignature table is created in the target database and this record is copied over. If multiple merge modules have been merged into a single target database, then that target database will contain a Module-Signature table with more than one row.

This table has these columns:

ModuleID (Identifier, K)   An identifier composed of the merge module name and the transformed GUID for the merge module.

Language (Integer, K)   A Language Identifier (LangID) specifying the language contained in this merge module. If the merge module is language-neutral, this column should contain zero.

Version (Version)   A string describing the version of the merge module.

Figure 11.2 shows a sample ModuleSignature table from a merge module for the Sys-Info ActiveX control.

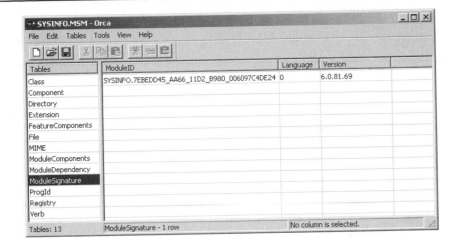

FIGURE 11.2
ModuleSignature table in a merge module

The ModuleComponents Table

The ModuleComponents table is a required table. This table performs a function similar to that of the FeatureComponents table in a regular Installer database. Instead of associating components with features, it associates components with the merge module itself. The Installer can use this table to track which components were added by which merge module.

This table has these columns:

Component (Identifier, K)   A foreign key to the Component table.

ModuleID (Identifier, K)   A foreign key to the ModuleSignature table.

Language (Integer, K)   A foreign key to the ModuleSignature table.

In a merge module, this table will contain a single record for each record in the Component table. The ModuleID and Language columns will be identical for every record in the table.

The ModuleDependency Table

The ModuleDependency table is an optional table that lists other merge modules that are required for the current merge module to function properly. It has these columns:

ModuleID (Identifier, K)   A foreign key to the ModuleSignature table.

ModuleLanguage (Integer, K)   A foreign key to the ModuleSignature table.

RequiredID (Identifier, K)   A foreign key to the ModuleSignature table of the required merge module.

RequiredLanguage (Integer, K)   This can be an exact Language ID to force a particular language version of the required merge module, a Language Group ID to accept any version in a particular language group, or zero to accept any language version at all of the required merge module.

RequiredVersion (Version, N)   This specifies the version of the required merge module. If it's null, any version is acceptable.

The ModuleExclusion Table

The ModuleExclusion table is similar to the ModuleDependency table. However, merge modules listed in the ModuleExclusion table are incompatible with the current merge module and cannot be included in the same Installer database. This table has these columns:

ModuleID (Identifier, K)   A foreign key to the ModuleSignature table.

ModuleLanguage (Integer, K)   A foreign key to the ModuleSignature table.

ExcludedID (Identifier, K)   A foreign key to the ModuleSignature table of the incompatible merge module.

ExcludedLanguage (Integer, K)   This can be an exact Language ID to exclude a particular language version of the required merge module, a Language Group ID to exclude any version in a particular language group, a negative Language ID to exclude everything other than the specified ID.

ExcludedMinVersion (Version, N)   Minimum version of the other module to exclude.

ExcludedMaxVersion (Version, N)   Maximum version of the other module to exclude.

The ModuleIgnoreTable Table

The ModuleIgnoreTable table lists tables within the merge module that should not be merged into the target Installer database. This table has a single column:

Table (Identifier, K)   Name of the table not to merge.

As an alternative, you may simply delete the table not to be merged from the merge module. This approach will also help minimize the size of the merge module.

The ModuleSequence Tables

A merge module may also contain up to six sequence tables to be merged with the sequence tables in the target Installer database. These are the ModuleAdminUI-Sequence, ModuleAdminExecuteSequence, ModuleAdvtUISequence, Module-AdvtExecuteSequence, ModuleInstallUISequence, and ModuleInstallExecute-Sequence tables. Each of these tables has the same schema:

Action (Identifier, K)   Name of a standard action, custom action, or dialog. If it's a custom action or dialog, the merge module must contain the necessary information in a CustomAction or Dialog table.

Sequence (Integer, N)   Sequence number of a standard action. Null for a custom action or dialog.

BaseAction (Identifier, N)   If present, a foreign key back into this same table indicating the action that this action is related to.

After (Integer, N)   0 if this action comes before any related BaseAction, 1 if this action comes after any related BaseAction.

Condition (Condition, N)   Value to be copied to the Condition column of the target database.

Other Tables

In addition to the tables listed in this section, a merge module may also contain other tables to be merged into the target database. For example, if a merge module installs a component that depends on Registry entries, it may contain a Registry table. The primary key columns in any such table must contain the merge module's GUID to ensure uniqueness.

MergeModule.CABinet

All of the files installed by a merge module must be included in the embedded `Merge-Module.CABinet` cabinet file stream within the merge module. As mentioned above, these files must use the same sequence and file names as they are listed with in the File table.

A `MergeModule.CABinet` stream may contain additional files that are not listed in the File table. These additional files are ignored when the module is merged. The purpose of this is to allow a single `MergeModule.CABinet` stream to be shared by multiple versions of a merge module. For example, you could use the same stream for the English and Japanese versions of a merge module, and you could use the File table in each merge module to list only the files that should be installed from the stream.

Because the files in a merge module are always stored in compressed form in the `MergeModule.CABinet` stream, it is not necessary to mark them as compressed in the File table.

Merging Merge Modules

When you're ready to add the components in a merge module to your Installer package, you need to use a merging tool. All of the major editing packages (see Chapter 12, "Installer Editing Tools") offer this functionality. There's also a utility named `MsiMerg` `.exe` that ships as part of the Windows Installer SDK. You'll find this utility in the Tools folder underneath the folder where you installed the SDK.

The help for the MsiMerg utility is limited to a single cryptic line:

```
msimerg (d).exe {base db} {ref db}
```

It turns out that the base database is the Installer package that you're merging to, and the reference database is the merge module that you want to add to the package. So, for example, you might construct a command line such as this:

```
msimerg HelloWin.msi sysinfo.msm
```

This will add the information from the sysinfo merge module to the HelloWin Installer package. If there are any errors during the merge, it will create a table named _MergeErrors that you can inspect for more information.

> **NOTE**   If possible, use a full-featured Installer editing tool instead of MsiMerg to perform merges. These tools will generally do a better job of explaining conflicts and checking for dependent modules.

Obtaining Merge Modules

If the Windows Installer Service is adopted as widely as Microsoft hopes, it should be possible to obtain almost any software component in the form of a merge module. We can look forward to the day when custom control manufacturers, for example, automatically include a merge module when you purchase a new control.

In the meantime, though, Microsoft itself is the only source of merge modules. Specifically, there are 43 merge modules available as part of the Visual Studio Installer package. I'll discuss the Visual Studio Installer in Chapter 12. Meanwhile, if you're a registered owner of Visual Studio 6.0, you can download your own copy from msdn.microsoft.com/vstudio/downloads/vsi/.

Table 11.2 lists the merge modules that are included with the Visual Studio Installer version 1.0.

TABLE 11.2: Merge Modules Included with Visual Studio Installer

Merge Module Name	Contains
ATL.MSM	Active Template Library
COMCAT.MSM	Microsoft Component Category Manager DLL
COMCT232.MSM	Microsoft Windows Common Controls (2)
COMCT332.MSM	Microsoft Windows Common Controls (3)
COMCTL32.MSM	Microsoft Windows Common Controls
COMDLG32.MSM	Microsoft Common Dialog Control
DBGRID32.MSM	Microsoft DBGrid Custom Control
DBLIST32.MSM	Microsoft DBList Custom Control
MCI32.MSM	Microsoft Media Control Interface
MDAC.MSM	Microsoft Data Access Components
MFC42.MSM	MFC DLL Shared Library (Retail)
MFC42U.MSM	MFC DLL Shared Library (Retail Unicode)
MSADODC.MSM	Microsoft ADO Data Control
MSBIND.MSM	Microsoft Data Binding Collection Object
MSCHRT20.MSM	Microsoft Chart Control 2.0
MSCOMCT2.MSM	Microsoft Windows Common Controls (2)
MSCOMCTL.MSM	Microsoft Windows Common Controls
MSCOMM32.MSM	Microsoft Communications control
MSDATGRD.MSM	Microsoft Data Grid Control
MSDATLST.MSM	Microsoft Data List Control
MSDATREP.MSM	Microsoft Data Repeater Control
MSDBRPTR.MSM	Microsoft Data Report Runtime DLL
MSDERUN.MSM	Microsoft Data Environment Runtime DLL
MSFLXGRD.MSM	Microsoft Flex Grid Control
MSHFLXGD.MSM	Microsoft Hierarchical Flexgrid Control

TABLE 11.2: Merge Modules Included with Visual Studio Installer *(continued)*

Merge Module Name	Contains
MSHTMPGR.MSM	Microsoft DHTML Page Designer
MSINET.MSM	Microsoft Internet Transfer Control
MSMAPI32.MSM	Microsoft MAPI Controls
MSMASK32.MSM	Microsoft Masked Edit Control
MSRDC20.MSM	Microsoft Remote Data Control
MSRDO20.MSM	Microsoft Remote Data Engine
MSSTDFMT.MSM	Microsoft Standard Data Formatting DLL
MSSTKPRP.MSM	Microsoft Stock Property Page
MSVBVM60.MSM	Microsoft Visual Basic 6.0 Runtime
MSVCIRT.MSM	Microsoft C++ Runtime Library
MSVCP60.MSM	Microsoft C++ Runtime Library
MSVCRT.MSM	Microsoft C Runtime Library
MSWCRUN.MSM	Microsoft Web Class Runtime
MSWINSCK.MSM	Microsoft Winsock Control
OLEAUT32.MSM	OLE Automation
PICCLP32.MSM	Microsoft PicClip Control
SYSINFO.MSM	Microsoft System Information Control
TABCTL32.MSM	Microsoft Tab Control

WARNING The MDAC.MSM merge module differs from the others in that it does not actually install the MDAC. Rather, it checks to see whether the MDAC is already installed on the user's computer, and if it isn't, it advises them to download it from the Microsoft Web site. To actually install the MDAC, you'll need to use a custom action, as detailed in Chapter 7, "Putting the Pieces Together."

No new merge modules have been released by Microsoft since the Visual Studio Installer shipped in the second half of 1999. As of this writing, it's not clear how (or whether) Microsoft will coordinate the release of merge modules by the development groups.

Understanding Transforms

Transforms provide a convenience for both the developer and the administrator. A *transform* is a file that contains a set of changes that will transform one Installer database into another. This is useful when you want to ship one basic Installer package and allow it to be customized in many ways.

For example, suppose your product includes a user management tool that should only be available to some users. One way to handle this would be to follow these steps:

1. Create an Installer package that installs everything except the user manager.
2. Create an Installer package that installs everything including the user manager.
3. Create a transform from the first package to the second.
4. Ship the first package and the transform to your customers.

An administrator at your customer sites would then have two choices:

- For regular users, just install the base package.
- For administrative users, apply the transform to the base package and install the transformed package.

In this section, I'll show you how to create and apply transforms, both using command-line tools and using the Installer automation model. I'll also discuss the security issues associated with transforms.

Creating Transforms

As an actual example of using transforms, I've created `HelloWinP.msi`. Figure 11.3 shows a dialog box from this Installer package in action.

As you can see, the user interface for HelloWinP has been partially converted from English to Pig Latin. I did this by making a copy of the `HelloWin.msi` package that I created for Chapter 10, "Creating and Using Patch Packages," and editing the Control and Property tables by hand.

FIGURE 11.3
Running `HelloWinP.msi`

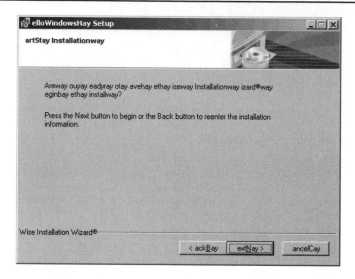

HelloWinP installs precisely the same files that HelloWin installs. To avoid shipping two entire Installer packages, I can create a transform that converts the English version of the package to the Pig Latin version. The Windows Installer SDK contains a command-line tool to create transforms named `MsiTran.exe`. The syntax of this tool is

```
MsiTran -g {base db} {new db} {transform} ⤶
    [{error/validation conditions}]
```

Here, the –g switch tells `MsiTran` to generate a transform. The base database is the "before" database that the transform will be applied to. The new database is the "after" database that the transform will create. The error conditions argument allows you to specify conditions that should not be treated as errors, even though they ordinarily would be treated that way. It can consist of any or all of these flags:

a   To ignore attempts to add an existing row.

b   To ignore attempts to delete non-existent rows.

c   To ignore attempts to add an existing table.

d   To ignore attempts to delete non-existent tables.

e   To ignore attempts to modify existing rows.

f   To ignore attempts to change the code page of the package.

You can also specify validation conditions are part of the same argument. Validation conditions specify things that the Installer should check when applying a transform. This argument can use these flags:

g To check the upgrade code.

l To check the language.

p To check the platform.

r To check the product.

s To check the major version only.

t To check the major and minor versions.

u To check the major, minor, and update versions.

v To force the applied database version to be less than the base database version.

w To force the applied database version to be less than or equal to the base database version.

x To force the applied database version to be equal to the base database version.

y To force the applied database version to be greater than or equal to the base database version.

z To force the applied database version to be greater than the base database version.

In this example case, you can generate the transform between HelloWin.msi and HelloWinP.msi with this command line:

```
MsiTran -g HelloWin.msi HelloWinP.msi HWPL.mst
```

Note the use of the .mst extension for a transform.

Transform Summary Information Stream

Like packages and merge modules, a transform file contains a summary information stream. The MsiTran utility will automatically create a summary information stream in the transforms it creates. Table 11.3 lists the properties stored in the summary information stream in a transform file.

TABLE 11.3: Transform Summary Properties

Property	Contains
Title	"Transform"
Subject	Short description of the transform
Author	Manufacturer property from the Installer database

TABLE 11.3: Transform Summary Properties *(continued)*

Property	Contains
Keywords	"Transform"
Comments	"This transform contains the logic and data needed to modify *<productname>*"
Template	Platforms and languages supported by this transform
Last Saved By	Platform and languages of the database after the transform
Revision Number	GUIDs of the old and new products
Create Time/Date	Time the transform was created
Last Saved Time/Date	Time the transform was last modified
Page Count	Minimum Installer version necessary to process the transform
Character Count	Error and validation flags
Creating Application	Software used to create the transform
Security	4 (Read-only enforced)

NOTE

MsiTran doesn't fill in all of these properties, but it does create them and fill in the ones that the Installer depends on for its internal processing.

Secure Transforms

There are times when you won't want the end user to be able to modify the transforms applied to an Installer package. For example, if you call for a transform named `foo.mst`, and the user can substitute their own file for the `foo.mst` you intended, they could cause the Installer to do anything. Remember, the Installer process runs with administrative privileges, so this would be a serious security hole. It's easy to imagine a trojan transform file that would invoke User Manager and add the current user to the Windows NT Administrators group.

For this reason, the Installer supports the notion of *secure transforms*. Secure transforms are simply transforms that are kept in a place where the user does not have write access. This might be the root of the location where an administrative installation of the package has been performed (*Secure-at-Source transforms*). It might also be a share or full path elsewhere on the network (*Secure-Full-Path transforms*). You can indicate that the Installer should use secure transforms by special characters in the TRANSFORMS property (discussed in the next section) or by setting the TransformsSecure or TransformsAtSource property within the Installer database to 1.

When the Installer uses a secure transform, it will cache a copy of that transform locally. If the local copy becomes lost or damaged, it will restore it only from the original location.

Applying Transforms

To apply a transform, you include it on the command line when you invoke msiexec, as a setting for the TRANSFORMS property of the Installer package. For example, this command line would invoke the English version of HelloWin.msi, but apply the transform to transform it into the Pig Latin version:

```
msiexec /I HelloWin.msi TRANSFORMS=HWPL.mst
```

Of course, you can set the TRANSFORMS property by making entries to the Property table within the Installer package instead of by using a command line. This is especially useful if you're a network administrator who wants to roll out a transformed Installer package for a group of users. By modifying the TRANSFORMS property internally to the Installer package, you can make sure that the transforms you choose are applied every time the package is installed.

When setting the TRANSFORMS property, the Installer recognizes a number of special symbols. Here are the various syntaxes you can use:

@ followed by a list of filenames without paths   Indicates a set of Secure-at-Source transforms, which must be located in the root of the source for the package itself.

| followed by a list of filenames with paths   Indicates a set of Secure-Full-Path transforms, which must be located exactly at the specified paths.

A list of filenames with no special character   Is treated as a list of Secure-at-Source transforms if the TransformsSecure or TransformsAtSource properties are set to 1, and as a list of unsecure transforms located at the root of the source if neither of these properties is set.

A list of filenames with paths, but with no special character   Is treated as a list of Secure-Full-Path transforms if the TransformsSecure or TransformsAtSource properties are set to 1, and as a list of unsecure transforms located at the root of the source if neither of these properties is set.

: followed by the name of a transform   Indicates a transform that is embedded in the package as a separate stream.

Transforms in the Object Model

The MsiTrans.exe program will probably cover most of the transform construction you need to perform, unless you're working on an Installer tool yourself. In that case, you may need to know that you can create transforms from within the Installer automation model. To do so, you use methods of the Database object. There are two methods involved, GenerateTransform and CreateTransformSummaryInfo. Both of these methods should be invoked from a Database object representing the transformed ("after") database.

The GenerateTransform method has this syntax:

```
Database.GenerateTransform(reference, storage)
```

The *reference* parameter should be replaced with the full path and filename of the reference ("before") database. The *storage* parameter should be replaced with the full path and filename where you want the transform file to be saved.

The GenerateTransform method returns True if it's able to create the transform, and False if the two files are identical (and so the transform isn't needed). If there's some other problem, it will raise an error.

Unlike MsiTran.exe, the GenerateTransform method doesn't create the summary information stream in the transform file. For that, you use the CreateTransformSummary-Info method:

```
Database.CreateTransformSummaryInfo(reference, storage, errorConditions, validation)
```

The *reference* parameter should be replaced by the full path and filename of the reference ("before") database. The *storage* parameter should be replaced with the full path and filename of the transform that should have the summary information stream added.

The *errorCondition* and *validation* parameters work similarly to the command-line arguments to MsiTrans. In the CreateTransformSummaryInfo method, these are combinations of constants. Table 11.4 lists the constants that you can use with this method.

T A B L E 1 1 . 4 : Constants for CreateTransformSummaryInfo

Name	Value	Type	Description
msiTransformErrorNone	0	E	Don't ignore errors.
msiTransformErrorAddExistingRow	1	E	Ignore attempts to add a row that already exists.
msiTransformErrorDeleteNonExistingRow	2	E	Ignore attempts to delete a nonexistent row.
msiTransformErrorAddExistingTable	4	E	Ignore attempts to add a table that already exists.

TABLE 11.4: Constants for CreateTransformSummaryInfo *(continued)*

Name	Value	Type	Description
msiTransformErrorDeleteNonExistingTable	8	E	Ignore attempts to delete a table that does not exist.
msiTransformErrorUpdateNonExistingRow	16	E	Ignore attempts to update a row that doesn't exist.
msiTransformErrorChangeCodepage	32	E	Ignore attempts to change the codepage.
msiTransformValidationNone	0	V	No validation.
msiTransformValidationLanguage	1	V	Default language must match base database.
msiTransformValidationProduct	2	V	Product must match base database.
msiTransformValidationMajorVer	8	V	Validate only major version.
msiTransformValidationMinorVer	16	V	Validate Major and minor versions.
msiTransformValidationUpdateVer	32	V	Validate Major, minor and update versions.
msiTransformValidationLess	64	V	Applied version must be less than the base version.
msiTransformValidationLessOrEqual	128	V	Applied version must be less than or equal to the base version.
msiTransformValidationEqual	256	V	Applied version must equal base version.
msiTransformValidationGreaterOrEqual	512	V	Applied version must be greater than or equal to the base version.
msiTransformValidationGreater	1024	V	Applied version must be greater than the base version.
msiTransformValidationUpgradeCode	2048	V	Transform must match the base upgrade code.

NOTE   You'll also find that the more full-featured of the third-party Installer editing tools are capable of generating transforms (see Chapter 12).

Localizing Packages

One of the most important uses of transforms is to localize Installer packages. It may not be completely obvious just what you need to change for localization to properly take care of all the places where the Installer can display text. Here's a list of what you need to change before you can generate a localization transform:

1. Import localized error and action text tables. The Windows Installer SDK supplies these tables for all the major languages that are supported by Windows.

2. Translate the user-interface text found in the Control, Dialog, and Property tables.

3. Set the ProductLanguage property to the LangID of the target language.

4. Set the Template summary information property to include the LangID of the target language.

5. Localize the descriptive text in the summary information stream.

6. Localize any messages provided by custom actions.

Of course, you should always test your localized package to make sure you haven't missed any English-language text.

NOTE	Some of the more sophisticated third-party editing tools offer built-in support for localization.

Installer Editing Tools

- MsiDb

- Microsoft Orca

- Microsoft Visual Studio Installer

- InstallShield for Windows Installer

- Wise for Windows Installer

For a young technology, the Windows Installer has spawned quite a number of tools. Some of these tools came directly from the Windows Installer group within Microsoft; they had to supply the necessary rudiments before anyone else could work with this technology. Some come from other groups within Microsoft. And some come from independent software vendors (ISVs), who recognize that any technology pushed this hard by Microsoft is bound to create a market. In this chapter, I'll review the available tools for editing Installer databases and try to give you a sense of where the tradeoffs lie between expense and power.

MsiDb

Before there was an editor for the Installer database, there was MsiDb. This tool, supplied by the Windows Installer team, performs imports to and exports from an Installer database. Thus, you can create an Installer database by building a series of tables as text files and importing them to a blank Installer database. Though tedious, this process still works, and sometimes it's still the best way to work with databases. For one thing, MsiDb has a complete command-line interface, so it can be integrated into an automated build process. Also, MsiDb can be used to import and export streams, a function that some other tools cannot perform.

Using MsiDb Interactively

MsiDb is installed as part of the Installer SDK. Unlike some of the other tools in the SDK, you do not have to run a separate program to install MsiDb; it's automatically placed in the Tools directory of the SDK. This tool has a graphical interface in addition to the command-line interface. If you run MsiDb directly from Windows Explorer, it will present the dialog box shown in Figure 12.1 to allow you to select an Installer database. Note that the dialog box caption refers to the program as MsiTable, which was its name in a previous version.

You use this same selection dialog whether you're planning to import or export data. You can select any Installer database to work with, or you can type in the name of a merge module.

If you want to create a new Installer database with MsiDb, start by making a copy of the schema.msi database that you'll find in the Database folder of the Installer SDK.

Once you've selected the database, the next step is to select the folder that will hold the text files containing Installer data. You can do this with the dialog box shown in

Figure 12.2. Once again, this dialog box is the same whether you're importing or exporting data.

FIGURE 12.1

Selecting an Installer database with MsiDb

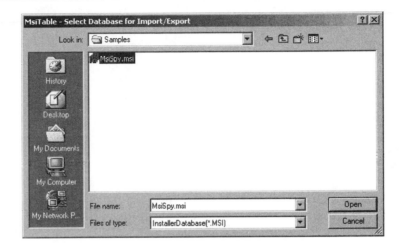

FIGURE 12.2

Selecting a location for text
files with MsiDb

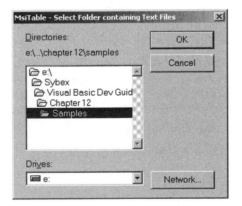

The final step is to tell MsiDb about the operation that you want it to perform. Figure 12.3 shows the dialog box used for this purpose. If you select the Import radio button, you'll be presented with a list of the text files in the selected directory. If you select the Export radio button, you'll be presented with a list of the tables in the selected Installer database. You can select as many of these files or tables as you'd like (the dialog box supports simple multiselect but not the extended multiselect shortcuts of Ctrl+Click and Shift+Click) and then click the OK button to complete the operation. When you're done, click the Quit button to dismiss MsiDb.

FIGURE 12.3
Selecting tables to export

The text files used by MsiDb have the extension .idt. These files start with three rows of metadata. For example, if you export the FeatureComponents table from an Installer database, the first three rows of the resulting FeatureComponents.idt file will be

```
Feature_    Component_
s32     s72
FeatureComponents    Feature_    Component_
```

The first row lists the column names in the table.

The second row lists the data types for the columns, in a code that MsiDb understands. Here the two columns are a string with a maximum length of 32 and a string with a maximum length of 72.

The third row lists the table name, followed by the names of the key columns in the table.

Because the format of these first three rows is completely inflexible, you should never edit these rows. If you want to create a new table to import, the simplest way to do so is to export an existing table and edit the resulting file.

After the three rows of metadata, the .idt file continues with the actual data from the table. This is dumped one row per line, with tabs separating the fields. If you want to edit an .idt file, you must use a text editor that does *not* convert tabs to spaces. Windows Notepad is one good choice for this. For longer files, you might find it convenient to use Microsoft Excel, which can read and write tab-delimited files.

For example, if you export the FeatureComponents table from the sample MsiSpy.msi database supplied with the Installer SDK, here's the entire FeatureComponents.idt file that you'll get:

```
Feature_      Component_
s32     s72
FeatureComponents      Feature_      Component_
HelpDeu      Help_Deu
HelpEnu      Help_Enu
SystemInterface      System_InterfaceAlpha
SystemInterface      System_InterfaceDebug
SystemInterface      System_InterfaceIntel
UIResourcesAra      Resources_AraAlpha
UIResourcesAra      Resources_AraDebug
UIResourcesAra      Resources_AraIntel
UIResourcesDeu      Resources_DeuAlpha
UIResourcesDeu      Resources_DeuDebug
UIResourcesDeu      Resources_DeuIntel
UIResourcesEnu      Resources_EnuAlpha
UIResourcesEnu      Resources_EnuDebug
UIResourcesEnu      Resources_EnuIntel
UIResourcesJpn      Resources_JpnAlpha
UIResourcesJpn      Resources_JpnDebug
UIResourcesJpn      Resources_JpnIntel
UserInterface      User_InterfaceAlpha
UserInterface      User_InterfaceDebug
UserInterface      User_InterfaceIntel
```

To add a new entry to the FeatureComponents table, you could just add one more row to this text file, and then use MsiDb to import the edited file back to the original database. Imported tables will automatically overwrite existing tables with the same name.

Tables that contain binary data are exported as a series of files. For example, if you export the Binary table from MsiSpy.msi, you'll get this binary.idt file:

```
Name    Data
s72     v0
Binary      Name
bannrbmp      bannrbmp.ibd
completi      completi.ibd
```

```
custicon    custicon.ibd
dlgbmp    dlgbmp.ibd
exclamic    exclamic.ibd
info    info.ibd
insticon    insticon.ibd
New    New.ibd
removico    removico.ibd
repairic    repairic.ibd
Up    Up.ibd
```

The Data column lists filenames (`bannrbmp.idb`, `completi.ibd`, and so on) for separate files that contain the actual binary data. These files will be found in a subdirectory named after the table—so, in this case, you'll find a Binary subdirectory containing eleven files. Although all of these files will have the extension `.ibd`, they have the original binary contents. For example, `bannrbmp.idb` is a bitmap file that can be opened with Windows Paint or another imaging program.

Using MsiDb from the Command Line

For use on the command line, MsiDb is called with a set of options and a set of tables:

```
MsiDb <option> <option> … <table> <table> …
```

Table 12.1 lists the valid options that you can use on the MsiDb command line. Command-line options for MsiDb are case-insensitive, and may be specified with either a dash or forward slash delimiter. The ? and * wildcards may be used when specifying tables to import, but only the * wildcard may be used when specifying tables to export.

T A B L E   1 2 . 1 :   MsiDb Command-Line Options

Option	Description
-?	Display command line help.
-A{file}	Add file as a new stream.
-C	Create a new database (overwrites any existing database).
-D{database file}	Database to use.
-E	Export files.
-F{folder path}	Specifies the folder containing streams and tables.
-I	Import files.
-J{storage name}	Remove the specified storage.
-K{stream name}	Remove the specified stream.
-M{merge file}	Merge the specified `.msm` file.

TABLE 12.1:   MsiDb Command-Line Options *(continued)*

Option	Description
-R{storage name}	Add storage.
-S	Truncate names to 8 characters on export.
-T{transform file}	Apply the specified transform.
-W{storage name}	Export the specified storage.
-X{stream name}	Export the specified stream.

A few examples will show how you can use MsiDb with a Windows Installer database. For example, to extract a copy of the Component table from a database, you could use this command line:

```
msidb -D product.msi -F c:\IDTs -E Component
```

If you then edited the file and wanted to replace the version in the database with the edited version, you'd use the corresponding import command line:

```
msidb -D product.msi -F c:\IDTs -I Component
```

If you have a cabinet file that you need to include in your Installer package, it's easy to insert it using MsiDb:

```
msidb -D product.msi -A cabfile.cab
```

> **TIP**   If you're inserting a cabinet file, you need to make the proper entries in the Media table to tell your database to use this cabinet for its files. See Chapter 3, "Basic Installer Concepts," for more details.

Microsoft Orca

Microsoft Orca is the next step up from MsiDb in terms of power and complexity. Orca is an editor that operates directly on the tables in your Installer database. It's available as part of the Windows Installer SDK, which means that any developer can get a copy for free. You've seen Orca in various examples earlier in the book, but now it's time to take a look at it in a bit more detail.

WARNING   Orca operates directly on the Installer tables with minimal validation. Before you try to do anything with Orca, you'd better have a good idea how the Windows Installer works. It's also a good idea to keep a backup copy of your database, just in case you make a serious mistake.

Using Orca

Figure 12.4 shows the basic Orca interface. You select a table to work with in the list on the left-hand side of the interface, and the table itself is displayed on the right-hand side of the interface. To edit an existing row, click in any cell on the right-hand side and start typing. To import binary data, click in a binary column (such as the Data column in the Binary table). Orca will prompt you for a filename to import directly into that column.

A shortcut menu on the editing area provides shortcuts for adding and dropping rows of data. When you elect to add a row, Orca presents a dialog box listing the data type for each column and showing you which are the key columns.

FIGURE 12.4

Using Orca to edit an Installer database

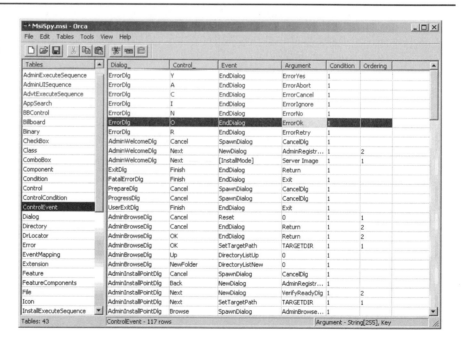

Edit ➤ Find or the Ctrl+F key combination will open a Find dialog box. This dialog box allows you to enter text, and it searches through every table in the database looking for that text.

There are several menu items available for dealing with tables. You can use the Tables menu to perform these operations:

- Add Table (Orca has available the definitions for all the standard Installer tables)
- Drop Table
- Import Table (from an .idt file)
- Export Table (to an .idt file)

Orca Tools and Options

Although the Orca editor is fairly primitive, it does offer some useful tools and options. These include validation, dialog preview, and summary information editing.

To validate an Installer database using Orca, choose Tools ➤ Validate. Orca will prompt you for the location of a .cub file containing the ICE tests that you wish to run (see Chapter 13, "Validating Installer Databases," for details of the validation process). You can enter a Web location here, such as `http://myserver/myice.cub`, to load a `.cub` file from a Web server. You can also type in a filename from the local file system.

To preview a dialog, choose Tools ➤ Dialog Preview. Orca will open a dialog box showing all of the dialogs in the current database. Select a dialog from the list and click Preview to see it, as shown in Figure 12.5. When you're done previewing dialogs, use the Done button on the Dialog Preview dialog box to dismiss all the open dialog boxes; the controls on the dialog boxes themselves are not functional in this state.

NOTE   Orca does not include any tools for constructing dialog boxes. You need to make entries directly in the appropriate database tables to create dialog boxes. If you're working on a complex user interface, you should consider using a different editor to create the user interface.

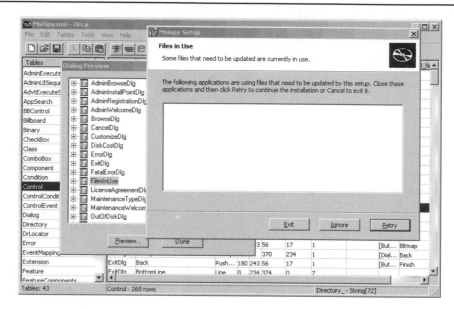

To view summary information from an Installer database, choose View ➤ Summary
Information. Orca will display the fields of interest from the summary information
stream on a dialog box similar to that shown in Figure 12.6. You can edit these properties directly in this dialog box.

TIP   The Windows Installer SDK, including MsiDb and the Orca editor, is available for download at
`msdn.microsoft.com/developer/sdk/wininst.asp`.

FIGURE 12.6
Summary Information
Stream in Orca

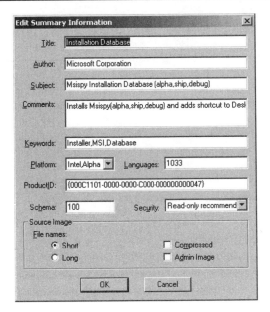

FIGURE 12.6
Summary Information
Stream in Orca

Microsoft Visual Studio Installer

The Microsoft Visual Studio Installer is also available for free online (msdn.microsoft
.com/vstudio/downloads/vsi/default.asp), although only for registered users of
the professional or enterprise editions of Visual Studio or its constituent products. This
tool, shown in Figure 12.7, is Microsoft's own entry into the high-end setup-creation
market.

The Visual Studio Installer seems to be largely the product of a series of compromises.
It's designed to work well with products created in the Visual Studio shell and to do
most of the work automatically. However, this means that it's not capable of editing
arbitrary Installer databases. Indeed, the Visual Studio Installer itself does not work
with Installer databases. Rather, it uses its own project files that are later compiled into
such databases.

FIGURE 12.7
The Visual Studio Installer

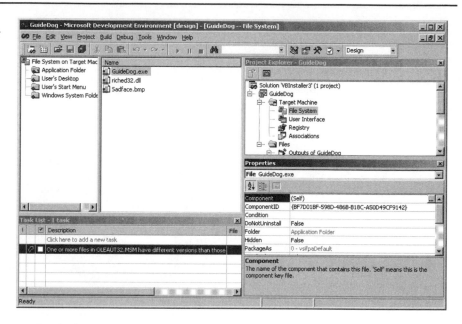

On the plus side, the Visual Studio Installer is integrated with the Visual Studio shell, and it knows how to import Visual Studio and Visual Basic projects. However, apparently in the interest of making the tool easy to use, Microsoft has chosen not to expose most of the power of the Installer through this tool. For instance, there is no user interface editor at all. You can choose from a set of dialogs, and you can set properties such as the background bitmap to use, but you can't design your own dialog boxes from scratch.

This tool can create Installer projects from scratch or from a Visual Basic project. If you create an Installer project from a Visual Basic project, the Visual Studio Installer will automatically add the necessary runtime files. If you start with an empty project, you proceed by adding files one at a time, specifying the folder where you'd like each file installed. The tool can edit the complex information needed to create COM objects, but it does not offer any facility for automatically generating this information.

There's also no support here for custom actions, which allow you to extend the Installer's functionality by calling entry points in an external library. With the Installer itself being a version 1 product, this is sometimes necessary, and the absence of custom actions from this product is troubling. You can manipulate products and features, but the interface for doing so is not especially obvious. If you want to do such tweaking, you might use the Visual Studio Installer to create the original project, compile it, and then use Orca for the final touches.

However, you may want to download a copy of the Visual Studio Installer even if you have no intention of using it. That's because this is also the way that Microsoft has distributed a few dozen merge modules for common components such as the Windows Common Controls or the System Information component. Those merge modules are necessary to properly install shared components produced by Microsoft, and should be in the toolbox of every Installer developer. You'll find a complete list of these merge modules in Chapter 11, "Merges and Transforms."

TIP   Microsoft is also allowing independent vendors to redistribute these merge modules. Currently, they're available with the latest versions of the InstallShield and Wise tools, as well as directly from Microsoft.

InstallShield for Windows Installer

InstallShield for Windows Installer is one of the two full-featured, ISV setup programs directed at Installer technology that's available today (the other is Wise for Windows Installer, which I'll discuss later in the chapter). Installshield integrates Best Practices, Help, and editing tools into one interface, and will guide you through all aspects of creating a logo-compliant Windows Installer setup for your application.

NOTE   For more information on InstallShield for Windows Installer, visit the InstallShield Web site at `www.installshield.com`. For this chapter, I used version 1.10 of the software.

Creating an Installer Package

InstallShield offers six distinct ways to get started:

- You can open an existing InstallShield setup.
- You can import an existing Windows Installer package.
- You can create a new, blank package.
- You can import a Visual Basic project to an Installer package.
- You can use the Project Wizard to create a package.

- You can use the included NetInstall Spy to create a package from another setup of any sort.

Of these, the Project Wizard (one panel of which is shown in Figure 12.8) is likely to be of the most help to the average software developer. As with most wizard software, the Project Wizard walks you through a series of panels that collect important information. At the end of the process, it builds your Installer package based on that information. The Project Wizard includes these seven panels:

1. Create or Open project
2. Application Information
3. Setup Languages
4. Application Features
5. Application Components
6. Setup Design (associating Components with Features)
7. Application Files
8. Create Shortcuts
9. Import Registry Data
10. Dialogs
11. Create Project

Once you've created a project, it will be open in the InstallShield workspace. This workspace contains six major areas:

- Project
- Setup Design
- Sequences
- Actions/Scripts
- User Interface
- Release

I'll consider each of these areas in turn.

FIGURE 12.8
The InstallShield Project
Wizard

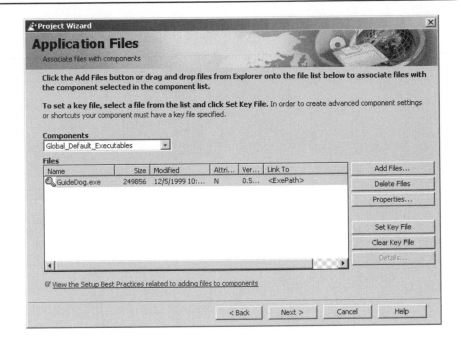

Working with the Project

Figure 12.9 shows the Project section of the InstallShield interface. As you can see, it integrates a treeview of the contents of this area with a property sheet and a help facility. From the Project section, you can set the project, product, and summary information stream properties, enter the information used by the Add/Remove Programs Control Panel applet, manage paths and properties, and manipulate the string table.

The string table deserves special mention. InstallShield incorporates the ability to use named strings everywhere that the user interface requires text and supports multi-language authoring. By making use of the built-in string table, you can make it simple to produce versions of your setup program in many different languages with a single build process. This is a good example of the added value that InstallShield brings to the process over what's built into the Windows Installer.

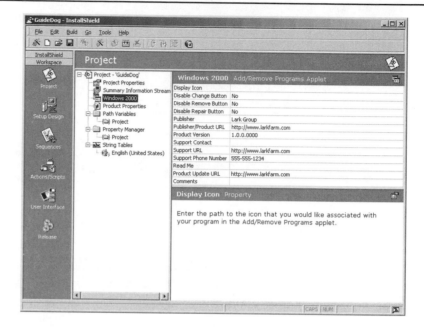

Working with the Setup Design

The Setup Design area of the InstallShield interface lets you manipulate features, components, and merge modules. It presents an integrated treeview that makes it easy to associate features with the proper components. You can also handle all the other functional areas of setup from here:

- Files
- Registry settings
- Shortcuts
- Paths
- COM registration
- File types
- Services
- Publishing

One very useful part of the setup design is the Component Wizard. The Component Wizard lets you select files and organizes them into components following the Installer "best practices." The Component Wizard delivers two key benefits. First, it makes sure you follow the Installer componentization rules. Second, it automatically extracts all the necessary information from COM Servers and places this information into the appropriate Registry tables. The Component Wizard can even be told to include all the files in an entire directory tree, and it will sort them out into components that follow the rules.

Working with Sequences

The Sequences area of the InstallShield interface lets you edit the sequence tables in your Installer database. You can combine dialog boxes, standard actions, and custom actions; you can also reorder them, and set their conditions. InstallShield will automatically set up the six standard sequence tables with Microsoft's recommended sequence of actions by default.

Working with Actions and Scripts

The Actions and Scripts area of the InstallShield interface is designed to let you edit custom actions. In addition to the custom action types that are directly supported by the Windows Installer, InstallShield lets you write custom actions using InstallScript. InstallScript is a BASIC-like scripting language that users of other InstallShield products will already be familiar with (in fact, you can even import your existing script files from older versions of InstallShield). By compiling InstallScript into custom actions, InstallShield makes the power of custom actions easier to tap.

Working with the User Interface

One of the strongest points of InstallShield is its editor for the user interface of your setup program. Visual Basic users will be right at home with the dialog designer that uses simple drag and drop functionality along with property sheets to specify control behavior. Figure 12.10 shows the dialog editor in action.

Of course, you can also edit the dialog events in the User Interface view. InstallShield provides a simple picking interface to make it quick and easy to assign events to controls.

FIGURE 12.10
The InstallShield dialog
editor

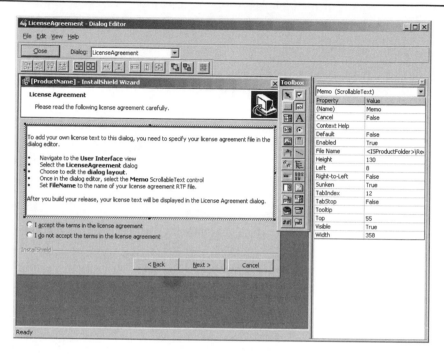

The InstallShield dialog editor also supports export to the RC format and import from the RES format. These are standard formats used for user interface resources by many Windows programs. What this means is that you can design dialogs in another tool you already know (for example, Microsoft Visual Studio) and then import them into InstallShield for final tweaking and incorporation into a setup.

Working with Releases

When you've finished creating your project within InstallShield, you still have to build it into a release using the Release area of the user interface. That's because InstallShield stores information in its own proprietary database and only creates an Installer database as a final step. While this is sometimes an annoyance, it lets InstallShield store things, like helpful comments, that the Installer itself doesn't make room for. It also simplifies the process of releasing multiple versions of a product, for example to support different languages. Overall the build process is a net gain rather than a loss.

The Release Wizard lets you manage multiple releases from a single project. You can control all aspects of an Installer package from this view, including the user interface language, whether source files should be compressed or included in cabinets, and whether there should be a bootstrap program to handle installing the Installer Service itself.

Other Features

InstallShield includes a Power Editor tool that lets you work directly in the Installer database tables, but you usually won't need this tool. Instead, you can use the more logical organization of the InstallShield interface, and trust the product to make the necessary database changes for you. Particularly if you're new to the Windows Installer, this reorganization will save you lots of time. Simple operations like adding a file, for example, would require several operations within the database but can be performed as a single step in the InstallShield user interface.

InstallShield has complete facilities for working with merge modules. You can include merge modules developed by other manufacturers and create your own merge modules. InstallShield also supports creating and applying transforms through a simple wizard interface.

InstallShield features a variety of levels of help that will be of great assistance to the setup developer who's perhaps feeling a bit overwhelmed by the Windows Installer. This includes animated demonstrations of key features, links to the InstallShield Web site, and integration of Microsoft's help from the Installer SDK, as well as extensive help both within the user interface and in a separate help library.

Wise for Windows Installer

Wise for Windows Installer also offers a complete solution for the developer who wants to rapidly create logo-compliant Windows Installer setup packages. Wise also integrates the entire setup process into a single interface and attempts to make sense out of the confusing tables of the Installer database.

NOTE For more information on Wise for Windows Installer, visit the Wise Web site at www.wisesolutions.com/default.htm. For this chapter, I used version 2.0 of the software.

Creating an Installer Package

Wise offers seven distinct ways to get started:

- You can open an existing Wise setup.
- You can open an existing Windows Installer package.
- You can create a new, blank package.
- You can import a Microsoft Systems Management Server (SMS) script.
- You can import a Visual Basic project to an Installer package.
- You can run an application and have Wise automatically record the files that it uses.
- You can use the SetupCapture Wizard to repackage any existing setup into an Installer script.

Wise does have its own .wsi file extension for projects that are later compiled into Installer packages. It also offers the ability to open .msi packages directly, making it a useful tool for quick edits to existing packages.

The Wise Installation Expert uses a flow metaphor to walk you through all the essential steps of creating an Installer package. As you can see in Figure 12.11, this flow has 6 steps:

1. Features and Files
2. System Additions
3. User System Checks
4. Wizard Appearance
5. Release
6. Finish

I'll review each of these steps in the remainder of this section.

FIGURE 12.11

Wise for Windows Installer

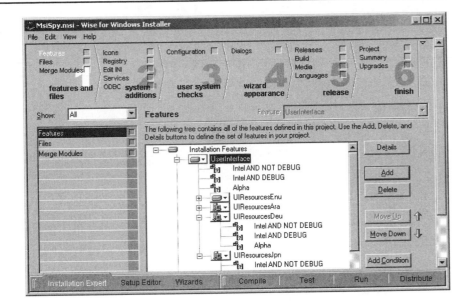

Features and Files

The Features and Files step lets you define the feature tree and the files to include in your installation. Features themselves are defined with a dialog box that allow you to choose all of the necessary information from combo boxes, as shown in Figure 12.12. Associating files with features is even simpler; just browse to the file and drag and drop it to the feature.

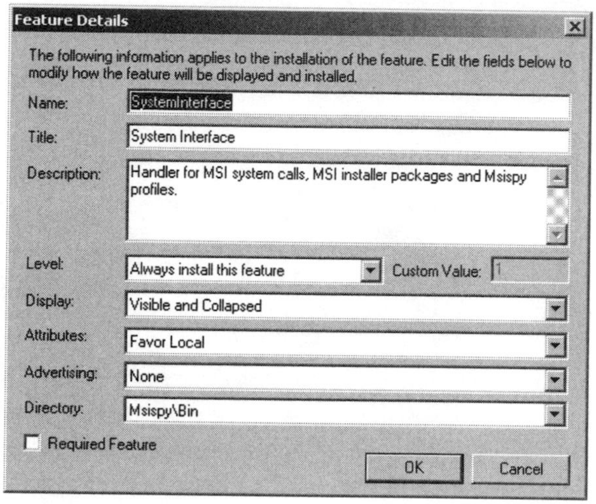

FIGURE 12.12
Setting properties for a
feature

This step also lets you choose merge modules to include in your installation, or create new merge modules.

If you add a file that's a COM server, Wise will automatically set it for self-registration. However, it does not have a built-in way to determine the settings required to use the Registry tables for registration instead.

Note that components aren't exposed at all when you're working with the Installation Expert interface in the Wise Installer. Assigning files and other objects to components is handled automatically and transparently in this mode.

System Additions

The System Additions step lets you specify the changes that should be made to the target system. This doesn't include files, which are handled on the Features and Files step. Instead, this is where you specify the other changes the Installer can make:

- Icons and shortcuts
- Registry keys and values
- .ini file changes
- Windows NT Services
- ODBC drivers and data sources

User System Checks

The User System Checks step allows you to specify conditions that should apply to the installation as a whole:

- Windows version
- Windows NT version
- Screen resolution
- Screen color depth

Wizard Appearance

The Wizard Appearance step lets you decide which dialog boxes should be displayed during the installation. This step also lets you edit the dialog boxes. Editing is done in the Setup Editor's Dialogs tab, as shown in Figure 12.13.

FIGURE 12.13
Editing a dialog box in Wise for Windows Installer

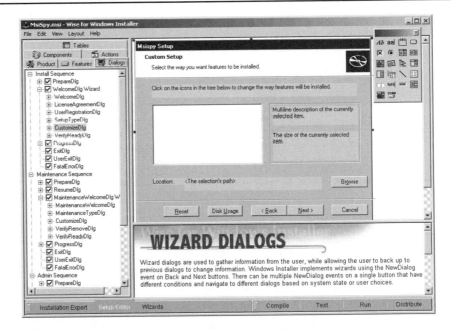

The dialog editor features drag-and-drop control creation and manipulation. Control properties are handled with property sheets rather than a property area, which is sometimes less convenient than being able to work with the control and its properties both visible. Events and conditions for controls are also handled on the control property sheets.

Release

In the Release step, you handle all the details of going from the design to the finished Installer package. This includes deciding the details of packaging and whether to include a bootstrap executable to install the Installer Service. You can choose to copy build settings from another release, which is handy when you're creating an upgraded package. This step also handles media and language-related settings.

Wise handles multiple-language builds by providing a facility to export and import the strings in the user interface as tab-delimited files. You can just send this file out to be translated into your target language, and then import the translated file. This allows the people doing the localization to work entirely without the Installer software.

Finish

The Finish step handles a number of final details for your package. These include the following:

- Project properties
- Summary Information Stream properties
- Upgrade information (making it easy to identify this package as an upgrade for a previous version)
- Add/Remove Programs applet information
- MIF and PDF creation (to interface with Microsoft Systems Management Server)
- Code signing

Once you've worked through all of the steps to create the project, you can then distribute it. The Wise interface sports separate buttons to compile, test, and run a package. You can interactively compile and test until you're sure you've got what you wanted.

Other Features

In addition to the Installation Expert mode, there's also a Setup Editor mode that allows editing directly in the Installer tables. This mode allows both editing in the raw tables and a number of more organized views that strike a balance between organization and power:

Product   For launch conditions, properties, and summary.

Features   To organize the feature tree and all of the other tables that are related to features.

Dialogs   For editing dialog boxes.

Components   Which provides a tree view of the components and their contents.

Actions   For editing the sequence tables.

Tables   For making direct changes to any table in the Installer database.

In addition to supporting the standard actions, Wise provides a wizard for creating custom actions.

Finally, two of the other useful wizards deserve mention. The first is a Patch Wizard, which provides you with an easy way to create patch files (see Chapter 10, "Creating and Using Patch Packages"). Wise is the first tool to offer this functionality, though, of course, you can use the Installer SDK tools to create patches in conjunction with other editing software.

Wise for Windows Installer also includes an Application Verification Wizard that will check your installation for logo compliance. The help file has further information on logo compliance so that you can check the parts of the specification that don't impact the Installer directly.

Validating Installer Databases

- The Three Types of Validation

- Internal Consistency Evaluators (ICEs)

- Standard ICEs

By now, you will have realized that the Windows Installer relies on a complex database for its operations. Perhaps this has made you wonder what happens if something in the database is incorrect? The short answer is that the Installer Service will happily do the wrong thing, perhaps locking up while trying to install software or (much worse) installing software incorrectly so as to break other software.

Fortunately, there is an alternative to remembering every single Installer rule when you're creating and modifying Installer databases. This alternative is called *validation*. The Windows Installer team has written a set of tests that can be used to check whether something is drastically wrong with an Installer database before you ship it. In fact, you should never ship an Installer package to a customer before the database that it contains passes every validation test.

In this chapter, I'll show you how the Installer handles validation, discuss the software involved in the process, and then review the specific faults that the validation process is designed to catch.

The Three Types of Validation

There are actually three different types of validation that you can use with Windows Installer databases:

- Internal validation
- String-Pool validation
- Internal Consistency Evaluators (ICEs)

Most of this chapter is devoted to ICE validation, which is capable of the most thorough and complex validity checking. But first, I'll briefly explain the other two types of validation.

Internal Validation

Internal validation is the simplest of the three types of validation. Basically, this validation checks that you haven't tried to store an integer in a String column, or vice versa. Internal validation can also check that an integer is within a particular range, that Primary Key columns are unique, and that all Non-nullable columns have assigned values in every record.

Although internal validation is important, it should be completely invisible to most developers working on Installer databases. That's because all of the Installer editing tools automatically call the internal validation functions whenever you add or modify a record in a table. This sort of validation happens continuously as you work with your Installer database, with the result that this simplest of validation checks should always be passed.

> **NOTE**   If you're writing your own tool to modify Installer databases, you may want to call the MsiViewModify API function to perform internal validation directly. You can find more information on using MsiViewModify for this purpose in the Windows Installer SDK.

String-Pool Validation

String-Pool validation is designed to verify two things:

- That there is no internal corruption in the storage area that the Installer database uses to hold text strings
- That the text strings in the database can be properly displayed

The Installer SDK includes a command-line tool, `MsiInfo.exe`, that can be used to perform String-Pool validation. To use this tool, you specify the database to be checked, along with the /D command-line option. If all goes well, you'll get output similar to this:

```
I:\MsiIntel.SDK\Tools>msiinfo e:\temp\data1.msi /D
String ID size: 2
Code page: 0
```

However, it's possible that you'll receive warnings from MsiInfo, as in this case:

```
I:\MsiIntel.SDK\Tools>msiinfo e:\temp\hellowin.msi /D
String ID size: 2
Code page: 0
String 315 has characters with high-bit set, ↵
but codepage is not set.
String 420 has characters with high-bit set, ↵
but codepage is not set.
String 435 has characters with high-bit set, ↵
but codepage is not set.
String 1479 has characters with high-bit set, ↵
but codepage is not set.
String 1556 has characters with high-bit set, ↵
but codepage is not set.
String 1684 has characters with high-bit set, ↵
but codepage is not set.
```

The warnings here indicate that the referenced strings contain special characters that cannot be displayed by the code page that the database is set to use. If you'd like to know which strings are causing problems, use the /B switch in conjunction with the /D switch to dump the String table:

```
I:\MsiIntel.SDK\Tools>msiinfo e:\temp\hellowin.msi /B /D
String ID size: 2
Code page: 0
...
Id: 1478  Refcnt:    1  String: ℘
[_WiseDialogTitleFontDefault]Select Features
Id: 1479  Refcnt:    1  String: ℘
[_WiseDialogFontDefault]Please, wait while t...
Id: 1480  Refcnt:    2  String: ReinstallFileExact
Id: 1481  Refcnt:    4  String: NameE
...
```

As you can see, the String table dump won't necessarily show you the entire string, but it should show you enough that you can use a tool such as Orca to locate the string in question.

WARNING   The output from dumping the String table will likely be quite long. You'll probably want to use the > command-line pipe to dump the results to a file instead of trying to view them on screen.

If MsiInfo reports codepage problems, there are two ways that you can fix them. First, and most portably, is to edit the strings in question so that they don't contain any extended characters (characters with an ASCII value over 127). This will ensure that your Installer package can be used on the widest variety of systems because the base codepage without extended characters is the same on every system.

Unfortunately, that approach won't work in all cases. For example, if you're creating an Installer package to run on a Japanese system, you'll need double-byte character set (DBCS) characters that aren't available on the base codepage. In that case, you'll need to set the codepage of the database to an appropriate value. You can do this by importing a file that specifies a table named _ForceCodepage into your database. Create a file consisting of two blank lines, then a line with the number of the codepage that you want to use, a tab, and the string "_ForceCodepage" (without the quotes). Then use MsiDb to import this table to the database. If you're using a commercial program to edit your Installer database, check the documentation to see whether it offers an easier way to set the codepage.

WARNING   MsiInfo also checks for reference count problems. For example, a string might be used in four places even though the String table thinks it's only used in three places. If MsiInfo reports any reference count problems, you should immediately use the MsiDb utility (covered in Chapter 12, "Installer Editing Tools") to export all the tables from the database and then import them to a new blank database.

Internal Consistency Evaluators (ICEs)

The most flexible and sophisticated of the three types of validation is validation via Internal Consistency Evaluator, commonly abbreviated to ICE. ICEs take advantage of the fact that the Installer Service can execute custom actions that actually inspect the contents of an Installer database. In fact, ICEs are stored in a special file with the same structure as any other Installer database. By default, this file uses the extension .cub. Figure 13.1 shows a .cub file open in the Orca editor. Note that the ICEs themselves are listed in the CustomAction table. The .cub file also contains extra files needed by particular ICEs, such as the _BadRegData table.

ICEs, like custom actions within Sequence tables, can be written in VBScript or JScript, or contained in DLLs with entry points that correspond to custom actions. And of course ICEs can use the Installer API and the Installer automation model to gain full access to the contents of an Installer database.

The Windows Installer SDK ships with a set of ICEs and a tool to run them. This tool is called MsiVal2, and it's installed by running the MsiVal2.msi installation in the Tools folder of the SDK. This will create both the MsiVal2.exe program that runs the ICEs and the darice.cub file that contains the standard ICEs.

FIGURE 13.1

Sample .cub file of ICEs

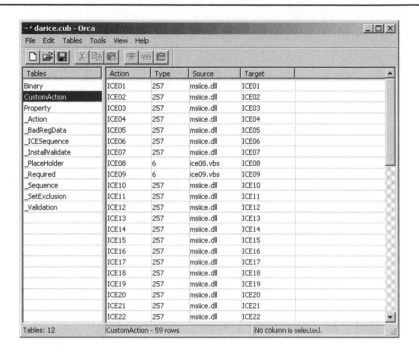

The Windows Installer SDK shows you how you can create your own ICEs for special situations. For most installations, the standard ICEs should be sufficient.

Running ICEs

If you've installed the Windows Installer SDK, you can run ICEs with the command-line tool MsiVal2. When you run MsiVal2, it takes the name of an Installer database and the name of a .cub file as arguments. Then it follows these steps:

1. It makes a temporary copy of the Installer database.
2. It merges the .cub file into the temporary copy.
3. It uses the information in the _ICESequence table in the .cub file to determine which ICEs to execute in what order.
4. It prints or saves any messages from the ICEs.
5. When the validation process is over, the temporary file is deleted. Neither the Installer database nor the .cub file is changed.

The formal syntax of `MsiVal2` is as follows:

```
msival2 {Installer Database} {cub file} [-F] ⏎
[-L {logfile}] [-I {ICE ID} [:{ICE ID}…]]
```

The optional arguments have these effects:

-F   Filters out information messages, printing only errors and warnings.

-L   Saves the results to a log file. If the log file already exists, the –L option is ignored; files will not be overwritten.

-I   Runs only the specified ICEs. If you omit the –I switch, all the ICEs listed in the _IceSequence table are run.

You can also execute ICEs from most of the available Installer editing tools. For example, Microsoft Orca can invoke validation from its Tools ➢ Validate menu item.

Orca itself ships with three different `.cub` files. You can choose between these files by description on the Validation Output dialog box, shown in Figure 13.2:

Full MSI Validation Suite   Includes all of the ICEs shipped by Microsoft.

Windows 2000 Logo Program Suite   Includes a subset of ICEs designed specifically to evaluate compliance with the Windows 2000 logo requirements.

Merge Module Validation Suite   Includes only ICEs that apply to merge modules.

Once you've chosen which set of ICEs to run and clicked the Go button, Orca executes each ICE in turn. Error and information messages are returned to the Validation Output dialog box. You can use the Copy Results button to place these results on the clipboard. When you close the dialog, any tables and rows within Orca that generated validation errors will be highlighted in red.

FIGURE 13.2
Validating an Installer database with Orca

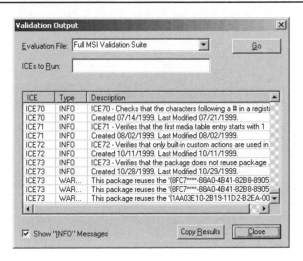

Standard ICEs

The Windows Installer SDK includes 71 standard ICEs, numbered from ICE01 through ICE73 (for some reason there is no ICE37, and ICE11 appears to be undocumented and uncalled). These ICEs can be divided into seven groups. I'll discuss the individual ICEs under these main groupings:

Base ICEs   Check the ICE system itself and the fundamental properties of the database. If any of these ICEs fail, the result is likely to be fatal for the Installer trying to deal with this database.

Feature and Component ICEs   Verify the proper functioning of features and components. Errors and warnings from these ICEs usually indicate that an installation will be incomplete or confusing.

File and Registry ICEs   Look at the low-level files and Registry entries that are assembled into components. Failures in these ICEs can result in unexpected behavior of the installed product.

Action ICEs   Verify the Sequence tables in the Installer database. Problems reported by these ICEs will usually keep the installation from completing properly.

Property ICEs   Inspect the Property table and the use of properties in other tables. Perhaps the most important one of these ICEs is the one that catches unintentional case mismatches between properties.

Dialog ICEs   Verify the proper operation of the Dialog, Control, and associated tables. Errors and warnings from these ICEs will usually translate into fatal errors attempting to display dialog boxes.

Miscellaneous ICEs   Check other parts of the Installer database. These include the Media table, shortcut advertising, stream names, merge module dependencies, and more.

Before you ship any product, your Installer database should pass all of these ICEs. That means that none of the ICEs should report an outright error in your database, and that you've inspected all of the warnings and satisfied yourself that the database is correctly formatted in those areas.

Base ICEs

ICE01 tests to make sure the ICE mechanism is functioning. All it does is return the time that it was invoked. ICE01 should never fail. If it does, something is wrong with the Installer Service on the computer where you're running validation.

ICE03 checks the basic items that internal validation should check during editing. It can detect a variety of conditions, including the following:

- Duplicate primary keys
- Nulls in non-nullable columns
- Foreign keys that reference nonexistent rows
- Values outside of acceptable ranges
- Invalid GUIDs
- Improperly formatted Condition columns
- Mistakes in the _Validation table itself

ICE06 performs a sanity check on the .cub file itself. It checks to make sure that the database being validated contains every column that is being checked by any of the ICEs. If this ICE fails, it most likely means that you're using a new version .cub file with an older version of the Installer database.

ICE32 looks at Foreign Key columns and makes sure that they are the same size and data type as the Primary Key columns that they're referencing. As long as you're only using the standard tables in your Installer database, this ICE should never fail.

Feature and Component ICEs

ICE02 checks to make sure that you've got the relations right between the Component, File, and Registry tables for KeyPath columns. You'll recall that the KeyPath column in the Component table points to either an entry in the File table or an entry in the Registry table. The corresponding entry in those tables must point back to the same record in the Component table that points to it. ICE02 verifies that this circular relationship has been properly set up.

ICE08 makes sure that there are no duplicate GUIDs in the Component table.

ICE09 checks that any component being installed into the SystemFolder folder has its permanent bit set. It's a violation of the Installer guidelines to install non-permanent components to this folder.

ICE10 looks at feature hierarchies and advertisement. If a parent feature is set to favor advertisement, all of its child features must be set to favor advertisement as well. If a parent feature is set to disallow advertisement, then all of its child features must be set to disallow advertisement.

ICE14 makes two checks in the Feature table. First, it verifies that the root feature is not set to "follow parent" status, because it has no parent. Second, it makes sure that no feature is its own parent.

ICE18 verifies that any empty directories used as the KeyPath column for a component are listed in the CreateFolder table.

ICE19 checks that advertised components use a file as their key path, rather than a folder or a Registry key.

ICE21 uses the FeatureComponent table to verify that every component in the Component table is assigned to at least one feature.

ICE22 validates that the FeatureComponent and PublishComponent tables do not conflict. The FeatureComponent table assigns components to features, and the Publish-Component does the same. The two assignments must be the same in all cases.

ICE35 checks components that are stored in compressed fashion in `.cab` files. In particular, it makes sure that these components are not set to run from source.

ICE38 checks components that are installed to a particular user's profile (for example, to the predefined StartMenuFolder or DesktopFolder). Such components must use a Registry key as their key path, and this Registry key must be located in the HKEY_CURRENT_USER Registry hive.

ICE47 looks at the Feature and FeatureComponents tables to locate features that refer to more than 800 components. Such features will cause trouble on Windows 9x systems. It also checks that no feature has more than 1600 components, which is the absolute limit on Windows NT and Windows 2000 systems.

ICE54 looks for components whose key path files are companion files (that is, whose key path files reference another file for version information). Key path files must have explicit version information in the File table.

ICE57 makes sure that components do not mix per-machine and per-user data. It checks the Component, File, Registry, and Directory tables. For example, a component that installs files to the DesktopFolder and Registry keys to the HKEY_LOCAL_MACHINE hive would fail this ICE.

File and Registry ICEs

ICE04 checks to make sure that all files have sequence numbers that make sense when compared to the information in the Media table. It finds the largest LastSequence value in the Media table, and makes sure that the value for the Sequence column in every row of the File table is less than or equal to this value.

ICE30 checks that the same file is never installed in the same directory by two different components in the same Installer package (doing so would break the reference counting scheme of the Installer). It considers both long and short file names, and looks at what will happen if Condition columns evaluate to either true or false.

ICE33 validates that all entries in the Registry table should be in that table. Some Registry information should be made through the more specialized tables in order to support advertisement and install-on-demand. This includes information that belongs in the Extension, ProgId, Verb, MIME, Class, Typelib and AppId tables. If this ICE detects any problems, it will tell you which entries you should move and which tables you should move them to.

ICE42 inspects rows in the Class table for InprocServer32 Registry entries. It makes sure that these rows do not refer to an .exe file in the File table because in-process servers must be .dll files.

ICE49 inspects the data type of default Registry entries (those with a null in the Name column). Such entries must use the REG_SZ data type.

ICE53 presents a warning if the Registry table tries to modify the Installer policy by writing to keys underneath Software\Policies\Microsoft\Installer. Any changes made to these keys are better made by setting the values of the properties that control the Installer's actions.

ICE60 looks at file version information in the File table. If a file is not a font and it has a version, then it must also have a language. If you ignore warnings from this ICE, then repairs will tend to reinstall files needlessly. That's because the file on disk will always have a language, even if the entry in the File table does not. The Installer will see this as the installed language not matching the language in the package, and so it will reinstall the file.

ICE70 checks Registry entries that write integers to make sure that the integers are specified properly. For example, ##5 or #x12A4 are valid, but #zzy27 is not.

Action ICEs

ICE12 is used to validate that type 35 and type 51 custom actions are properly positioned with respect to the CostFinalize action in any Sequence tables. Type 35 custom actions must come after the CostFinalize action, and type 51 custom actions must come before the CostFinalize action.

ICE13 checks for dialogs in the Execute Sequence tables. Dialogs can only appear in the UI Sequence tables.

ICE26 checks the Sequence tables to make sure that all of the required actions are present. It also makes sure that no Sequence table contains an action that is disallowed for that table.

ICE27 verifies that every entry in every Sequence table is either a standard action, a custom action, or a Dialog name. It also checks the organization of each Sequence table to be sure that actions are being performed in the proper order.

ICE28 looks at ForceReboot actions, and makes sure that they are not being called in inappropriate places.

ICE63 checks the sequencing of the RemoveExistingProducts action. This action may be placed in several spots in the Sequence tables, but there are other spots where it is invalid.

ICE68 checks the Type column in the CustomAction table. Only some numbers are valid custom action types. For example, a value of 82 in this column (which is not a valid custom action type) would generate an error from this ICE.

ICE72 checks the AdvtExecuteSequence table to make sure than any custom actions it contains are type 19, 35, or 51. If this table contains other types of custom actions, advertisement may fail.

Property ICEs

ICE05 checks to make sure that required properties, including ProductName, ProductLanguage, ProductVersion, ProductCode, and Manufacturer are present in the database.

ICE16 checks the length of the ProductName property to make sure it does not exceed the maximum allowed 63 characters.

ICE24 checks the data types of the ProductCode, ProductVersion, and ProductLanguage properties.

ICE46 looks at the database for properties that differ only in case (for example, "MyProperty" and "myProperty"). Because the Installer is case-sensitive, such properties are treated as two distinct properties. This is usually not what the developer intended. If you really did want to have separate MyProperty and myProperty properties, you can ignore the warnings from this ICE.

ICE52 checks for private properties in the AppSearch table. All properties in the AppSearch table must be public properties (that is, their names must be entirely upper case).

ICE69 inspects strings of the Formatted data type, looking for [$componentkey] substrings. These substrings must refer to the same component that is referenced in the Component column of the table being inspected.

Dialog ICEs

ICE17 checks for some common problems with the Control table, including the following:

- PushButton controls without entries in the Event table
- Bitmap or Icon controls without entries in the Binary table
- RadioButtonGroup, ListBox, ComboBox, or ListView controls without entries in the corresponding tables

ICE20 verifies that required dialogs are present and that they have the required controls. For example, there must be a FilesInUse dialog box and it must have a Listbox control and three PushButton controls with specific properties set.

ICE23 checks that the tab order is correct for every dialog. That is, it makes sure that there is a Control_First control specified for every dialog, and that the Control_Next properties for each dialog form a single closed loop.

ICE31 validates that any text styles used in the Control table are actually defined in the TextStyle table.

ICE34 checks for inconsistencies in the RadioButton table and the corresponding RadioButtonGroup controls. For example, it makes sure that the default value of the control is one of the values listed in the RadioButton table.

ICE44 checks the NewDialog, SpawnDialog and SpawnWaitDialog rows in the ControlEvent table to be sure that these rows reference dialogs that actually exist in the Dialog table.

Miscellaneous ICEs

ICE07 checks that all fonts are being installed into the Fonts folder on the user's computer.

ICE15 verifies the necessary reciprocal relationship between the MIME table and the Extension table. Every entry in the MIME table must refer to an entry in the Extension table in its Extension_ column. The referenced entry in the Extension table must refer back to that same entry in the MIME table through its MIME_ column.

ICE25 checks merge module dependencies. It checks to be sure that all of the merge modules listed in the ModuleDependency table are present, and that none of the merge modules listed in the ModuleExclusion table are present.

ICE29 verifies that all stream names within the Installer package are unique, even after possible name truncation (the Installer stores a maximum of 62 characters for a stream name).

ICE36 checks the database for *icon bloat*—that is, for icons that are stored in the database but that are never used anywhere during the installation. If this ICE detects unused icons, you should remove them to shrink your Installer package.

ICE39 validates the Summary Information Stream in the database. It checks to make sure that all of the required properties are present in the stream, and that they have the appropriate data types.

ICE40 does three miscellaneous validations:

- It checks to be sure an Error table is present in the database.
- It checks the Property table to make sure you have not defined a property named REINSTALLMODE.
- It checks the RemoveIniFile table to be sure that any Delete Tag entries specify the tag to delete.

ICE41 checks the Class and Extension tables to make sure that they do not conflict with the FeatureComponent table. The Class and Extension tables specify the Component and Feature for each row, and this information must match the associations between components and features in the FeatureComponent table.

ICE43 validates that non-advertised shortcuts refer to components that use a Registry entry in HKEY_CURRENT_USER as their key path.

ICE45 compares Bit Field columns to the bit fields that are defined for the current release of the Installer. It makes sure that none of the bits that are currently reserved is set to 1. It performs this check in these tables:

- BBControl
- Control
- Dialog
- Feature
- File
- MoveFile
- ODBCDataSource
- Patch
- RemoveFile
- ServiceControl
- ServiceInstall
- TextStyle

ICE48 looks at the Directory table, checking for paths that are hard-coded to local drives (for example, c:\Temp). Such paths can cause problems because the target machine won't necessarily have such a path available. This is not a fatal error because in some cases (for example, when installing to computers where you control the directory structure), this may be acceptable.

ICE50 warns you if you have an icon stored in files that do not have the extension .exe or .ico. Such icons won't be correctly displayed by Windows. It also warns you if you have an icon for a shortcut that does not have the same extension as the target for that shortcut, because this would cause the shortcut to have an incorrect context menu.

ICE51 checks for problems with font titles. Fonts stored in .ttf or .ttc files (True-Type fonts) should have a null value in the FontTitle column of the Font table, because these fonts have a name embedded directly in the font file. Fonts stored in other types of files (such as .fon files) should have an entry in the FontTitle column of the Font table, because these fonts do not contain embedded names.

ICE55 validates that all files and other objects referenced in the LockObject column of the LockPermissions table actually exist in the installation.

ICE56 checks the Directory table for several possible problems:

- There should be a single root directory.
- The root directory should be the TARGETDIR property.
- The SourceDir property should occur in the DefaultDir column.

ICE58 checks to make sure there are not too many entries in the Media table. The Media table is limited to 80 rows.

ICE59 verifies that advertised shortcuts belong to components that are installed by the target feature of the shortcut. If this ICE fails, then advertised shortcuts will not function properly. Instead, they will launch the Installer to install the necessary component, but because the component isn't associated with the feature that the shortcut calls, the Installer will be unable to locate it.

ICE61 inspects the Upgrade table to make sure that upgrades will not try to remove themselves or perform other illegal operations.

ICE62 checks the IsolatedComponent table for entries that might cause unexpected behavior. For example, it will detect isolated-shared components that are not properly set up for refcounting.

ICE64 checks for directory entries that will not be properly removed if an application is uninstalled.

ICE65 validates the format of entries in the Environment table.

ICE66 checks the database version (contained in the PageCount property of the Summary Information Stream) to make sure that it does not conflict with other information in the database. For example, the Upgrade table is processed by the version 1.1 Installer but not the version 1.0 Installer and so should not occur in version 1.0 Installer databases.

ICE67 checks that the target of a non-advertised shortcut belongs to the same component as the shortcut itself.

ICE71 validates that the Media table contains a row where the DiskID column has a value of 1. This entry is necessary because the Installer itself always assumes that the .msi package is on disk 1.

ICE73 checks the product code, package code, and upgrade code in your Installer database to make sure that these codes do not match any of those used in the Windows Installer samples. Copying the samples without changing the codes they contain is a common mistake, but doing so breaks the rule that Installer packages should not reuse product, package, or upgrade codes from another product.

Meeting Windows Logo Requirements

- The Windows Logo Program

- Windows Fundamentals

- Windows Installer Service

- Component Sharing

- Data and Settings Management

- User Interface Fundamentals

- OnNow/ACPI Support

- Application Migration

For several years, Microsoft has sponsored a variety of "Designed for Windows" and "Certified for Windows" logo programs. Applications that met a set of requirements and passed independent verification of their compliance were allowed to display the Windows logo on their packaging and advertising. In this appendix, I'll show you how you can use Visual Basic along with the Windows Installer to meet the most recent version of these requirements.

The Windows Logo Program

The requirements for the current logo program are contained in a document titled "Application Specification for Microsoft Windows 2000." (Actually, there are both desktop and distributed versions of this document; I'll concentrate on the desktop specifications.) You can download a copy of this document yourself from Microsoft's Web site at `msdn.microsoft.com/winlogo`. Version 1.0a of this specification was released in January 2000, just before the release of Windows 2000 itself.

Applications which comply with this specification are eligible to display the "Certified for Windows" logo, along with a list of the Windows platforms that the product is certified on. However, before an application can display the logo, its compliance must be verified. Verification is performed by an independent company named VeriTest. The VeriTest Web site is at `www.veritest.com/mslogos/windows2000/`.

The basic fee for logo compliance testing starts at $5,200 and goes up from there, though both Microsoft and VeriTest have offered discount coupons from time to time. This is obviously more than you'll want to spend for many internal applications. But you should consider the logo guidelines even if you're not interested in applying for the actual logo. That's because, as you'll see in this appendix, these guidelines are not simply arbitrary hoops to jump through. Rather, they represent the state of the art in designing applications that run well and interact smoothly with the Windows operating system.

In an appendix this size, I can only summarize the guidelines. If you're interested in seeing how Microsoft says you should write Windows applications, I encourage you to download the full application specification for yourself.

The application specification is broken up into seven major areas, which in turn contain 40 separate requirements:

- Windows Fundamentals
- Windows Installer Service
- Component Sharing
- Data and Settings Management
- User Interface Fundamentals

- OnNow/ACPI Support
- Application Migration

I'll consider each of these areas in turn in the rest of the appendix. As you'll see, you can meet most of the logo requirements "for free" simply by using Visual Basic 6.0 as your development platform and the Windows Installer as your setup platform.

Windows Fundamentals

The Windows fundamentals group of requirements includes 10 areas that your application should pass to be certified. These areas represent basic functionality:

- Provide primary functionality and maintain stability
- Provide 32-bit components
- Support long file names and UNC paths
- Support printers with long names and UNC paths
- Do not read or write certain files
- Associate types with your data files
- Perform Windows version checking correctly
- Support AutoPlay of compact disks
- Install only verified Kernel Mode drivers
- Install only (Windows Hardware Quality Labs) WHQL-tested hardware drivers

Provide Primary Functionality and Maintain Stability

What this requirement really says is that your application should not crash Windows and that Windows should not crash your application. For the most part, Visual Basic applications should be safe here because the Visual Basic runtime protects you from most unusual techniques that could get you in trouble. Errors such as trying to write to a nonexistent drive letter, or trying to create a file larger than a drive, will be caught by the runtime library and be returned to your program as an error.

This requirement does emphasize the need for your application to contain thorough and consistent error trapping. Even if something goes wrong, your application must not collapse entirely. This means that every procedure except the most trivial (one-line calls to another procedure, for example) must contain an error handler, and that error handler must contain a `Case Else` to manage the response to unexpected errors.

You can also use the resiliency functions of the Windows Installer to help make your application more robust. For example, you can use the Installer automation model or API to check the path to a component that the user might have installed anywhere, or to request that a copy of a missing component be reinstalled from the source media.

Provide 32-Bit Components

Certified applications must use 32-bit executables. If you're using Visual Basic 6.0 as your development environment, you get this automatically. All executables compiled by Visual Basic 6.0 are 32-bit.

Support Long File Names and UNC Paths

Logo-compliant applications that allow users to enter file names (for example, when they choose a file to open) must support both long file names (LFNs) and Universal Naming Convention (UNC) paths. This should not be a problem for applications written in Visual Basic, because Visual Basic itself understands LFNs and UNCs consistently.

One minor area that may cause a problem in Visual Basic applications is the Common Dialog Control. If you allow the user to multiselect files, and specify that you want long file names, it uses a null-separated format to return file names:

```
Path<null>Filename1<null>Filename2<null> …
```

You can use the `InStr()` function to break this string apart at the nulls and reassemble it.

The Windows Installer Service supports both LFNs and UNC paths as installation locations. For full support of LFNs, you should specify long names for all of your files in the File table inside of your Installer database.

Support Printers with Long Names and UNC Paths

Logo-compliant applications must be able to use printers with long names or located at UNC paths. Again, if you use Visual Basic and the Common Dialog control to handle your printing, you get this functionality automatically.

Do Not Read or Write Certain Files

There are four files that you should not read from or write to on Windows NT or Windows 2000 systems:

- `autoexec.bat`
- `config.sys`
- `win.ini`
- `system.ini`

This requirement comes about because those files may not exist on all operating systems and users may not have the necessary permissions to write to their default locations. Fortunately, you've got several easy alternatives for storing information: the Registry or private `.ini` files.

To use the Registry from Visual Basic, you can use the SaveSetting, GetSetting, and GetAllSettings functions. To use a private .ini file, you can use the WritePrivate-ProfileString and GetPrivateProfileString API calls.

Of course, the Windows Installer also supports writing information to the Registry via the Registry table (and associated special tables for COM information). It also supports the use of private .ini files through the IniFile table and associated tables.

So, using the combination of Visual Basic and the Windows Installer, you can set up your application with its configuration information in approved locations and then read and write that data as necessary from those same locations.

Associate Types with Your Data Files

To be more precise, if your application creates non-hidden files outside of its own directory, these files must be associated with icons, file type descriptions, and default actions.

The simplest way to conform to this requirement, of course, is to just not create files outside of your application's own directory. This may not be feasible, of course, especially if your application needs to save files for later use and prompts the user for their location.

An alternative strategy is to use a file extension that's already sure to be registered on the target system by Windows itself. For example, if you save your application's files with the extension .txt, they'll appear as normal text files in the operating system. However, with this approach you'll have to figure out what to do if the user attempts to open a text file that doesn't contain data usable by your application or wasn't created with your application.

Probably the better approach is to actually register a distinct file type with your application for its data files. The Windows Installer can help you do this when you install your application. All the information to handle the needs of data files is contained in the Registry table group in the Installer database.

Perform Windows Version Checking Correctly

This is a relatively simple requirement, but it causes problems for many applications. If your application is meant to run on Windows NT 4.0 or higher, you should check that the Windows version number is greater than or equal to 4.0, not that it's exactly equal to 4.0, because if it is, when a new version of Windows is released, your application will fail. Checking for exact equality has broken hundreds of applications in the past, despite the fact that this should be obvious.

Listing 2.1 in Chapter 2, "Running the Installer," shows how you can use the Get-VersionInfoEx() API call from Visual Basic to determine the Windows version.

If you need to know the Windows version while installing, the Windows Installer Service provides the VersionNT and Version9*x* properties.

Support AutoPlay of Compact Disks

Logo-compliant applications distributed on CD-ROM or DVD-ROM must use the Windows AutoPlay feature to launch the application setup when they're inserted into the CD-ROM drive for the first time. If you're using a professional Installer editing package, your package may create an AutoPlay program for you. Otherwise, you can create your own `autorun.inf` file on the CD to take care of this detail. The simplest possible `autorun.inf` file looks like this:

```
[autorun]
open=setup.exe
```

That tells Windows to run the `setup.exe` program in the root directory of the CD when that CD is inserted into the drive.

NOTE　For more information on the possible options you can specify in an `autorun.inf` file, refer to the MSDN Web site article "Creating an Autoplay-enabled CD-ROM Application" at `msdn.microsoft.com/library/psdk/shellcc/shell/Shell_basics/Autoplay_intro.htm`.

Install Only Verified Kernel Mode Drivers

If your product installs kernel mode drivers, those drivers must pass the tests administered by the Windows 2000 Driver Verifier Manager tool. If you're writing your product in Visual Basic, you're not going to be writing kernel mode drivers, so you don't need to worry about this requirement.

Install Only WHQL-Tested Hardware Drivers

If your product installs hardware drivers, those drivers must pass the tests administered by the Windows Hardware Quality Labs. This requirement is also unlikely in the extreme to apply to Visual Basic products, because it's pretty much impossible to write a hardware driver in Visual Basic.

Windows Installer Service

The second set of requirements refer to proper use of the Windows Installer Service itself. Naturally, using the Installer to install your software is the first step towards meeting these seven requirements:

- Install using a validated Installer package
- Observe the componentization rules
- Identify shared components
- Install to Program Files by default
- Support Add/Remove Programs
- Support advertising
- Ensure correct uninstalls

Install Using a Validated Installer Package

That's right, to gain the Windows Certification logo an application must use the Windows Installer Service for its setup. That's one reason why all of the major setup tools vendors are now supporting the Windows Installer (and perhaps one of the main reasons that you bought this book).

Note that the Installer package must pass validation. At a minimum, this means that you must run msival2 on the package using the standard set of ICE tests that ship with the Installer SDK and not get back any errors. Refer back to Chapter 13, "Validating Installer Databases," for more details on package validation.

Observe the Componentization Rules

I covered the rules for determining what should be in a component in Chapter 3, "Basic Installer Concepts." Those rules must be followed for a logo-compliant product. Additionally, it just plain makes good sense to follow those rules because they'll help the Windows Installer correctly install and uninstall your application without breaking other applications.

Identify Shared Components

Properly identifying shared components is a matter of properly using the Windows Installer Service. Be aware of the following two cases:

- If a component is composed entirely of files that are only installed by the Windows Installer, your job is done. You don't have to do anything special to have the Windows Installer handle the shared components in this case.

- If a component includes files that are shared with older applications (ones that do not use the Windows Installer Service), you need to set the SharedDllRefCount bit in the Attributes column of the Component table for that component.

Install to Program Files by Default

Logo-compliant applications must be installed to a subdirectory under the user's Program Files directory by default. You can accomplish this easily with the Windows Installer. Just use the property ProgramFilesFolder as the DirectoryParent value for the directory that's the root of your application's installation. The Installer will determine at runtime how to resolve this to the user's actual program files directory.

Support Add/Remove Programs

To properly support the Add/Remove Programs applet, an application needs to write certain values to the Windows Registry. The Installer will automatically write these values if you set the necessary properties in the Property table in your Installer database:

- ProductName
- ARPINSTALLLOCATION
- Manufacturer
- ProductVersion

In addition, you may want to set the rest of the properties whose names begin with ARP (see Chapter 7, "Putting the Pieces Together") in order to provide additional information to the user when they use the Add/Remove Programs applet to modify your application's installation.

Support Advertising

If your application installs its own file types, it must support advertising for those file types. This requires filling in the Shortcut, Icon, Extension, and Verb tables within the Installer database.

Of course, the Installer makes it possible to go beyond this minimal standardeasily. You may wish to consider whether it makes sense to break your application up into components that are installed on demand, and to make use of the Installer API or automation model to call chunks of your application in when they're needed. But that's optional as far as the logo requirements are concerned.

Ensure Correct Uninstalls

Logo-compliant applications can be installed cleanly and correctly. If you use the Windows Installer to install your application and do not include any custom actions, you get this behavior "for free." This is one of the chief benefits of the Windows Installer.

If your Installer package does include custom actions, you'll need to consider their effects. The uninstallation process must remove any files that these custom actions installed. This may require you to write a second custom action with conditional execution in the appropriate sequence table to make sure that it only runs when the application is being uninstalled.

Component Sharing

The third group of requirements have to do with Windows own requirements for component sharing. There are four requirements in this group:

- Do not attempt to defeat Windows File Protection
- Build side-by-side components
- Install side-by-side components
- Install shared files to the correct locations

Do Not Attempt to Defeat Windows File Protection

Windows File Protection is a new feature of Windows 2000 that prevents attempts to overwrite most files that Windows 2000 itself installs. This feature is designed to increase the stability of Windows by preventing other applications from overwriting necessary system files with newer but potentially conflicting versions.

If you properly follow the Installer rules for componentization, you won't run afoul of system file protection. That's because you're only allowed to create components from files that you produce, and all of the files protected by system file protection are produced by Microsoft. When those files need replacing, Microsoft will do so via a service pack for Windows 2000 only.

Build Side-by-Side Components

Side-by-side components are a new attempt on the part of Microsoft to avoid the "DLL Hell" syndrome in which upgrading a shared library would break older applications that depended on the old version of the library. Windows 2000 and Windows 98SE support side-by-side components. Basically, this means that you can install .dlls in the same folder as their parent application, and the operating system will allow multiple versions of the .dll to be loaded at one time.

If you're using the Windows Installer to install your application, and you install a .dll to the same folder as your application, it will automatically do the right thing.

Install Side-by-Side Components

This is the flip side of the previous requirement. If you build side-by-side components, you must use them. The Windows Installer will make the correct Registry entries for side-by-side .dlls to ensure this.

Install Shared Files to the Correct Locations

If your application installs shared files for older operating systems, you must put them in one of two places:

```
Common Files\<company name>
Program Files\<company name>\Shared Files
```

The Windows Installer provides built-in properties to locate the Common Files and Program Files directories, so installing files to these locations is just a matter of making the right entries to the File and Directory tables.

Data and Settings Management

The next group of requirements contains six requirements that relate to properly handling your application's data and persistent settings:

- Store data in My Documents
- Classify and store application data correctly
- Degrade gracefully on Access Denied
- Run in a secure Windows environment
- Respect Group Policy
- Properly store .adm file settings

Store Data in My Documents

The first time that a logo-compliant application displays the Common File open or save dialogs, it must default to the user's My Documents folder. You can accomplish this by using the Windows Installer automation model directly from Visual Basic. For example, using a Common Dialog named dlgCommon, you could execute this code to open a file:

```
Dim objInstaller As WindowsInstaller.Installer
Dim objSession As WindowsInstaller.Session
Dim strGUID As String
```

```
Set objInstaller = _
 CreateObject("WindowsInstaller.Installer")
objInstaller.UILevel = msiUILevelNone
strGUID = objInstaller.Products(0)
Set objSession = objInstaller.OpenProduct(strGUID)

dlgCommon.InitDir = _
 objSession.Property("PersonalFolder")
dlgCommon.ShowOpen
```

WARNING   Note that the My Documents folder may have different names depending on the operating system. It's not safe to make any assumptions about its location.

Classify and Store Application Data Correctly

Application data (files created by your application, as differentiated from files that the user saves) should also be saved in the proper places. There are three separate places to do this, depending on the type of data. Fortunately, the Windows Installer provides properties for all three of these special folders, so you can use the same code as shown in the previous section (but with different folder names) to retrieve the required locations:

- AppDataFolder for per-user data that should roam with the user
- LocalAppDataFolder for per-user data that should not roam with the user
- CommonAppDataFolder for per-machine data

Degrade Gracefully on Access Denied

Despite your best efforts, users will attempt to do things that Windows doesn't allow. For example, you can't prevent a non-administrative user from browsing to the Windows System directory and trying to save their files in that location. When they try, though, Windows will raise an error since regular users aren't allowed to write to that folder.

Degrading gracefully in this situation means that your application should continue to run and should inform the user that something went wrong. With Visual Basic, you can accomplish this by making sure that there's an error handler in any procedure that writes data. The error handler should pass the error message received from Windows back to the user.

Run in a Secure Windows Environment

This requirement is really a special case of the need to degrade gracefully when access is denied. Your application should be functional for a regular user under Windows NT.

This means that the application must work if the user is only allowed to write to three specific locations:

- The HKEY_CURRENT_USER Registry hive
- Their own My Documents directory
- The Common Documents directory

Ensuring this is usually just a matter of ensuring proper defaults for file save dialogs and not hard-coding any paths for saving information. Note also that the user can work with sub-keys and sub-folders of these three locations.

Respect Group Policy

Group Policy settings allow the system administrator to remove potentially dangerous items from access by regular users. Most applications won't need to worry about these settings at all. If your application contains any of these functions, though, you'll need to read a Registry key and disable them if the group policy says they should be disabled:

- Run arbitrary applications
- List drives and files other than through the common dialog
- List recently opened files
- Shut down Windows

The Windows Installer automatically checks the appropriate group policies when displaying file dialogs, as does the Common Dialog control in Visual Basic.

Refer to the Windows 2000 application specification for a full list of group policies and the Registry keys that you can check to determine their status.

Properly Store *.adm* File Settings

.adm files are administrative templates for manipulating group policy settings. If your application creates such files, they must be stored under either HKEY_CURRENT_USER\Software\Policies or HKEY_LOCAL_MACHINE\Software\Policies. You're extremely unlikely to need to create such files in a Visual Basic application.

User Interface Fundamentals

When the Windows logo requirements were first issued for Windows 95, they were largely concerned with the user interface. Now that most applications use the "new shell" interface, there are only seven UI requirements to adhere to:

- Support system size, color, font, and input settings
- Support High Contrast

- Provide keyboard access
- Expose the focus
- Do not rely on sound
- Do not clutter the Start Menu
- Support multiple monitors

Support System Size, Color, Font, and Input Settings

Your application's forms and dialog boxes must respect the settings that the user makes with the Control Panel Display applet. This automatically happens if you restrict yourself to the controls that ship with Visual Basic. For third-party custom controls, you can check by running a form with the control and then using the Control Panel to change to a different color scheme and default font. The control should automatically be updated when you save the settings.

One non-obvious consequence of this requirement is that you should make your controls bigger than seems necessary when you're using default Windows settings, so that there's still room for all the text if the user chooses one of the larger font settings.

The controls used by the Windows Installer in making its dialog boxes also automatically support system settings.

Support High Contrast

As an additional requirement, your application should remain usable if the user selects one of the high contrast settings from the Control Panel Display applet. Again, the standard controls shipped with Visual Basic support this setting automatically. You should test-drive your application under this setting to be sure that you can still find everything without undue difficulty.

Because the high contrast schemes are monochrome, this means that your application can't depend exclusively on color to convey information. For example, if you use red, yellow, and green boxes to indicate the status of items, you should also provide an alternative way (such as a tooltip or status bar message) for the user to retrieve the status.

Provide Keyboard Access

Your application must provide keyboard shortcuts for all functionality. This is easy to accomplish when you use Visual Basic for designing the application. Just remember to include accelerator keys in the caption properties of labels and menus. You'll also want to double-check that you don't accidentally use the same accelerator key twice on the same form.

For the Installer interface, you can ensure keyboard accessibility by including accelerator keys in the Text property of all the controls in the Control table.

Expose the Focus

For the benefit of those using screen-reader and magnifier software, your application must clearly indicate the location of the input focus at all times. This is another feature that's built into the controls that ship with Visual Basic, and to the controls that are used by the Windows Installer.

Do Not Rely on Sound

Because some users do not hear well, or do not have sound cards, you should never rely exclusively on sound for feedback. Always display a prompt or other visual cue any time you're conveying information with sound.

The Windows Installer doesn't use sound at all (except for system sounds that the user may have associated with messages), so it's automatically compliant with this requirement.

Do Not Clutter the Start Menu

Logo-compliant applications add as few items as possible to the Start Menu. In particular, you're not allowed to add these things:

- Help files (The user can get to Help from within the application.)
- Document files (Readme documents should be displayed during installation. You can do this with an RTF control on an Installer dialog.)
- Uninstall shortcuts (The Control Panel Add/Remove Programs applet will take care of this.)

You're also not allowed to add things to the top portion of the Start Menu (above Program Files), as this is meant to be reserved for personal use.

You can follow this requirement by being careful with the entries you make into the Shortcut table in the Installer database.

Support Multiple Monitors

Now that Windows supports multiple monitors, you should be able to run your application on a multiple monitor system without problems. Both Visual Basic and the Windows Installer support multiple monitors natively, so this should not be a problem.

One thing to watch out for in this regard is a technique that was once popular for hiding controls on Visual Basic forms: setting their Left property to a negative number. With a multiple monitor system, it's possible for negative Left coordinates to still be displayed on a monitor. The correct way to hide controls is to set their Visible property to False.

OnNow/ACPI Support

Five of the logo requirements relate to the new OnNow and Advanced Configuration and Power Interface (ACPI) interfaces in Windows:

- Indicate busy status
- Allow sleep and resume
- Handle sleep notifications when connected
- Handle wake without losing data
- Handle wake from critical sleep

Indicate Busy Status

Some applications may be busy but appear to Windows as being idle. These applications are required to call the SetThreadExecutionState API in a particular way to tell Windows that they're not really idle. Because Visual Basic isn't thread-aware, this option isn't open to applications written in Visual Basic.

Fortunately, an active application in Visual Basic won't appear idle to Windows. So you can generally ignore this requirement for Visual Basic applications.

Allow Sleep and Resume

The application must allow the user to suspend the computer and later resume without losing data. This interaction with the operating system is handled by the Visual Basic runtime library, so it's not something that you need to worry about.

Handle Sleep Notifications When Connected

The application must respond to suspend notifications even when it's connected to the network. This interaction with the operating system is handled by the Visual Basic runtime library, so it's not something that you need to worry about.

Handle Wake without Losing Data

The application must wake up from a suspend state without losing data. This interaction with the operating system is handled by the Visual Basic runtime library, so it's not something that you need to worry about.

Handle Wake from Critical Sleep

The application must wake up from emergency suspension (for example, a sudden loss of power) without crashing. This interaction with the operating system is handled by the Visual Basic runtime library, so it's not something that you need to worry about.

Application Migration

The final Windows logo requirement concerns application migration. This requirement states that if an application is installed on Windows 9x, or Windows NT4, and the system is upgraded to Windows 2000, then the application will continue working. Put another way, applications should not have platform-specific behavior. Because Visual Basic creates applications that use a single binary format regardless of the operating system, you're covered in this regard.

The Windows Installer saves Control Panel Add/Remove Program information in such a manner that it's also available after an operating system upgrade.

INDEX

Note to Reader: In this index, **boldfaced** page numbers refer to primary discussions of the topic; *italicized* page numbers refer to figures.

K

L

P